EMERGING HUMAN RIGHTS

EMERGING HUMAN RIGHTS

The African Political Economy Context

Edited by
George W. Shepherd, Jr.,
and Mark O.C. Anikpo

Studies in Human Rights, Number 8
George W. Shepherd, Jr., Series Editor

Published under the auspices of the
Consortium on Human Rights Development

GREENWOOD PRESS
New York • Westport, Connecticut • London

Library of Congress Cataloging-in-Publication Data

Emerging human rights : the African political economy context / edited
  by George W. Shepherd, Jr. and Mark O.C. Anikpo.
    p. cm. — (Studies in human rights, ISSN 0146–3586 ; no. 8)
    Bibliography: p.
    Includes index.
    ISBN 0–313–26853–3 (lib. bdg. : alk. paper)
    1. Human rights—Africa, Sub-Saharan. 2. Distributive justice.
  3. Social justice. I. Shepherd, George W. II. Anikpo, Mark O.C.
  III. Series.
  JC599.A38E44 1990
  323.4'9'0967—dc20   89–12037

British Library Cataloguing in Publication Data is available.

Library of Congress Catalog Card Number: 89–12037
ISBN: 0–313–26853–3
ISSN: 0146–3586

First published in 1990

Greenwood Press, Inc.
88 Post Road West, Westport, Connecticut 06881

Printed in the United States of America

The paper used in this book complies with the
Permanent Paper Standard issued by the National
Information Standards Organization (Z39.48–1984).

10 9 8 7 6 5 4 3 2 1

Copyright Acknowledgment

Chapters 2, 6, and 8 originally appeared in *Africa Today* Vol. 34, Nos. 1 & 2, pp.
13–26, 27–47, 69–84. Copyright © 1987, *Africa Today Associates*.

Contents

Acknowledgments

This book on human rights was initiated by the Port Harcourt University in Nigeria and the University of Denver collaboration in two conferences, the first in Denver (November 9–10, 1984) and the second in Port Harcourt (June 7–11, 1987). This book deals with important theoretical considerations about emerging rights from the standpoint of political economy.

The editors are especially grateful to the Social Science Research Council, Ford Foundation and Rubin Fund for making the conferences and subsequent publications possible.

The political economy approach to human rights studies is growing, but the African contribution has been especially significant and will doubtless grow in some of the directions touched on in these pages.

We especially acknowledge the support of the former dean of the Graduate School of International Studies, University of Denver, Professor James Mittelman, and the present dean, Professor E. Thomas Rowe. Professor S.J.S. Cookey, the vice chancellor of the University of Port Harcourt, Professor K.L.S. Kodjor, former dean of the Faculty of Social Sciences, University of Port Harcourt, and Dr. Olatunde Ojo played vital roles in the successful organization of the conference. To all the Nigerian government officials, the University of Port Harcourt students, and the U.S., European, and African scholars who helped make the conference a memorable event, we express our appreciation.

Many other men and women contributed immensely to the success of the Port Harcourt Conference and the publication of this book. Space does not allow us to mention all their names here. If this book contributes in any way to a better understanding and respect for the rights of African peoples, individually and collectively, everyone's effort will have been rewarded.

Africa Today has granted permission to include the chapters by George Shepherd, Michael Schultheis, and O. Nnoli in revised form.

EMERGING HUMAN RIGHTS

Introduction: The Political Economy of Universal Human Rights: The African Context

George W. Shepherd, Jr.

The African contribution to our understanding of emerging human rights has been enormous. They have helped to take us another stage beyond the eighteenth-century natural rights philosophers and the nineteenth and twentieth century neoclassical economists and lawyers to a new level of consciousness that is more completely universal. This has been a product of both intellectual thought and political struggle as in other parts of the world, from the French, American and British to the Russian and Chinese revolutions. In Africa, this globalization of human rights began with the self-determination movements against colonialism under activist leaders who, by 1989, established 53 new states. Today the process has continued with the African contribution to the formulation of International Political Economy (IPE) critique of the existing world system. This new paradigm of thought has many contributors from all over the world but this book is concerned with the particular African contribution. In the field of human rights IPE's central concept is people's rights, though there are other terms applied to it such as solidarity rights or emerging rights. The most prominent of these new rights is the right to development.[1] Neither international political economy nor people's rights has as yet won much favor in the Western world, where the right to development is regarded as an unjustified political demand.[2] And in the Second World it is seen as an offspring of dependence and other unorthodox Marxist ideas.[3] These major centers of power have preferred to continue their own approaches to the field of human rights. The West has long given priority to civil and political rights while the command economies have focused on economic and social justice. Of course, the Communist states have undergone an important shift toward democratization (Glasnost) that can conceivably take them in the direction of a more comprehensive and universal concept of human rights. And development of the global economy is forcing a greater recognition in all parts of the world of international political economy. Still, the West enjoys such a dominant position it is reluctant to accept the idea of structural redistribution in favor of the less fortunate parts of the world, and, as yet, there is little movement.

Thus, the idea of an international political economy that recognizes the injustice of the current distribution of opportunity and resources is more easily grasped in the Third World and Africa. People who live in weak states and who are the subjects of continuing exploitation in the international division of labor are more likely to recognize people's rights first.

There are deprived persons in the affluent societies as well, especially minorities and the homeless. And advocates of people's rights among the Churches, universities, and critical social movements are gaining ground; but they are not in a position to secure these rights at this point in history.

The political economy approach in contrast to the modernization school has helped provide the methodological bridge to this new consciousness. Political economists have been less ethnocentric and bound to prevailing legal norms. They have perceived that the allocation of resources in society are controlled by political decisions and that political choices are not independent from economic choices. Moreover, in extending this thinking to the world they have maintained that new states are dependent upon the international economy that often deprives them of their capacity to protect their citizens or provide for their welfare. This in turn has led to the realization that the distribution of wealth and the rights associated with basic human needs are closely related to the international political system. Therefore, the concept of people's rights has emerged from the recognition that such inequities will need to be dealt with on a global scale. But the world's people cannot rely on their states for such freedom and will have to find the means themselves to change these structures of power in order to strengthen the democratic institutions capable of providing and protecting universal human rights.

Africans have contributed to the idea that the emergence of these new rights depends upon global structural change which will come as a result of the growing consciousness of common humanity that transcends the limitations of the nation-state international system.

CHARACTERISTICS OF THE POLITICAL ECONOMY APPROACH

The characteristics of the political economy approach to human rights range from the universality and legal basis for rights that are agreed upon in international covenants to the democratic participation and redistribution of basic human needs of people struggling to achieve their rights against a global system of injustice.

1. *Universality* is the recognition that human rights are not the preserve of one part of the world, but rather are the possession of all people regardless of color, class or status, or national origin.[4] They find their expression at points of historical progress, such as the American and Russian revolutions, but they are also defined by the Universal Declaration of Human Rights, adopted by the United Nations, and by the Freedom Charter of movements like the African National Congress.

2. *Solidarity* refers to the rights that groups of disadvantaged people share for equitable integration into the world economy. These claims may be expressed in terms of traditional communality or modern class consciousness[5] and across national boundaries.

3. *Participation* involves not only the protection of individual rights to express opposition and dissent, but also a right of participation and control over the important sources of power in society, including both economic and political decisions.[6]

4. *Redistribution* is based upon "basic human needs," especially for the poor.[7]

5. *Self-Reliance* is a popular form of democracy, which extends representative rule into the national and world economy.[8]

6. *The modern state* is often the primary violator of rights rather than the protector and provider of the means of realization. Therefore, human rights cannot simply be the subject of the law, but the law itself is subject to the judgment of its compliance with the rights of people.[9]

This last characteristic challenges the international legal interpretation that human rights are only what international law or the state provides because the law itself is made by the dominant political forces of the world.[10] These forces frequently violate basic concepts of justice. According to this perspective, structural change is necessary if human rights are to be achieved by peoples everywhere, but especially those in the most repressive and disadvantaged circumstances.

This view would seem to lead to the overthrow of the existing world order. But the political economy approach does not repudiate the international system. It transforms the international legal debate. With the addition of "people's rights" it makes use of the conventional international human rights concepts, together with the addition of "the new human rights."[11]

People's rights are sometimes referred to as the "third-generation" human rights. The idea is not widely accepted in the United States, but some international lawyers use the term to express the difference with "civil and political" and the "economic and social" generations that followed it. These third-generation rights are not meant to replace or even supersede the rights of the first two generations. They simply add another dimension. For example, the right to development is not new, considering the various economic rights that are commonly accepted such as those that specify the second generation's rights as basic human needs. What is new is the idea that certain groups of people in a disadvantaged context, such as those in states below the poverty line, have a special claim on the world community for assistance in achieving their development goals. Thus a generational view leads to the conclusion that with time, a more universal concept of human rights will emerge which will provide for redistributive justice in an unjust and unequal world.

THE PORT HARCOURT PAPERS

Professor Claude Ake in his keynote address to the Port Harcourt Conference was generally skeptical of Africa's new interest in human rights because of the cynical way in which this concept has been used in the past. He argued for democracy within Africa: "The way I see it, we ought to be interested in human rights because it will help us to combat social forces which threaten to send us back to barbarism. Because it will aid our struggle for the social transformation while we need to survive and flourish."[12] Ake's approach to achieving human rights in Africa, which he claims is where the critical issues will be fought out, is through the continuing struggle of people for these rights.[13]

From these Port Harcourt papers two basic perspectives emerged on how to deal with the forces which Ake believes threaten Africa with barbarism. The first is a global distributive justice view, and the second is a neo-Marxist paradigm. Each perspective treats the origins of the problem quite differently. Yet each argues that the world forces of inequality have created conditions of injustice that make it impossible for the average African to achieve significant human rights.

Obed O. Mailafia of the National Institute of Policy and Strategic Studies in Jos, Nigeria, attacks the prevailing realism of Western political science from the standpoint of a Rawlsian demand for a new "distributive justice." He sides with Ali Mazrui in the debate over the New International Economic Order (NIEO) in which Mazrui criticizes Robert Tucker and others who justify the existing inequality of states in terms of order and efficiency. Mailafia represents an eloquent new voice in the search for a new basis for a just world order:

The problems of realism are many. Once a respectable, even fashionable school, it now suffers from certain fundamental problems, both epistemologically and philosophically. . . . Humankind is today confronted with predicaments that by their very nature call for multilateral cooperation and coordinated global planning and management. These, in turn, presuppose a new outlook that is universalist and planetary. It requires no less than international solidarity.[14]

Mailafia then focuses on an alternative paradigm that he believes can provide global justice: "In confronting the crisis of North-South negotiations, we need a normative philosophy that is sufficiently world-encompassing to address the imperatives of global distributive justice."[15]

By this statement Mailafia means the application of the Rawlsian "principle of difference" to states. Applied to the international sphere, John Rawls' theory supposes that international relations can be considered "just" only when the sum total of inequalities of the constituent states are arranged in such a way as to maximize the expectations of the least well off. Thus, Rawls concludes that a great power can be considered just only if it uses its power for "massive resource transfers, monetary and trade reforms, debt cancellation and massive aid, in order to effectuate massive re-distribution of global wealth."[16]

In contrast to this Rawlsian view of the need for structural change is the neo-Marxian critical view of human rights. This perspective has become widely accepted in African social science, with considerable differences of emphasis. The view was presented most clearly at Port Harcourt by a young political scientist, Julius O. Ihonvbere. On the surface, his view appears to reject the whole discussion of human rights for Africa as an attempt to reintroduce Western political values as part of continuing imperialism.

We contend that a proper analysis and understanding of human rights in any society can only be made by looking at the socioeconomic or material foundations of society. Hence, political institutions and processes, the existence of more than one political party, periodic elections, and constitutionally guaranteed rights mean very little because they all depend on the patterns of production and exchange, the relations among and within social classes, and the location of social formations in the international division of labor.[17]

It is a widely held view that no development can occur in Africa until the people in the African states deal with the international economic exploitation. But this is not the familiar argument of the Third World that development must take place first before political liberties can flourish. Ihonvbere, like Ake, maintains that the democratic struggle must be carried out against regimes that do not grant rights easily. Then and only then can underdevelopment be reversed and human rights begin to thrive.

Both of these political economy perspectives argue in Africa the state is primarily the repressive instrument of neocolonial elites who victimize their opponents. Only structural change through democratic movements that transform both the state and the international system can improve human rights conditions. At present, violations are to be protested and rights protected, but the essential task of building a new social order must be accepted.

Considerable attention has been given to the violations generally known as "political killings" by police and the military. The Nigerians themselves led the criticism of military repression in their own country and did not spare the Babangida government itself from these protests. Professor Osita Eze, a distinguished professor of law, and Judge Akinola Aguda of Lagos University are among these critics.[18] Significantly Nigerian intellectuals have not been intimidated or decimated as much as counterpart groups in many other African states. Professor J. D. Etuk, from the University of Cross River State at Uyo, has produced an important set of particulars about the way in which the police and the military should be restrained in Nigeria.[19] In addition, there is general recognition of the unfortunate and extensive experience of other African states with political killings.

At Port Harcourt, however, little belief was expressed that the new African Charter on Human and Peoples' Rights would do much to prevent these violations. In fact, Dr. K. Mathews, from Nsukka, argued that the Organization of African Unity had a miserable record of concern with human rights of this nature, and that some basic changes in political leadership would have to take place before international law and organization could improve the situation.[20] African scholars appear to have little faith in the power of international organizations like the UN Human Rights Commission or even Amnesty International to do much about their present predicament. Instead, it is widely believed in Africa that the only remedy lies in a new movement of workers, peasants, and petite bourgeoisie, including teachers, some lawyers, and businessmen, who will demand democratic reforms and new methods of redistribution.

REFUGEES

Support for a new international organizational effort to protect the rights of refugees was expressed at Port Harcourt. As is well known, Africa's longstanding political conflicts and famine situation have made its refugee problem the worst in the world.

Michael Schultheis of the Jesuit Refugee Services Committee argues that a major international program is needed to combat this problem. First, the refugees must receive protection, and then the world system of injustice that produces the refugee flows must be restructured. Refugees have not always fled their own lands out of a "well-founded fear for their lives," but rather because their right to survive has been endangered. Although international action, along with African state programs, have done much to protect their rights, as Barbara E. Harrell-Bond and Roxanne Dunbar-Ortiz show, they are increasingly vulnerable, as their numbers continue to grow and the sanctuary states become less able to provide for them.[21]

Schultheis estimates that 10 million Africans have been uprooted from their homes in an alarmingly growing pattern. He proposes both greater African state protection and international solidarity, chiefly through the churches and other Nongovernmental Organizations (NGOs). But he warns that this problem should be viewed as a global problem of inequity and injustice:

The methodology employed is to view migrants not simply as individuals and families who move to survive, but as symptomatic of deeper problems in the institutions and structures of the African countries and in the world systems of which they are a part. This chapter proposes and develops the general thesis that migration in Africa today can be understood only in the context of poverty and underdevelopment.[22]

In these terms, the claims of refugees or migrants as deprived groups within the world system clearly concur with the third-generation perspective of African scholars. These scholars have maintained that the needs of refugees cannot be met without peace and without an end to the wars of intervention, the exploitation of economies leading to unemployment, destruction of the environment, and the loss of food production.

APARTHEID

Apartheid is as reprehensible to those who see it as a denial of political rights and racial discrimination by South Africa as it is to those who view it as the personification of international unequal hegemony. The two groups differ, however, in their views of the most effective means of ending such violation. The suggestion that South Africa's white domination of blacks has decreased has been refuted. Professor O. Nnoli of the University of Nigeria at Nsukka, like many of his peers, sees the problem in terms of an international system of exploitation based on Western capitalism. He is not impressed with the so-called change of heart expressed by South African capitalist leaders such as Sir Harry Oppenheimer, who now propose reforms short of majority rule. They see change as coming only through the strengthening of the liberation movements, trade unions, and internal struggles against the power of the white establishment.[23]

The one implementation proposal on which all parties at Port Harcourt agreed was the strengthening of sanctions. Dr. Sanford Wright's proposal of universal compulsory international sanctions was well received. Professor Wright, a black American scholar from Indiana, presented a proposal for comprehensive sanctions that would affect the economy of South Africa by including major items in the embargoes such as oil and technology which U.S. and Commonwealth programs currently excluded. He also pointed out the need to bring all states into the embargoes through the United Nations.[24]

Africans are, of course, skeptical that the enforcement measures instituted will be sufficient to assure the effectiveness of these sanctions. In the past, many Third World and African countries have helped South Africa break embargoes, especially over arms. Nevertheless, responsibility for enforcement is the task of South Africa's primary trading partners, the United States, the United Kingdom, Japan, and Europe. Dr. Haider Khan argues that a sophisticated economics model enables the outside world to accurately assess the impact of sanctions on various communities in South Africa. He concludes that comprehensive sanctions will have the greatest impact on the agricultural and mine operators of the white section of the economy.[25]

Manyonzwa Hamalengwa of the York University Law School at Toronto discussed the problems of implementation from the standpoint of national and international law in the case of Canada. He demonstrated how domestic legislation to implement enforcement had been adopted and how it arose out of citizen action but required primarily a friendly administration.[26] African skepticism about sanctions at Port Harcourt, as elsewhere, arose over the sincerity of Western intentions to use effective economic force. Neither Prime Minister Margaret Thatcher nor former President Ronald Reagan gave any indication that either would lead the world against apartheid. However, the new Bush administration has accepted sanctions as part of a wider and more comprehensive policy.

ASSESSMENT OF PEOPLE'S RIGHTS

First, the African Charter does not, in itself, establish the claim of the third generation's rights. It does, however, provide a clear step in that direction under the rules of international law. This is the first regional charter to go this far.[27] Second, many issues remain to be resolved, and new steps must be taken before the third generation can become clearly established. These are issues of theory as well as implementation.

Several theoretical issues need to be discussed. The major criticism is that the third generation's rights, especially the African formulation, is based on a questionable ground of ethnicity that gives the group priority over the individual. To be sure, much of the earlier justification of this special African cultural viewpoint was enunciated by Keba M'Baye and Franz Fanon. But the more recent political economy approach is more conscious of the economic inequalities of power. The African state is seen not as some kind of Negritude sovereignty in the international arena but as a comprador client of Western interests. While Nyerere's "Ujamaa" (familyhood) has failed in some respects, it is not appropriate to dismiss group rights as an example of African chauvinistic collectivism, or elitist exploitation.

In International Political Economy the dichotomy between individualism and the group is as misleading as the division of the political and economic. The Rawlsian principle of "difference" which Obed Mailafia has demonstrated is applicable to groups and individuals. It has application to states in the world order, as much as to individuals within the social context. If an individual is disadvantaged by his or her membership in a particular group, then the claim of equality arises under human rights. A member of a poor state torn by civil war or a person born black in South Africa or born a woman in Saudi Arabia are examples. Religious minorities such as the Kurds in Iran or the southerners in the Sudan suffer similar

stigma, and the individuals who comprise these groups are victim-
ized as a consequence.

The capacity to realize rights is determined by the groups and
stratification patterns of which the individual is a part. Through
their experience of exploitation and their tradition of collective life,
Africans, as Mark Anikpo demonstrates concerning self-reliance,
have a clearer perception of this reality. Equality of individuals, when
most members of a differentiated group live under daily conditions
of injustice, can only be achieved when "people's rights" are fully
recognized.

NOTES

1. "Report of the Working Group of Governmental Experts on the Right
to Development," Commission on Human Rights, 35th Session, February
1-March 12, 1982, UN E/CN 1489, January 25, 1982.

2. Jack Donnelly, "In Search of the Unicorn: The Jurisprudence and
Politics of the Right to Development," *California Western International Law
Journal* 15, no. 3 (Summer 1988).

3. Valdimir Kartashkin, "The Socialist Countries and Human Rights,"
Karel Vasak and Philip Alston, eds., *The International Dimension of Human
Rights*, vols. 1 & 2 (Westport, Conn.: Greenwood Press, 1982), pp. 631–44.

4. Warren Lee Holleman especially brings out the tendency toward eth-
nocentricism in the concepts of human rights in *The Human Rights Movement* (New York: Praeger, 1987).

5. Hassan Faroq, "Solidarity Rights: Progressive Evolution of International Human Rights Laws," *Human Rights Annual*, Vol. 1 (New York: New
York University Press, 1983), pp. 71–74.

6. Osita C. Eze, *Human Rights in Africa: Some Selected Problems* (Lagos: Nigerian Institute of International Affairs, 1984), pp. 62–63.

7. Henry Shue, *Basic Rights: Subsistence, Affluence and U.S. Foreign
Policy* (Princeton: Princeton University Press, 1980).

8. George W. Shepherd, Jr., "Global Majority Rights: The African Context," *Africa Today* 34, nos. 1 & 2 (1987), p. 16.

9. Richard Falk, *Human Rights and State Sovereignty* (New York:
Holmes and Meier Press, 1981), p. 51.

10. David Forsythe, "Human Rights Is What the Law Says It Is," *Human
Rights and World Politics* (Lincoln: University of Nebraska Press, 1983),
p. 3.

11. "African Charter on Human and Peoples' Rights," Organization of
African Unity, in Vasak and Alston, eds., *The International Dimension of
Human Rights*.

12. Claude Ake, "The African Context of Human Rights," *Africa Today*
34, nos. 1 & 2 (1987), p. 7.

13. Ibid., p. 11.

14. See Chapter 1 of this volume.

15. Ibid.

16. Ibid.

17. See Chapter 3 of this volume.

18. See Chapter 5 of this volume.

19. J. D. Etuk, "Human Rights Issues and Violations: The Nigerian Experience." Unpublished manuscript, Port Harcourt Conference, 1987.

20. K. Mathews, "The OAU and Political Economy of Human Rights in Africa: An Analysis of the African Charter on Human and People's Rights, 1981," *Africa Today* 34, nos. 1 & 2 (1987).

21. Roxanne Dunbar-Ortiz and Barbara E. Harrell-Bond, "Africa Rights Monitor: Who Protects the Human Rights of Refugees," *Africa Today* 34, nos. 1 and 2 (1987).

22. See Chapter 8 of this volume.

23. See Chapter 6 of this volume.

24. Sanford Wright, "Comprehensive International Sanctions Against South Africa: An Evaluation of Costs and Effectiveness," *Africa Today* 33, nos. 2 & 3 (1986).

25. Haider Ali Khan, "Measuring and Analyzing the Economic Effects of Trade Sanctions Against South Africa: A New Approach," *Africa Today* 33, nos. 2 & 3 (1986).

26. Manyonzwa Hamalengwa, unpublished Port Harcourt paper, June 1987.

27. Faroq, "Solidarity Rights."

PART I

THEORY

1

The Right to Global Distributive Justice: An Inquiry into the Problems and Prospects of Creating an Equitable World Order

Obed O. Mailafia

One of the most remarkable developments of our time is the emergence of formerly colonized peoples on the stage of world politics. The peoples of Africa, Asia, and Latin America are asserting themselves with increasing forcefulness and are demanding their right to participate as free and equal members in the councils of the family of nations. They are calling into question the inequitable global political economy that condemns the vast majority of humankind to the state of servitude, starvation, and dehumanization, while the rich play in the carnival of affluence.

Granted that such sentiments underlay the earlier anticolonial struggle, the novelty of today's clamorings is that they take such an insistent and uncompromising tenor, for real independence and autonomous development, for self-reliance and social progress. The demand for a New International Economic Order (NIEO) is a call by the underdeveloped countries of Africa, Asia, and Latin America to redress the centuries of human degradation and economic exploitation under which they have been subjected by the affluent nations of Europe and North America. They have called into question the structure, institutions, and principles that sustain the present world order, which have come to be seen as both unjust and irrational.

It is now more than a decade since the international community, under the aegis of the United Nations General Assembly, embarked on the search for a New International Economic Order. The international media have reported the spate of bilateral and multilateral conferences that have been held on the subject both within and outside the forum of the UN system. Research activities and volumes of publications have also been undertaken on various aspects of the NIEO. But the prospects for a more equitable global order seem farther away than ever before. Indeed, hopes for global reform have been replaced by protectionist policies, political conservatism, and growing cynicism.

It is not surprising, therefore, that the NIEO has been dismissed in some quarters as a dream deferred, a moribund monologue among the deaf, where "Immobility and stalemate have become the norm, tempered by occasional counterfeit arguments to provide some illusions of progress and to keep the game going."[1] Indeed, observers such as George Abbott are right in saying that, today, "very little is now heard of the NIEO."[2]

Underlying the inability to develop a new order of world relations is the fundamental problem of evolving a "common minimum standard" for the pursuit of global equity. What is at issue is how to create, in a world of competing states and conflicting normative claims, what Professor Ali Mazrui has termed a theory of "normative convergence," a "shared framework of social reasoning and social calculation," for a more equitable ordering of international relations.[3]

This consideration takes us inevitably into one of the major moral philosophical debates of our time: the debate about morality and justice in international politics. This debate is traceable to the legal-political writings of the medieval Christian thinkers, notably Hugo Grotius, who was largely relegated to the backwaters of intellectual thinking (excepting, of course, Kant's eighteenth-century reflections), when thinkers such as Hobbes and Machiavelli celebrated the emergence of the sovereign states system as the new constitutional principle of international politics.

The emergence of the NIEO in the contemporary international diplomatic agenda has contributed to the reappearance of this perennial debate. It has spurred fundamental discussions among economists, jurists, political scientists, and philosophers about the place of justice and morality as norms of international relations and especially about the moral obligations of states with respect to distributive justice, and the implications of all these to the abiding question of international order.

In this chapter, therefore, we will attempt to address a set of interrelated questions: Do the poor countries reserve a right, based on international morality, to demand from the rich a just redistribution of the world's resources and power, of which the rich have enjoyed such unequal and unchallenged monopoly for centuries? Indeed, what is the place of moral norms in a competitive, sovereign states system? Can one speak of the moral obligations of states and of the right to distributive justice in international relations? If not, why not? If so, in what does it consist, and how can it be brought about in the present global political economy?

SOME CONSIDERATIONS OF THEORY

The noted German sociologist, Ralf Dahrendorf, has called for an "intellectual pause," a fundamental reassessment and reformulation of our current intellectual categories and sociopolitical values to cope with the unprecedented challenges of our epoch.[4] This reassessment is perhaps even more required in the social sciences today. With specific reference to international relations, we are beset with a profound paradigmatic disarray and an increasing irrelevance to the demands of twentieth-century global society. The absence of a universal theory of international politics, is, at bottom, a philosophical problem. What is at stake is the absence of a philosophical common ground for the understanding of international reality. In the words of E.B.F. Midgley: "The initial and primary problem concerns the recognition of fundamental criteria of truly rational human activity: criteria which, once they have been found, may be applied in the determination of norms for action in the international scene.... The lack of such a philosophy is, indeed, the reason why so many occasional writings on international relations are ultimately trivial or futile."[5]

To decry the absence of a common philosophical framework is to invoke the significance of political theory, at least in its internationalist tradition. At the heart of this preoccupation is the tension between the objective world as it is and the categorical imperative of what it ought to be. Those scholars who see the scientific value of their work only in terms of empirical analysis are quite mistaken: They understand neither the nature of science nor the political meaning of the social sciences. Similarly, those who are preoccupied with idealism are the now-discredited apostles of Utopia. They do not understand "the world outside, a battlefield given over to conflicts of the gods, laid waste by prophets and demagogues, a terrain where one must choose between undemonstrable values."[6] In order to avoid the moral nihilism that is inherent in both approaches, we need a normative framework that helps us understand the objective world and to be more rational with regard to universal imperatives.

ORDER, MORALITY, AND JUSTICE IN INTERNATIONAL POLITICS

Having disposed of these preliminaries, we will proceed to address the models of order in world politics and to see how they relate to concepts of morality and justice in the international system. But first we will discuss three models of world order, namely, the natural law tradition, the model of evolutionary progress, and the model of fragmentation.

The natural law school is perhaps among the oldest conceptions of world order, going back as far as the pre-Socratic Greeks, to Zeno and the Eleatic school of natural philosophy. This model makes a number of propositions about the brotherhood of humankind, universalism traversing political boundaries and a transcendant justice that applies to all people as people, regardless of their origin, status, or race.

The natural law model assumes the existence of two relatively autonomous worlds, one spiritual and the other human. The one is the *Civitas Dei*, the divine realm, in which there is perfect justice and eternal harmony; the other is the *Civitas Terrena*, the human community, which is bound together under natural law and is itself a product of the individual's participation in the divine reason. In its more spiritualized version, this model assumed a political role for the Church as the guardian of the natural law from the ever-recurrent susceptibilities of sinful humans. Even in war, there are supposed to be normative standards that no states or armies may violate. The principle of nationalism and the ethic of the reason of states or political expediency are rejected as the bases of interaction between political communities. This tradition resonates in the numerous human rights declarations of this century, particularly in the Universal Declaration of Human Rights.

Second, there is the model of evolutionary progress. As its name suggests, this model assumes an ultimate progress in the cataclysmic unfoldings of history, an inevitable, albeit slow, march from the irrationalities and inequities of past eras toward a future of greater rationality and justice in the organization of human society. This model is an intellectual byproduct of the European Renaissance and Enlightenment, which Kant celebrated as the emergence of the individual from self-imposed tutelage. Inherent in it is the belief in progress, in rationalism, in the efficacy of human institutions, and in an ultimate harmony of interests among the various competing members of the states system. This model abounds in the works of modernists such as Norman Angell and the contemporary philosophers of international organization.[7]

Immanuel Kant can be singled out as the originator of this essentially optimistic model of international order. In his classic essay on Eternal Peace, Kant saw in human nature the root cause of the tumultuous character of world events.[8] As a solution to his perennial problem, he advocated a *foredus pacificum*, a league for peace, which he believed would guarantee a pacified world community and ensure an unprecedented amity among the nations. Many contemporary writers see in this great German philosopher the forerunner of modern international organization, particularly the defunct League of Nations and the United Nations.

Finally, there is the model of fragmentation. This pessimistic viewpoint is by far the most dominant paradigm in the theory and practice of contemporary international politics. Stanley Hoffmann discerns its earliest origins in Thucydides' historical accounts of the Peloponnesian Wars. In giving the account of these wars, the ancient Greek historian presented a dramatic portrayal of the clash between universal human passions such as honor, fear, interest, and power in the violent interplay between warring principalities.

The root causes of war are said to lie in the "fragmentation" between the domestic and external universes that underlie the foundation of the states system itself. Within the state there is order, authority, and law. Outside it, law is weak, authority and order are virtually nonexistent, and morality is meaningless. Under this condition, power and interest constitute the *ultima ratio* (basic rule) of interstate relations and recourse to self-help is the natural means of survival.[9]

The model of fragmentation has its disciples in the so-called realist or power approach to international thought. Realism stresses power and the reasons of state as the fundamental principles in world political relations, principles that are said to derive from human nature and from the essence of politics as a primary human activity. The realists denounce the optimistic rationalism of the progressive evolutionists as resting on a spurious political theory and dismiss the notion of transcendent goodness or morality in a world in which the statesman, if he is not to surrender to self-delusion or suicide, must scrupulously observe the laws of realpolitik. It is argued that moral claims cannot be made on a fragmented international system without the existence of a superordinate authority and an overarching morality. David Fromkin makes this point based on what he calls "the independence of nations": "there are limits to the freedom of action of independent states, but from the point of view of justice and morality, these limits are irrelevant. They do not correspond to the limitations that domestic societies impose upon their members, because they are not imposed by a superior authority, let alone a superior authority that is morally purposeful."[10]

Rousseau can be regarded in many ways as the philosopher of this basically pessimistic model of world society.[11] For him, civil society rather than human nature (as Kant thought) is the root cause of war. He reasoned that in the state of nature the individual is essentially timid and peaceable, and that only as human beings enter into civil society do they invent war as an instrument of policy. Rousseau concluded that the only possible solution to this problem might be the establishment of a powerful world confederation able to enforce a system of peace among states. However, he himself doubted the political feasibility of such a global institution.

Underlying this viewpoint is a radical despair over the allegedly irredeemable irrationality of the universe and the ill-fatedness of the human condition itself. Not only is there presumed to be no discernible progress in human history, but also the familiar norms of international politics—law, morality, and justice—are considered tenuous, delusive, or irrelevant.

There are two variants of the model of fragmentation, namely, the model of "troubled peace" and the model of the "state of war." In the first, the distinction between the domestic and external universes is said to be only in terms of degree rather than of kind. International politics is regarded not as a system of pure anarchy since it has within it a modicum of order, rules, and norms that regulate interstate relations. Order is weak only because the system is lacking in a centralized machinery to enforce the institutions of order. In the other variant, however, the system of world politics is alleged to be predominantly a system of war. Rules and norms of morality are believed to be a mere mirage, and peace is only a temporary convergence between power and interests, a brief respite from war. It is the system in which the dictum *si vis pacem para bellum* remains a paramount doctrine.

The three models discussed above relate directly to differing conceptions of morality in international politics. The models of natural law and evolutionary progress can be regarded as the idealistic perspective, while the other, fragmentation, can be seen as the realist. One's conception of the place of moral norms in international politics depends on which of these schools of world order one subscribes to.

Realism does not recognize the existence of universal moral norms in interstate relations. Such norms are either said to be fictitious or are assumed to be a mere rationalization of underlying national interests. According to Werner Levi:

History provides at best an inconclusive answer to the question. There is evidence that in the course of time men have attempted to humanize their relations. There is the counter-evidence also that they have treated each other with increasing dishonesty and cruelty. The same civilization which raised the status of the common man has also perfected his destruction. Still, until that destruction takes place, from time to time statesmen appear to find it necessary to justify their international acts in moral terms. The records of international agencies abound in moral appeals and moral justifications of international actions.[12]

Adele Jinadu has argued that realists such as Machiavelli were not altogether denying the important role that accepted canons of morality could and should play in both domestic and international politics. Rather, they saw the issue of morality in terms of the "conscience casuisty problem," that is, in terms of situation ethics: Morality was to be defined in terms of the national interest, and whenever it conflicted with that interest, the moral imperative was to be abandoned. The national interest is thus prior to any universally accepted canons of morality. Jinadu himself has clearly raised the problems that such a position incurs:

First, the assumption that the preservation of the state is an end in itself is questionable. It is quite possible for other ends to be valued and pursued. The problem here is compounded by the fact that it is unclear whether the claim is that the preservation of the state ought to be the end of political action or that it is in fact the end. Secondly, we are not sure how the conflict is to be resolved in situations where the national interest and the personal interest of the ruler conflict. This turns in part on the definition of the national interest—whether there is some objective measure of it that distinguishes from the interest of the rulers or ruling class.[13]

In contrast with the moral pessimism of the realists, the idealist position holds that there exists an international community of states bound together by universal moral precepts. Although not denying the fact of the existence of independent, sovereign states, idealists do not subscribe to the Hobbesian vision of international politics. Rather, they believe that power and interest should be subordinated to the overriding demands for order, peace, and justice.

It was Kant who expounded the idea of an overarching and universal morality and the obligation of states to subject their action to the judgment of that higher morality. Indeed, he lifted morality in interstate relations into a categorical imperative to serve the higher ends of justice, equality, liberty, and international amity. Of this contribution, Professor Gallie has observed:

He [Kant] had made the first significant attempt . . . to construct a framework of ideas within which the generally acknowledged rights and duties of states vis-à-vis their own citizens can be shown to require, logical acknowledgment of certain equally important rights and duties towards each other and each other's citizens if their traditionally recognized tasks are ever to be effectively discharged.[14]

The German philosopher was a believer in the unity of the human race, although he realized fully well the arduous difficulties of building such unity and of guaranteeing an enduring peace among the nations. The idealist position is thus in sharp opposition to the realist. While it recognizes the fact of power and interest as central elements of the sovereign states system, it rejects power calculations and the reasons of state as the *ultima ratio* of interstate relations. Rather, the bonds of our common humanity are posited as the foundation of a universal morality and the basis on which states could work together in the pursuit of their common good.

It should be clear from the foregoing that we are in sympathy with the idealists. This is not to say that, through some kind of existential choice, we have become idealists ourselves. It is simply that, in exploring the kind of ideas we wish to develop in this study, the realists can offer us very little. However, we cannot overlook some of the fundamental and valid points made against the idealist scheme, and how these set the limits on whatever one might imagine to be practicable. The practice of politics is to be properly understood as the art of the possible.

Our exploration of the concept of justice occupies an important place in the history of political philosophy. It dates back to the pre-Socratic philosophers and the Hebrew prophets. As a concept, justice usually relates to the idea of cosmic or natural order and is designated in various terms, *ordo naturalis* (natural order), *lex naturalis* (natural law), *lex aeterna* (eternal law), and so on. Among the ancient Hellenic and Hebraic sages, justice was the ultimate in all human virtues.

Definitions of justice abound. It is not our intention to add to the confusion that already surrounds the concept. For Aristotle as well as Cicero and Augustine, justice relates to "the conservation of organized society, with the faithful discharge of obligations assumed."[15] Within the international sphere, Frederick Bonkovsky sees justice as implying that "the nation, while primarily concerned with its own interests, will give positive attention to the concerns and purposes of others" and will "restrain one's hubris and the pursuit of one's own desires" for the sake of the interests of others.[16]

For centuries, justice, however defined, has been an ideal of most polities, but it has been slow in becoming an ideal of interstate relations. Even Aristotle, in *The Nicomachean Ethics*, maintained that justice was possible only within the polis—that community of free and equal citizens—but not outside it, where reigned the law of anarchy and brute force.[17] This notion is echoed in Hobbes' *Leviathan*, where justice is said to be irrelevant beyond the confines of the state.[18]

By 1945, however, justice began to feature more prominently as a desirable ideal in the system of international politics. As understood in this period, it was seen in the narrow sense of strengthening international institutions and enforcing the international rule of law. That was an understanding of justice in the procedural sense, that is, in the impartial application of the rules and norms between states. Today, however, the concept of justice has shifted from the procedural to the distributive sense, that is, in terms of the achievement of more equitable ends. This idea relates to the redistribution of the world's material resources in accordance with egalitarian norms. However, it does not necessarily exclude the importance of procedural justice in terms of impartial application of the rules and the right to fully and effectively participate in the process of their formulation.

The call for an NIEO by the poor nations can be regarded as demand for distributive justice in the international system. The inequalities in wealth and power between the North and South are seen as a manifestation of injustice. But the poor do not seek only a massive transfer in wealth; they also demand the right to participate effectively in formulating the rules and managing the institutions of the international system. In brief, they are also demanding procedural justice in the structure of world relations.

It remains to say a word about the relationship of justice to international order. Any talk about justice presupposes a stable political order. In other words, no one would dare to complain about injustice in a condition of social breakdown or anarchy. Ian Clark has pointed out the dialectical nature of the conflict between order and justice: "A warless world may not only be a just one, it may in fact prevent the creation of a just one. And conversely, a just world may not only not be a peaceful one, it may in fact prevent the emergence of a peaceful one."[19] F. O. Bonkovsky has also alluded to this dialectic, whereby "perceived injustice is so psychologically and politically unsettling that it prohibits stable rule. On the international level, injustice (sometimes) legitimates severe conflict and war."[20]

Order and justice are therefore not necessarily coequal ideals, since the pursuit of one could upset the existence of the other. This dilemma may be said to be inherent in the nature of politics itself.

Politics as a human activity arises precisely because social order must always be achieved and maintained under the constant threat of disorder, while justice as a human ideal always remains imperfect.

Any claims to global justice should therefore take account of the structure of power in the world system and critically outline the anatomy of order in that system. A rational approach is to opt for a system of justice that will not hinder an enduring peace, a just peace that will neither humiliate the rich nor set the lowly as the new oppressors.

THE DEBATE ABOUT GLOBAL JUSTICE

The point of departure on the contemporary debate about global justice might be taken from the famous intellectual quarrel between Harry Johnson and Richard Cooper on the one hand and Ali Mazrui on the other. During one of the first international seminars on the NIEO, held at the Massachusetts Institute of Technology in the summer of 1976, a rather philosophical argument exploded on the place of morality and justice as norms of international relations. Johnson and Cooper argued that the demand of the Third World for global distributive justice is quite out of place in a fragmented international system and that such ethical imperatives can apply only to individuals and not to such collectivities as nation-states. Cooper maintained that

Much recent discussion on transfer of resources falls uncritically into the practice of anthropomorphizing nations, of treating nations as though they are individuals. . . . This is not legitimate. If ethical arguments are to be used as rationale for transferring resources, either a new set of ethical principles applicable to nations must be developed or a link between resource transfers must be made back to the individuals who are the ultimate subjects of standard ethical reasoning.[21]

Johnson was even more caustic in his polemic. He dismissed the NIEO as a kind of "imperialism in reverse" which the developing countries have come to regard as a matter of right: "from the collection of imperial tributes regarded as a matter of right, to the freedom of the imperial rulers to waste the tribute in lavish and wasteful consumption. . . . The new empires of the poor nations are hoped to be built by political majority in the United Nations and kept by moral blackmail."[22]

Ali Mazrui, the only voice to speak in defense of the Third World position, sharply reacted to these criticisms first by pointing at the collectivist tradition in Western political thought that goes back to

Plato, Rousseau, Bentham, and Marxian ethics. He distinguished between charity, which can be justifiably regarded as a moral demand at the interpersonal level, and economic and social justice, which does exist as a moral imperative between collectivities. Second, he alluded to the historical process underlying the gradual emergence of "a new international moral order," a process that dates back from the Peace of Augsburg (1555) and the Treaty of Westphalia (1648) to the trials of the Nazi war criminals at Nuremberg after the Second World War. He argued that such a normative shift justified the universalist framework of ethical reasoning, and he berated the intellectual opportunism inherent in the Western position: "Those who claim that the workers of Detroit should not be forced (compelled?) to subsidize the ruling elites of Kenya or Zaire, are, unfortunately, the same ones who would be alarmed by the ruling elites of Kenya and Zaire going socialist. Salvador Allende paid with his life not because he was getting too elitist but because he was trying to transcend elitism."[23]

Realism remains the most powerful normative argument against global distributive justice, with perhaps its most sophisticated formulations in writers such as Robert W. Tucker, David Fromkin, and Terry Nardin.

Robert Tucker has marshalled arguments against the NIEO from the viewpoint of the natural inequality of states and the anarchical character of the international states system. He maintains that nations are, as it were, "born unequal" and that the ultimate arbiters in the international system are power and self-help. He refers to the famous statement from the Athenians to the Melians as recorded in Thucydides, that the powerful take what they can and the weak grant what they must. In this context, moral claims to equality and distributive justice are quite meaningless in

a system of inequality par excellence. If there is a limited truth in the contention that the institution of international society—the balance of power, international law, diplomatic practice—served to moderate the extreme consequences of self-help, and thereby to provide a semblance of order, the larger truth is that these institutions functioned on balance to legitimize power and inequalities power created. . . . The only equality this society has known has been a rough and precarious equality of the strong.[24]

Similarly, David Fromkin, has advanced an argument against claims of international morality and justice from the point of view of the sovereign independence of states: "there are limits to the freedom of action of independent states, but from the point of view of justice and morality, these limits are irrelevant. They do not correspond to the limitations that domestic societies impose upon their members, because they are not imposed by a superior authority, let alone a superior authority that is morally purposeful."[25]

Some scholars within this tradition are fundamentally opposed to the principle of distributive justice in itself, with reference both to domestic society and to the international system. Terry Nardin, for example, drawing largely from Michael Oakeshott's philosophy of civil association and echoing Robert Nozick's anarchist principles and August von Hayek's conservative political economy, has argued that if the international system is approached as a form of civil association, the only valid concept of justice is in respect of the rules of the game. It cannot, he insists, apply to the pursuit of substantive ends such as the redistribution of wealth or the welfare of the underprivileged. Questions of substantive ends are alleged to be outside the purview of the philosophy of civil association.[26]

The problems of realism are many. Once a respectable, even fashionable school, it now suffers from certain fundamental problems, both epistemologically and philosophically. Just as the Aristotelian system persisted as an intellectual anachronism even after the cosmological revolution brought by Galileo, realism has persisted in spite of the profound transformations that now characterize the physiognomy of contemporary world politics. Granted that the territorial state is still the primary unit of political interaction, it is today saddled with fundamental and unprecedented crises.[27] The global political economy has become one of complex interdependence, and we now have what is called a "global village." There are powerful transnational corporations capable of wielding independent economic and political power. There are also the demographic explosion, the ecological crisis, the problem of starvation and poverty, and it is no longer considered an exercise in cheap sentimentality to lament the grim prospects of a thermonuclear holocaust. Humankind is today confronted with predicaments that by their very nature call for multilateral cooperation and coordinated global planning and management. These in turn presuppose a new outlook that is universalist and planetary. It requires no less than international solidarity and the unity of the human race. Indeed, one of the most well-known realists of our time, John Herz, has called for a new attitude of universalism, "a minimum ethics of human survival."[28]

It is clear that the philosophy of naked power and self-help is of less relevance to political policy, given the new realities of contemporary international society and the complexity of its problems. The challenge for political science, as indeed for international relations, is to evolve a paradigm that is directly relevant to the needs of today's world. Central to this challenge is the need to overcome what George Modelski has termed "the Aristotelian paradox" in political science, that is, the persistence of realism, in spite of the globalization of world events:

For too long now, political science has been the hand-maiden of the nation-state system. It has made great strides ... in the world of learning but it has not moved much beyond Aristotle and his pre-occupation with the small scale *polis*. Paradoxically, Aristotle's greatest pupil was Alexander the Great, founder of the first universal empire, but one would not know that from reading the politics. The old world of city-states was fast crumbling all around him, yet Aristotle provided no guidance to meet the problems of organizing a new world.[29]

TOWARD A THEORY OF GLOBAL JUSTICE

In confronting the crisis of North-South negotiations, we need a normative philosophy that is sufficiently world-encompassing to address the imperatives of global distributive justice. We need a philosophy that emphasizes global solidarity and the global common good as opposed to one that emphasizes power, self-help, and competition and is supportive of the negative trends toward injustice, self-destruction, and nihilism.

In the search for an alternative vision of international society, the work of E.B.F. Midgley is particularly enlightening. He has contributed considerably in clarifying the relevance of the law of nations tradition in the search for a minimum standard for the pursuit of the world common good, based on reason, morality, and justice. In positing the primacy of the world common good, Midgley made specific reference to the teachings of the medieval jurist, Vittoria, "who taught most explicitly not only that the common good of the state is superior to the private good of an individual but also that the common good of the whole world is superior to the common good of the individual state. He held that this hierarchy of common goods was the true basis on which justice and order in global society could be rightly promoted."[30]

VITTORIA'S HIERARCHY OF GOODS
WORLD
STATE
INDIVIDUAL

While the overall good of the state is prior to that of the individual, the global common good is also prior to that of the individual states that make up the constituent units of world society.

Based on Vittoria's notion of the primacy of the world common good, John Rawls' theory will be explored in relation to the problems of global distributive justice. Rawls' famous book, *A Theory of Justice*, has been widely acclaimed as an important milestone in the revival of classic political philosophy which an earlier epoch had pronounced dead.[31]

Rawls' approach saves us from the essentialist pitfall of trying to define justice. He starts from the vantage point of social contract theory and identifies two fundamental principles which rational or reasonable people would regard as necessary for the distribution of "primary social goods" and for the attainment of "self-respect" by the overwhelming majority:

1. Each person will have a right to the most extensive total system of basic equal liberties compatible with a similar system of liberty for all.

2. Social and economic inequalities are to be arranged so that they are both (a) to the greatest benefit of the least advantaged and (b) attached to positions open to all under conditions of fair equality of opportunity.

The first principle seeks to safeguard the fundamental rights of freedom and political liberty of the citizens. It does not, however, include the right to economic liberties of property, contract, or inheritance, which writers like Milton Friedman, August von Hayek, and Robert Nozick would consider equally important. The first part of the second principle allows for the "difference principle," which does not require an absolute equality in the distribution of wealth and authority. It does, however, demand that all inequalities should be distributed to improve the life chances of the poorest. As to which of the two principles has precedence over the other, Rawls argues that priority should be given to the first, whenever a minimum level of welfare has been attained. For the entire system of inequalities to be regarded as just, it must be so arranged that it maximizes the expectations of the worst off.

While assigning a priority to the principle of freedom, Rawls gives two conditions under which it may be curtailed: First, basic liberties may be restricted whenever necessary to strengthen the total system of liberty; and, second, it may be curtailed in societies that have not yet attained a certain level of material wealth in which these liberties can be effectively exercised. However, there must be a guarantee that the long-term benefits will transform a backward society into one in which civil liberties can be meaningfully exercised.

The nonideal theory is the principle that Rawls posits to solve the problem of anomalies that may arise in nonideal situations. It has to do with the issues of punishment, compensation, and various forms of activities against unjust regimes.

Rawls assumes a "natural duty of justice" on the part of the original contractees: They would agree on the principle of supporting and promoting conditions of justice and of working to create them in conditions that are nonideal. He opts for nonviolent civil disobedience as the method of struggle, particularly in the context of nearly just societies. He favors the use of violence in radically unjust societies but insists that this must be calculated only to achieve certain definite ends and must eschew the use of terror.

Applied to the international sphere, Rawls' theory would suppose that international relations would be considered just only when the sum total of inequalities of the constituent states are arranged in such a way as to maximize the expectations of the least well-off. This assumes that a state may be just in terms of its domestic social organization but may be constitutively unjust if its condition vis-à-vis other states is not arranged in such a way as to optimize the life-chances of the poorest among them. The difference principle would therefore require massive resource transfers, monetary and trade reforms, debt cancellation, and massive aid in order to effect a large-scale redistribution of global wealth.

Under the difference principle, what is at issue is not who or what was historically responsible for the conditions of global inequities and would be responsible for paying indemnity for past wrongs. (The position of the socialist countries has always been that they are absolved of the duty of implementing the demands of the NIEO on the grounds that they did not partake in imperialism and colonial exploitation.) That is quite irrelevant for Rawls. The imperative for redistribution simply arises from the difference principle and is aimed at improving the long-term life-chances of the underprivileged.

With reference to the principle of nonideal action, the inhabitants of the poor nations ought to take certain steps to right the evils of international injustice. They are, first of all, to engage in peaceful dialogue, in the use of nonviolence, in the appeal to the sense of justice of the rich. When these fail, it is permissible to explore alternative courses of action that are likely to yield meaningful results. While the use of violence and even war may be justified if peaceful methods have been exhausted, terror or nuclear blackmail, which "encourage contempt for human life," should not be applied.

Rawls has, of course, been criticized on a number of fronts. One of the most well-known criticisms is that his model is rather too abstract to be applicable to the real world of human affairs. The other is that, in fact, using this same model, it is possible to justify the grossest inequalities in society.[32]

From the tradition of the law of nations we have derived the notion of the primacy of the world common good and from Rawls the imperative for sustained global action under the difference principle.

The ultimate claims for global justice can thus be said to derive from the simple fact of our common humanity, whereas the praxial imperative to struggle for a more equitable international system derives from the stark reality of a situation in which the vast majority seems condemned to a life of destitution while a minority thrives in affluence. "Two worlds now confront each other," Maurice Duverger has reminded us, "one rich, the other poor. While the former sees on the horizon the society of abundance, the latter remains close to the Middle Ages, with its famines, epidemics and human misery."[33]

There are those who will argue that the notion of a social contract cannot be applied to the international system and that the difference principle cannot therefore be applied globally. There are also those who will insist that economic efficiency will be threatened by redistributive schemes. To the first, one can only say that the globalization of world affairs in our time does, in fact, support theoretical reasoning from the viewpoint of a putative international society. There is also the natural law tradition from which the unity of the human race is posited. To the second charge, about the problem of maintaining economic efficiency, one can only say that efficiency itself cannot override human values and cannot therefore be approached in ethically neutral terms. Hitler's war machine, for example, could be regarded as a model of technical efficiency. But it is quite another thing to suppose that it was an efficiency geared to positive human purposes. The point being made is that, under the difference principle, the question of economic efficiency cannot be approached in the abstract. Rather, it must be seen in relation to the irreducible minimum of liberty and the well-being of the least advantaged in society.

CONCLUSIONS

The search for a more equitable global system will be one of the most enduring issues before the international community. We have tried to highlight some of the moral philosophical obstacles militating against the creation of the NIEO. Given the resurgence of neoconservatism as the dominant political ideology in the West in recent times, the odds against the new international order seem even more relentless.

It is pertinent to stress that it is the Western bloc—the vestige and purveyor of the world capitalist system—which poses the greatest obstacle to the emergence of a new order of relations among the nations. We are not, of course, arbitrarily including in this group the radical and enlightened populace in the West—from whom we have received promising signs of solidarity. We have in mind the vested interests who see the struggle for a just and peaceful world as a threat to the so-called ideals of Western civilization. With the advent of regimes such as those of Reaganism, we have witnessed what Senator William Fulbright called "the Arrogance of Power," the glorification of the militarist ethos—facts that can only portend a gathering storm.

The socialist countries, on the other hand, have made loud protestations about their support for the cause of the Third World. Indeed, there is much to be said for the positive role of the Soviet Union, particularly in the anticolonial struggle. However, in the quest for the NIEO, the lofty protestations of the socialist countries have not been borne out by the rather curious anomaly of Soviet trade relations with the noncommunist developing countries, whereby armaments exports far exceed the outflow of other goods— a fact that does no good to the already serious crisis of Third World militarism. One is not, of course, suggesting that the Soviet bloc is alone guilty of arming the Third World. Rather, the socialist countries should strive to bridge the hiatus between rhetoric and reality in their relations with the developing countries and should make good their claim to being their natural allies in the quest for peace, development, and social progress.

As for the developing countries, they have all but lost the diplomatic initiative and fervor of the early 1970s. Indeed, with the passing of time, legitimate doubts have come to be cast about whether Third World leaderships are really serious about their call for fundamental global reforms. In particular, they have not been able to preserve their diplomatic cohesiveness and single-minded devotion to a common purpose. This is manifested in the crisis that has bedevilled the Organization of Petroleum Exporting Countries (OPEC) as well as in the protracted immobility of regional organizations such as the Organization of African Unity (OAU) and the Arab League.

The problem of Third World disunity reflects real diversities and conflicting interests among these countries themselves: between the newly industrialized and desperately poor; between oil producers and nonoil producers; between "Third" and "Fourth" worlds. With a rather fragile basis for unity, the developing countries have been unable to sustain their collective bargaining strength, to formulate a common set of goals, to agree on priorities, to coordinate their policies, and to map out a common program of action.

This problem has been exacerbated by the Western diplomatic offensive. It has been part of Western global strategy to weaken or even destroy the basis of Third World cohesion. An example of this was the so-called Kissinger Plan, by which the West intended to weaken the solidarity among the developing countries by infiltrating organizations such as the OAU, destabilizing the collective power of OPEC, and coopting such regional powers as Mexico, Saudi Arabia, Brazil, and Nigeria.

Part of the problem rests, of course, in the rather amorphous character of the NIEO provisions. It is quite clear, at least, that what the Third World political elites are challenging is not the worldwide system of dependence it has engendered. Far from seeking what has been termed in some circles "an exit visa," the advocates of the NIEO seek greater participation and more integration into the world politico-economic system. Samir Amin has raised this issue with perhaps a tinge of hyperbole:

NIEO is then a programme perfectly in conformity with all the sacrosanct principles defended by the wisdom of the liberal West. It is a programme which places higher than ever the objective of intensified links of world economic interdependence and which aims at basing it on comparative advantage—a programme which ought to have been devised and proposed by the economics professors of the most conservative academies rather than the governments (of the Third World). It is the irony of history that this initiative came from the "nationalist" Third World and that it was unanimously rejected by the apostles of the principles on which it was based.[34]

Even granting the reformist spirit of the NIEO, we are yet to see decisive and concrete action by Third World leaders in terms of structural reform of the domestic national orders as the corollary of international reform. Except for a few who have taken genuine steps toward self-reliance, social justice, and autonomous development, most of these countries are hardly more than neocolonial outposts of international capitalism. Rarely does one come across leaderships that are not reactionary defenders of unjust social orders—which constitute the linkages in the unjust international order.

So, where do we go from here? One thing is clear: conferences rarely settle the fate of nations. It cannot be expected, therefore, that mere conference diplomacy, no matter how intensive or lofty the goodwill of the actors, would bring about an NIEO. The rich in particular will not give up their privileges simply on the basis of moral appeals to their sense of charity. To quote the noted Nigerian economist, Onyekaba Nwankwo: "the developing countries must realize that the diplomacy of international development is not an exercise in charity; it is not a game of wits or reason; it is rather a game of power. And they must realize that nowhere in history is power surrendered freely. Power is acquired or lost by sheer force of subjugation."[35]

It may well be that, with time, the NIEO will simply disappear from the international agenda, with all its rhetoric and summitry approach. There are indeed contemporary trends that are supportive of such a pessimistic assessment: There is the new wave of conservative regimes in Western countries; the continuation of the arms race despite arms limitations talks; a self-preoccupation of the superpowers with issues of national security as opposed to those of international justice and world development; and there is also the increasing tension between the underdeveloped countries themselves—despite the settlement in the Gulf War between Iran and Iraq. On the other hand, the liberation struggle in southern Africa has begun to achieve some successes with the easing of cold war tensions.

It is at this point that the need for a new paradigm in academic international relations becomes such a pressing epistemological imperative. On our part, we have attempted to explore the relevance of the intellectual tradition known as the law of nations and the notion of human society as a social contract. With specific reference to Vittoria, we have seen how the world common good takes precedence over the private good of the individual nation-state, a principle that sets limits to hard-headed realpolitik and the reasons of state as the basic operative principles of international politics.

Applied to the context of present North-South economic negotiations, this notion of the primacy of the world common good implies that the negotiators will give ultimate priority to the world interest in seeking a rational and equitable approach to global reform and global economic management. This, in turn, implies a de-emphasis on the exclusive doctrine of the national interest, and in its place, the evolution of a comprehensive and well-coordinated international public policy.

This doctrine of the primacy of the world common good is palpably in conflict with the widely held assumptions about the sanctity of the sovereign state, a principle that is most cherished by advocates of the NIEO. Far from seeking an erosion of their hard-won sovereign nationhood, the leaders of the Third World want to guarantee permanent sovereignty over the natural resources within their jurisdiction and to ensure effective control over their own sovereign nationhood. Indeed, this principle is well enshrined in the Charter of Economic Rights and Duties of States and is implied in the legal right of states to nationalize foreign enterprises whose activities run at cross-purposes with the national interest.

It may therefore well be that the task of global reform will require a redefinition of national sovereignty in such a way as not to compromise the priority of the world common good. In this regard, international jurists can play an important role in enunciating principles of a new international law.

From the social contract model of Rawls we also derive an international minimum standard for the pursuit of global equity. The categorical imperative is derived from Rawls' difference principle. Under this principle, the developing countries will formulate their demands based on the moral imperative that existing global inequities do not maximize the chances of the least well off. What is at stake is not absolute equality among nations. Such a demand in any case would have amounted to an absurdity, since certain natural factors—including population, size, geography, and availability of resources—set limits to the principle of the equality of states. Rather, what would be sought is a Pareto-optimal allocation of global resources so as to ensure a basic minimum of welfare for the most marginalized groups in the international system.

Under Rawls' "nonideal" principle, there is an imperative to enter more decisively into the struggle for international justice, which also happens to be the cause of the Third World. Such an imperative may in fact entail the abandonment of the NIEO and its substitution with concerted efforts by Third World leaders in exacting maximum concessions from an unjust world system. This, of course, presupposes that the leaderships are themselves committed to radical reform within the domestic order. Ultimately, the initiative will have to come from the people of the Third World themselves, in alliance with the enlightened populations in the developed countries.

On the international front, enlightened leadership would explore further the basis for Third World unity and cohesion so as to strengthen their diplomatic leverage in the global negotiations. To achieve this end, they will have to strengthen such international institutions as OPEC, the Non-Aligned Movement, and other regional organizations aimed at collective self-reliance.

The suggestion for the establishment of a Third World Secretariat is especially worthy of serious consideration. Such an institution will considerably enhance Third World bargaining power and will reduce some of the handicaps that the developing countries face in negotiating under the auspices of the UN system—a system that has been much criticized for its infiltration and domination by Western-oriented personnel and Western-oriented values. Such a Secretariat should be manned only by citizens of the Third World and should serve as a forum for coordinating their policies and for presenting a common intellectual and diplomatic front in the North-South negotiations.

The creation of a Third World Secretariat should be pursued as part and parcel of the quest for a more viable system of international organization as espoused by the NIEO. Third World states should press harder for a fundamental restructuring of the United Nations system so as to serve the interests of the poor and weak states.

The rich countries will, of course, resist most of these measures, sometimes even resorting to the use of force to maintain the status quo ante. It will be remembered that at the height of the oil crisis in 1973, prominent figures such as Henry Kissinger, then American secretary of state, and Robert W. Tucker, a political scientist at the Johns Hopkins School of Advanced International Studies in Washington, had openly mooted the possibility of forcibly taking over the Gulf oilfields and entrusting their governance to the hands of an "international" agency so as to guarantee Western supplies of petroleum.

The struggle will therefore have to be seen for what it is: a revolutionary struggle. As such, revolutionary violence may not be ruled out. However, as Rawls would caution, such violence should be proportionate to clearly perceived gains. It should not negate just principles, and above all, it must be wary of the use of terror or nuclear blackmail, which would only amount to contempt for human life and a denial of human dignity and liberty.

In conclusion, it must be stressed that the struggle for global justice will be a long and hard one. It will certainly not be won on a platter of gold; it may not exclude acts of international civil disobedience, even revolutionary violence. In conformity with the non-ideal principle, the developing countries can legitimately engage in international civil disobedience. This may take the form of unilateral disengagement from international institutions such as the World Bank and the International Monetary Fund (IMF) whose roles in the Third World are at best questionable ones. Countries gasping under the weight of massive foreign debts may also take measures toward declaring a unilateral moratorium on these debts. The protest demonstrations against external debts by citizens of some Latin American countries in the recent past are a welcome gesture in this regard, as is the courageous decision taken by leaders such as Dr. Alan Garcia of Colombia, by which they would devote no more than 10 percent of their foreign earnings to debt-servicing.

The words of the great German sociologist Max Weber, addressed
to a different generation and in a different context, may not be com-
forting but they are relevant and timely:

Ahead of us is not the bloom of summer, but first a polar night of icy
darkness and hardship, whichever group may win the battle of the day. For
where there is nothing, not only the emperor but the proletarian too has
lost his chance. Once this night slowly begins to recede, who then is going
to be alive of those whose scent has now apparently blossomed in such
abundance? And what will have become of all of you within yourselves?
Embitterment or barbarism, simple dumb acceptance of the world and
man's place in it.[36]

It is thus evident that the times ahead will not be times of cele-
bration. They will be times of struggle, when those sections of humanity that have hitherto borne the burden of the centuries assert
their right to become masters of their own historical destiny. A major
part of the challenge of the new international order will require a
shift in political sensibilities toward an awareness of the world common good. As early as 1949, the British historian, Sir Alfred Zim-
mern, echoed the same point when he called for a new "global public
spirit" as the basis for an international civic community. The late
Hedley Bull, Montague Burton Professor of International Relations
at Oxford, also spoke in terms of the emergence of a universal and
all-embracing "cosmopolitan culture":

The future of international society is likely to be determined, among other
things, by the preservation and extension of cosmopolitan culture, embrac-
ing both common ideas and common values, and rooted in societies in general as well as in their elites, that can provide the world international society
of today with the kind of underpinning enjoyed by geographically smaller and
culturally more homogeneous international societies of the past.[37]

At the widest level, this sense of cosmopolitan identification might
be said to be inchoate in the contemporary universalization of human affairs; in the belief in progress; in secularization and modernity; in scientific and technological advancement; in economic
interdependence; and in the universal aspiration toward development and social upliftment.
    Part of the challenge of the new international order is to encourage
this sense of universality among the world's peoples. This is a critical
role for enlightened statesmanship, for cultural action, and for political education in our time, so that, to quote the late French political
thinker Raymond Aron: "The nations will gradually surmount their
prejudices and their egoism, fanatics will cease to incarnate their

dreams of the absolute in political ideologies, and science will give humanity, grown conscious of itself, the possibility of administering the available resources rationally, in relation to the needs of the many."[38]

NOTES

1. R. L. Rothstein, "The North-South Dialogue: The Political Economy of Immobility," *Journal of International Affairs*, 34, no. 1 (Spring/Summer 1980), pp. 1–17.

2. G. C. Abbott, "Rhetoric and Reality," *International Journal*, 34, no. 1 (Winter 1978–1979), pp. 1–15.

3. A. A. Mazrui, "World Culture and the Search for Human Consensus," in S. H. Mendlevitz, ed., *On the Creation of a Just World Order* (New York: Free Press, 1975), pp. 1–37.

4. R. Dahrendorf, in an interview with the journalist Altaf Gauhar, *Third World Quarterly* 11, no. 1 (January 1980), pp. 1–13.

5. E.B.F. Midgley, *The Natural Law Tradition and the Theory of International Relations* (London, 1975), p. xvii.

6. S. Hoffman, "Theory and International Relations," in J. N. Rosenau, ed., *International Politics and Foreign Policy* (New York: Free Press, 1969), pp. 30–39.

7. Cited in E. H. Carr, *The Twenty Years Crisis* (New York: Harper and Row, 1964).

8. For an interesting discussion of the Kantian position, see A. L. Jinadu, *Human Rights and U.S. African Policy Under President Carter* (Lagos: NIIA, 1980), pp. 4–6.

9. S. Hoffman, *Primacy of World Order: American Foreign Policy Since the Cold War* (New York: McGraw-Hill, 1979), p. 107.

10. D. Fromkin, *The Independence of Nations* (New York: Praeger, 1981).

11. One writer had contended that the whole of international relations could be conceived of as a debate between Rousseau and Kant. See I. Clark, *Reform and Resistance in the International Order* (Cambridge: Cambridge University, 1980.

12. W. Levi, "The Relative Irrelevance of Moral Norms in International Politics," in Rosenau, ed., *International Politics and Foreign Policy*.

13. Jinadu, *Human Rights*.

14. Ibid.

15. F. O. Bonkovsky, *International Norms and National Policy* (Grand Rapids, Mich.: Eerdmans, 1980).

16. Ibid.

17. For a discussion of Aristotle's position, see G. Modelski, *Principles of World Politics* (New York: Free Press, 1972), pp. 314–55.

18. Ibid.

19. Clark, *Reform and Resistance*.

20. Bonkovsky, *International Norms*.

21. See J. N. Bhagwati, ed., *The New International Economic Order: The North-South Debate* (Cambridge, Mass.: MIT Press, 1977), p. 355.

22. Ibid., p. 360.

23. Ibid., p. 374.

24. R. W. Tucker, *The Inequality of Nations* (London: Robertson, 1977), p. 15.

25. Fromkin, *The Independence of Nations*, p. 19.

26. T. Nardin, "Distributive Justice and the Criticism of International Law," *Political Studies* 29, no. 2 (September 1981), pp. 232–44.

27. An entire journal volume has been devoted to the review of the current crisis of realism. See *International Studies Quarterly* 25, no. 2 (June 1981), pp. 182–97.

28. J. H. Herz, "Political Realism Revisited," *International Studies Quarterly* 25, no. 2 (June 1981), pp. 182–97.

29. Modelski, *Principles of World Politics*, p. 358.

30. Midgley, *The Natural Law Tradition*, p. 242.

31. J. Rawls, *A Theory of Justice* (Cambridge, Mass.: Harvard University Press, 1971).

32. See, for example, R. Amdur, "Rawls' Theory of Justice: Domestic and International Perspectives," *World Politics* 29, no. 3 (April 1977), pp. 438–61.

33. Maurice Duverger, *Modern Democracies: Economic Power versus Political Participation* (Hinsdale, Ill.: Dryden Press, 1974).

34. S. Amin, *Unequal Development* (London: Harvester, 1976).

35. G. O. Nwankwo, *The New International Economic and World Monetary System* (Lagos: NIIA, 1976).

36. Quoted in R. Dahrendorf, *The New Liberty: The BBC Reith Lectures* (London, 1975).

37. Hedley Bull, *The Anarchical Society* (London: Oxford University Press, 1980).

38. Raymond Aron, *Peace and War* (New York: Free Press, 1962).

2

African People's Rights: The Third Generation in a Global Perspective

George W. Shepherd, Jr.

Human rights are first conceived in the hearts and minds of people. Only later are they recognized in political-economic covenants. They then promote the fulfillment of the physical, intellectual, and spiritual nature of humanity, which change and evolve in history. One major recent historical change has been the decolonization of Africa. Out of this change has come the realization of a new dimension or generation of human rights called people's rights.[1] The recognition and implementation of these third-generation rights are crucial to the advancement of human rights in Africa.

PEOPLE'S RIGHTS

The struggle for self-determination and liberation of the African people has been a long one. From the outbreak of the decolonization and liberation struggle in the early part of this century, and the formation of the United Nations after World War II, to the intervention of numerous transnational nongovernmental organizations to assist in this major movement for freedom of Third World people in the latter part of the twentieth century, the issue has risen.

The recognition of global rights today has emerged from the earlier movements of the seventeenth and eighteenth centuries which established individual rights and state constitutions to protect civil and political liberties. Later, in the nineteenth century, collective rights to life-enhancing social and economic conditions became recognized.

These earlier rights were largely the product of the nation-state system in which the state was seen first as protector of rights and then later as *provider* of economic and social opportunity. People's human rights are the result of the recognition of the Third World in the global system in which the nation-state is either too weak or too much the instrument of the ruling class to protect or provide the conditions for achievement of first- or second-generation rights.[2] Therefore, these people's rights are the claims of the world's poor and deprived majority against the injustice of the global power system and their own tributary states.

These are not simply abstract rights because they are the basis of major liberation movements. They are increasingly being recognized in international declarations and covenants,[3] and reluctantly recognized by policies of powerful states themselves, which attempt to coopt the revolutionary force which this movement represents.

Solidarity unites the periphery with the poor and minorities of the center powers in the struggle to obtain the rights of self-determination, representation, and equality. It is therefore a transnational rights movement. Racial equality and fraternity are closely linked. State boundaries of geography and ethnicity are secondary to the bonds of humanity. Franz Fanon has given classic Third World expression to these ideas of the inevitable struggle of the poor to decolonize:

Decolonization . . . transforms spectators crushed with their inessentiality into privileged actors, with the grandiose glare of history's floodlights upon them. It brings a national rhythm into existence. . . . Decolonization is the veritable creation of new men . . . the thing which has been colonized becomes man during the same process by which it frees itself.

. . . the last shall be first and the first, last. Decolonization is the putting into practice of this sentence.[4]

Liberation theologians such as Gustave Gutierrez have also given a revolutionary expression to this movement against the unjust world:

It is becoming evident that Latin Americans will not emerge from their present status except by means of a profound transformation, a social revolution, which will radically and qualitatively change the conditions in which they now live. The oppressed sectors within each country are becoming aware—slowly, it is true—of their class interests and of the painful road which must be followed to accomplish the break-up of the status quo. Even more slowly, they are becoming aware of all that the building of a new society implies.[5]

In Africa, Colin Morris aptly termed the dominant system to be "the unyoung, the unpoor, and the uncolored":

... the unpoor have settled down to a long siege, grimly determined to hang on to what they've got to the last drop of blood of the mugs they pay to do their fighting for them. Heart-rending propaganda will not shame them out of their near-monopoly of this world's goods. Governments don't feel shame, and it is government by the rich for the rich that guards the gap between the Haves and the Have-nots against shrinkage during our lifetime or anyone else's short of bloody revolution.[6]

From another standpoint, Walter Rodney has clearly laid out the basis of solidarity rights against the continuing system of neocolonialism and underdevelopment which has deteriorated values and standards of life throughout the Third World. He represents a school of dependence scholarship which includes Gunder Frank, Samir Amin, and Claude Ake, who have documented in various ways the process of unequal trade, capital accumulation, and peasant and working-class marginalization that has characterized the deterioration of the conditions of life of the majority of poor, colored, and landless of this world.[7]

THE UNDERDEVELOPMENT OF AFRICA

The solidarity rights movement is the unity of the poor and exploited of the world against the injustice of the rich. It is the phenomenon Marx predicted would take place in industrial Europe but has emerged in the peasant-based mercantile feudal economies of the Third World, where capitalism has failed to become the dominant mode of production. The struggle is a transnational popular one which is not racial but multiracial and involves not one class but several, with representatives of peasants, workers, the petty bourgeoisie, and the middle classes. However, within each state, the class struggle is beginning, as Gutierrez observed, as part of the global solidarity struggle, against the comprador class which sides with privilege. According to Amilcar Cabral, this progressive coalition was the basis for the liberation movements of Africa.[8]

Thus, the African economic crisis has brought out the claim of people faced with famine and declining living standards to a more equitable share of the world's productive system. Adebayo Adedeji and Timothy Shaw have described this African economic decline:

The African economy particularly since 1980 has been characterized by a persistent fall in the overall output of goods and services. The crisis has had its most devastating impact on the directly productive sectors. The fall in the outputs of food and agriculture and of mining and manufacturing sectors has been the most spectacular manifestation of the crisis.[9]

The crisis is used here in a particular way to describe the breakdown in the equilibrium provided by the colonial and postcolonial state as a prelude to the formation of new relations with the world system. The African crisis and that of the Third World are thus seen as part of the world crisis as best described by Gunder Frank in respect to Latin America and as used by Nzongola-Ntalaja and Ilunga Kabondo in their work on Zaire. They consider the crisis in Gramscian terms as a "fundamental breakdown in the equilibrium of social structures whose peak is reached in an impasse: as the group holding this structure together is falling apart, no other political force is viable enough to take it over."[10]

The cause of this breakdown lies in the conflicts of the world system between the center and the periphery and within the periphery itself between the comprador rulers of the tributary states and the assertive national bourgeoisie and the working classes. Because these new self-reliance forces are not yet strong enough to provide a realistic alternative and are constantly being undercut by the dominant interests of world powers, the state in Africa has become predatory and repressive, serving the interests of the dominant and external powers rather than providing development and human rights. This particular social formation I have recently labeled the "tributary state" in my work, *The Trampled Grass: Tributary States and Self-Reliance in the Indian Ocean Zone of Peace.*[11]

Our tendency to view human rights within the context of a successful struggle for self-determination and the establishment of new state constitutions is a reflection of Western modernization political science. In Africa, as elsewhere, the self-determination movements have been largely coopted by the comprador groups which have failed to establish viable independent states. For that reason, the issue of how a new equilibrium can be found for the majority of Africans is far from settled. It is within this context that the subject of human rights in Africa needs to be examined.

At the outset, we need to carefully define this conflict and identify the principal contenders. The struggle is over which human rights will be recognized, if any. In the tributary state, there is a nominal constitutional provision for human rights generally, based on Western and, to a lesser degree, socialist state concepts.[12] But the capacity to implement these rights is very low as Osita Eze observes, and this limitation contributes to the crisis. The state is not autonomous, and those who control the political economy use its power to enforce their interests against the demands of the majority for wider recognition of political and economic rights.

Therefore, in the context of the African crisis, the struggle for human rights is still primarily one of self-determination for control of the state and the economy by a representative majority of the people. In one sense, this is not very different from the period of the American, French, and Russian revolutions (1776–1917).

The struggle for decolonization resulted in a number of independent "sovereignties"; but as the recent political economy analysis has demonstrated, the transfer of power was largely a chimera as hegemonic blocs have created tributary states, dependent on superpowers and their international interests. The effect of international corporate and financial intervention as well as security systems has created a neocolonial system that has deprived former colonial people of any real benefits of self-rule. The internal class conflict of African society has added to the control of the state by a comprador bureaucratic, military, and business class. The repressive rule of this class, in different guises, has become the central human rights crisis from the Cape to Cairo.

This widespread repression has given rise to a new liberation movement which perceives the struggle in its total terms. South Africa's enormous reaction and devastating counterrevolutionary tactics, supported by Western interests, has led the repression of movements for liberation—notably Southwest African Peoples Organization (SWAPO), the African National Congress (ANC), Front for the Liberation of Mozambique (FRELIMO), and Popular Movement for the Liberation of Angola (MPLA). These movements, which represent recognized self-determination claims, established solidarity in the world centers of power with the human rights movement.

Self-determination, in its contemporary form in Africa, has therefore become the right of the poor and repressed majority to participation in and control of their resources and the environment. This is the people's right to the development of their economy for the enhancement of basic life requirements. In the debates during the past decade at the United Nations, these are called "solidarity rights," and in Africa they have been called "people's rights."

The process of recognition of human rights under international law has been called the accumulation of statist rights.[13] It is the result of new conditions that have given rise to international declarations and conventions and treaties.[14] Each of the three generations of human rights has contributed to this process. This accumulation of international law and practice has already begun for majority human rights in Africa.[15]

The Swedish jurist, Peter Nobel, in discussing the Banjul Charter of the Organization of African Unity (OAU), observed that the African Charter on Human and Peoples' Rights has explicitly listed the people's rights:

The catalogue of these "all people's" rights includes the equality of all peoples and the principles of nondomination, the right to free themselves from colonial or other oppression, the right to dispose of their wealth and natural resources which right shall be exercised in the exclusive interest of the people, the right to economic, social and economic development, the right to national and international peace and security and the right to a satisfactory environment.[16]

There is a dispute among human rights specialists over whether these majority claims have any basis in theory or any standing in law. The denial of their existence is rooted in a Western positivist view of law and hegemonic power interests.[17] The new claims regarding human rights have emerged out of a nonaligned perspective in international law as argued by Professor Vojin Dimitrijevic of Yugoslavia:

There is a moment when a right passes from the moral to the legal stage, from the realm of "natural law" to the realm of positive law. A right emerges in its embryonic form as a political claim, which is then strengthened by being presented as something self-evident, inherent in human nature, just or ordained by some superior authority or order of things. Even when expressed in legal language and accepted by some legislative or quasi-legislative body it is initially contained in acts of declaratory or pragmatic nature, some rights retain such nature in constitutions. In the United Nations, there has been a rule that a right has to pass the stage of declaration before it is included in the convention.[18]

This is the process that these majority rights have undergone in order to find acceptance and be initiated in Africa in specific legal form. The next question we will consider is, how have these rights been implemented within African states, between them, and in the international system?

THE VIOLATION OF PEOPLE'S RIGHTS IN SOUTHERN AFRICA

Claude Ake, Samir Amin, and numerous other African writers contend that the right to choose one's own national form of production has been violated by the international capitalist system. International capitalism has, in general, not developed greater equality for most people; rather, it has encouraged the reverse—underdevelopment.[19] The dominant interventionary forces of finance, technology, and capital have imposed external controls over the mode of production. The impact varies from country to country, but the consequences have been devastating to the economic self-determination of African states. Ann Seidman's studies of South Africa demonstrate the importance of multinational corporations (MNCs);[20] Samir Amin emphasizes capital accumulation in West Africa;[21] and others have analyzed the role of international financial agencies.[22]

Not the least important objective of the international system in South Africa is the security and preservation of Western interests in Southern Africa, with the help of South African hegemony. This objective has provided the rationale for continuing financial and economic ties with a system of apartheid which so obviously denies the self-determination of its citizens. In fact, the whole debate over the role of American and Western corporations in South Africa has revealed the way in which major economic investment can be rationalized at the expense of the majority of the inhabitants and the continuation of a system of racial discrimination.[23] Perhaps the Sullivan companies have honestly believed that they contributed to development, jobs, and welfare for all races in South Africa and even to the reform of apartheid. But the outcome of the period of rapid industrial growth (1960–1980) has been underdevelopment for Africans and political instability for all. Over one hundred of these same investors have now withdrawn from South Africa. Reports of widespread unemployment and poverty in that country are not proof of development or change but rather constitute evidence of deteriorating standards.[24]

In a new South Africa ruled by the majority of its inhabitants perhaps the dominant mode will be a mixed economy under the African National Congress (ANC). The Freedom Charter, adopted by the ANC in 1955, states: "The people shall share in the country's wealth," and "The land shall be shared among those who work it."[25] The ANC and other opponents of the present regime insist that there will be much wider public control and access to the land and other resources of South Africa. The Freedom Charter shows that they will adopt a gradualist socialist mode as in the case of Zimbabwe. Within this context for change in South Africa, we can expect an acceptance of economic rights for all workers and a floor of welfare for all citizens.

REPRESSION OF MINORITY GROUP RIGHTS

Minority groups within African states are frequently the victims of global power structures, based on neocolonial interests and comprador ruling classes. The domination of the Matajiri in Kenya, the Arabs in the Sudan, and the political power exercised by northerners in Nigeria are a product of the continuation of the ethnic-class system established under colonial rule. Little has changed with independence.[26] Within this colonial system was a dominant mode of production that benefited traditional elites and external capital. The shift from the settlers in Kenya to the black bourgeoisie did not alter this dependence. The support of the Western security system first for Kenyatta and then for President Moi reinforced the capacity of the tributary state to control the opposition.[27]

Lately, considerable attention has been given to the denial of individual liberties to opponents of the Moi regime in Kenya.[28] In a state structured to maintain privilege, this is inevitable. Too frequently, political genocide has been the case in Africa. Too often whole groups of people are alleged to be the source of disloyalty, intellectuals are condemned, and university students, dispersed. Indians or other expatriates have been expelled, and political arrests and killings have been directed at certain tribal groups. In Uganda since the 1970s, hundreds of thousands of citizens have been slaughtered, and there are estimates that in a total population of 15 million, close to a million people have died as a result of regime repression. In the Lowero Triangle, north of Kampala, one of the greatest mass killings took place under the Obote regime.[29] Both civilian and military regimes have committed these crimes against the people. Similar reports have come out of Zaire, the Central African Republic, Guinea, and Ethiopia.[30] The rights of religious, ethnic, gender, and class groups first to participate equally and then to be protected in their differences of opinion have become a chronic human rights problem for Africa. They are identified by the bonds of kinship or religion. Respect for and protection of these differences is a human right that has been written into international covenants and the OAU Regional Charter, the African Charter of Human and Peoples' Rights.

Under the repression of the tributary state, this tolerance has been ignored and destroyed. Communal strife has grown, along with fear of the state. Both the Sudan and Nigeria have experienced different forms of civil strife as communal fears and hatreds have erupted. In the Sudan, it has become a chronic civil war, while Nigeria has contained but not solved the violence.

In all probability, this situation will not improve simply by a change of leadership, unless that change is accompanied by structural changes that produce new social formations. How far and fast that should proceed is difficult to judge, but various analysts of human rights in Africa have suggested a change away from the new colonialist relationship mode to a socialist model that incorporates greater democratic participation in and control of the political economy. As Professor Osita Eze stated:

The net effect of neo-colonialism is that in spite of formal independence, the ruling classes at the national level are not free agents. It would thus seem that in order to achieve the objective of national liberation, the neo-classical structures must be dismantled, and this can best be done by a class—peasants and workers—who, under a socialist government, provide the most effective challenge to imperialism.[31]

THE NATIONAL QUESTION

Two other states with outstanding problems of group denial of rights are Ethiopia and the Sudan on the Horn of Africa. Several countries have major minority problems that have arisen from their failure to recognize the legitimate claims of large numbers of people to some form of either real autonomy or separation. Self-determination implies the right to establish a separate self-governing political unit under a federal or confederal form of government. Decentralization of power leads to greater confidence in state authority. In several cases, this recognition of group autonomy has worked well. The best example is the position of Zanzibar within Tanzania.[32] The Berbers of Algeria have fared less well, and the Watutsi of Burundi have established a peace of the grave with the Bahutu. There are certain conditions under which a group's right to self-determination extends to secession. Ironically, this has been generally denied in Africa where decolonization and separation have led to the greatest acceptance of this right in the history of the world. The two most chronic cases are the Sahrawi in North Africa and the Eritreans on the Horn. The earlier colonial history of both peoples provides ample justification for nationhood, according to the criteria established under the United Nations in the self-governing debates. In both cases the conflicts have grown into international issues, and their resolution can be achieved only with the application of full self-determination.[33]

The national question can be dealt with properly only when the rights of indigenous and former colonial peoples are treated on their own merits rather than as part of an external power's interest in a region. The case of Ethiopia was determined first by U.S. intervention and later by that of the USSR. The human rights dimension of this problem has grown enormously, with millions of refugees fleeing flagrant violations. This political ethnocide can no longer be ignored by either the superpowers or the African states.

From its inception as an independent state, the Sudan has been plagued by the southern question. Despite repeated attempts to deal with it from the formation of the southern legislative seats to the Southern Council after the Addis Ababa agreement, the problem has remained unresolved. In the later stages of his rule, Jaafel el Nimeri greatly aggravated the situation by applying the Sharia Law to the South. The widespread revolt led by Colonel John Garang has reached a point that clearly demonstrates internal grievances. The legitimacy of many of these southern claims to a control over their own resources, nondiscrimination in education, and participation in production must be recognized. Only a major change in the attitudes of the dominant Arabs can assure a solution. Many Muslim leaders have protested the imposition of Sharia Law; its reapplication by Sudan under another form cannot be termed progress. As Professor Mohammed O. Beshir and his colleagues in the Sudanese Organization of Human Rights have proposed, a federal system with real autonomy for the southern provinces is the only way to avoid a new secessionist movement by the southerners.[34]

There is considerable danger that these minority group issues may become far more numerous, not only because of the growing violations in Southwest Sahara or the Horn of Africa, but also because they are neglected and not addressed in their full political economic dimensions as a continuation of the self-determination crisis, and the principle of majority human rights.

IMPLEMENTATION OF PEOPLE'S RIGHTS

There has been a major focus on third-generation rights both in UN debates and in the formulation of regional human rights charters such as the African Charter on Human and Peoples' Rights. These are important sources for validating a new claim, but in the last analysis they have force only insofar as they reflect the basic changes of a new consciousness among people in a region such as Africa and in the world. Even more important is the change in power structures within the states themselves. Under new direction, the states become the major means of implementation for their own citizens and for other members of the tributary system not yet freed from domination and exploitation.

A process of change with regard to the acceptance of people's human rights cannot be expected to take place within an international system dominated by the interests of the hegemonic powers. It is remarkable that within a system so totally subordinated to major power interests there have emerged such forthright statements of human rights as the Universal Declaration of Human Rights, the two major Covenants on Human Rights, the Declaration Against Racial Discrimination and Apartheid, and the Indian Ocean Zone of Peace, as well as the regional charters such as the OAU Charter. It is perhaps a reflection of the self-determination crisis itself which even dominant powers cannot entirely suppress. But it would be quite misleading to suggest that even important new international regimes can be the primary instrument to lead the world in accepting one of the most basic human rights revolutions in history.

Even so, a very significant solidarity consciousness across national boundaries has emerged. It has come into existence because human rights are inherent and have a universal basis that enables transnational groups to evolve under the most difficult circumstances and to provide some of the important means for bringing about needed changes in the world. This can be misleading, for certain groups which perpetuate dominance may generate a false international consciousness. Some fundamentalist Christian and Islamic movements promote communal conflict, but as important secondary effects they have provided education and the means by which new ideas and movements have taken root in African societies. Far more important are the numerous new international nongovernmental organizations (NGOs) that have provided specific assistance to the liberation and human rights struggle, both internal and external, to Africa.[35] In my own work, I have attempted to distinguish some of these groups in the struggle against apartheid. On the one hand there are the gradualists who, in the main, have accepted continued dependence, and on the other there are the abolitionists who have backed the liberation movements of the ANC and SWAPO which will bring structural change. The liberation movements themselves have indicated that, while they intend to be the primary architects of the freedom struggle, they welcome more support from abroad.[36] This NGO assistance has flowed from both the East and West and is a prime example of the solidarity of the people's rights struggle.

The power of human rights consciousness in the United States today is so strong that the right wing, despite its earlier opposition to human rights, has attempted to use it for its own interventionary policies. The most outstanding example has been the Heritage Foundation in Washington, D.C., which has advocated the support of the National Union for the Total Independence of Angola (UNITA) in Angola and the Mozambique National Resistance (MNR) in Mozambique, thus substituting ideology and Cold War criteria for internationally defined and accepted self-determination. However, other NGOs with major transnational constituencies—from Amnesty International to the International Defense and Aid Fund and the American Committee on Africa—have played a major role in building communities for protecting and implementing human rights in the new African states. These groups have growing NGO counterparts in Africa. While they are not members of the establishment or close to the centers of power, they have significant support and are growing in influence, despite the repression in Africa and the power of the right-wing leadership of Western neocolonialism.

In the final analysis, the crisis of self-determination can only be resolved by Africans themselves, as they come to recognize the nature of that crisis and find ways to create solidarity and support for global majority rights and respect for minority rights within their own countries and transnationally. The first step is to recognize the depth and scope of the continuing flagrant violations in Africa. The second step is to encourage liberation groups to build on the opportunity for solidarity and class struggle within their own societies. This process has already begun in Africa through the self-reliance movement. We should realize that the world power system has intervened against the attempts of several states such as Tanzania, Zimbabwe, and Angola to build self-reliant socialist production systems.[37] The people's rights solidarity movement is the best assurance that Africans will ultimately succeed, despite this new form of hegemony.

CONCLUSIONS

Several schools of thought have helped formulate people's rights— from liberal anti-imperialism to neo-Marxist, Christian, Judaic, and Islamic theologies. It cannot be characterized as only one philosophical tradition or ideology such as Marxist or liberal. As third-generation thought, people's rights have combined the northern contribution of individualism of the West, and collectivism of the East with the world majority claims of the South, to produce concepts that come much closer to a universal basis for human rights than had previously been achieved.

It has become increasingly apparent that human rights cannot be limited to the civil and political priorities of Western capitalism which exploits minorities at home while carrying out flagrant violations abroad. This has been amply expressed by Western legal critiques of such violations as the invasion of Grenada.[38] As is now clear to many Eastern Europeans, the socialist version of collective economic and social rights does not justify concentration camps and the repression of dissent by a police bureaucracy, and torture in any part of the world is a flagrant violation.[39]

If the majority of the world are to be given their rights by states and the world system, their claims to political and economic participation and the redistribution of the world's wealth will need to be universalized. Otherwise, the propositions about the equality of all people and the unity of the human race are simply hypocritical propaganda, promulgated by a ruling class that coined the Universal Declaration of Human Rights at a moment in history when they simply wanted to rally the world against fascism to preserve their privileges. The colonial world, however, took these ringing phrases very seriously. In 1948, people's rights as a part of universal human rights broke through the world consciousness and became a movement. "Everyone is entitled to a social and international order in which the rights and freedoms set forth in this Declaration can be fully realized."[40] This declaration inaugurated the solidarity movement, which gave rise to the liberation struggles and then were written into the new state constitutions, beginning with India in 1947. International treaties and UN covenants have since been adopted and have given specific law and authority to these old and new claims.

Solidarity in global human rights cannot be used to paper over real differences in conditions for life-fulfillment and injustices. It is both a divisive concept of struggle against privilege and a hope for a better world in which humanity is not fundamentally exploited by a few. Equality is genuinely the goal of all members of the human race, and authority is held responsible for making progress toward specific new human rights conditions. Thus, people's human rights are the basis of the new liberation movement which has broken out of the narrow group consciousness of religion or state to a recognition of the common humanity from which we come. The claims of the poor on the rich, the landless on the capitalist, the tortured on the contented, the starving on the affluent, and the derelicts without meaning in their lives on the committed—all have a concrete basis for recognition.

These third-generation rights are not simply populist aspirations. There has emerged a revolutionary and legal process for their recognition and implementation under international law. They have moved from declarations at the United Nations and international meetings to covenants and treaties. National leaders have expressed these ideas, and constitutions and courts have recognized them.

International lawyers, professors, and movements have worked for their adoption. Though often ignored and violated by state authority, their advocates have grown in number and power. Today, the human rights movement has spread to all parts of the world, from the Mothers of the Plaza, the Black Sash, to the Palestinian Nationalists, the African National Congress and the Philippine National Peasants' Union (NPU). The nonviolent resistance movements in the superpower nations against the nuclear arms race and the concentration camps are also part of this solidarity.

In the final analysis, the global human rights movement in Africa can only be built by Africans themselves as they come to recognize the nature of that crisis and find ways of building a third-generation leadership which reflects this new thinking. We outside of Africa should give greater attention to the new ways Africans have found to understand and express their concept of human rights claims.

NOTES

1. Hassan Faroq discusses this third generation as found in the sequence of liberty, equality, and fraternity from the French Revolution to the African and Third World. See "Solidarity Rights: Progressive Evolution of International Human Rights Law," *Human Rights Annual* 1 (1983), pp. 71–74.

2. Richard Falk terms this the populist view of human rights and cites the Algiers Declaration of Rights in *Human Rights and State Sovereignty* (New York: Holmes and Meier Press, 1981), pp. 51–53.

3. Faroq, "Solidarity Rights," p. 52.

4. Franz Fanon, *The Wretched of the Earth* (New York: Grove Press, 1965), pp. 36–37.

5. Gustavo Gutierrez, *A Theology of Liberation* (Maryknoll, N.Y.: Orbis Books, 1973), p. 88.

6. Colin Morris, *The Unyoung, the Unpoor, and Uncolored* (London: Zed Press, 1962).

7. Claude Ake, *A Political Economy of Africa* (London: Longman Group, 1987).

8. Amilcar Cabral, "Return to the Source: Selected Speeches," ed. Africa Information Service. (New York: Monthly Review Press, 1973), pp. 54–55.

9. Adebayo Adedeji and Timothy Shaw, eds., *Economic Crisis in Africa: African Perspectives on Development Problems and Potential* (Boulder, Colo.: Lynne Rienner, 1985), pp. 9–10.

10. Nzongola Ntalaja and Ilunga Kabondo, eds., *The Crisis in Zaire: Myths and Realities* (Trenton, N.J.: Africa World Press, 1986), p. 5.

11. George W. Shepherd, Jr., *The Trampled Grass: Tributary States and Self-Reliance in the Indian Ocean Zone of Peace* (New York: Praeger, 1987), pp. 6–7.

12. Osita C. Eze, *Human Rights in Africa: Some Selected Problems* (La-

gos: Nigerian Institute of International Affairs, in cooperation with Macmillan, Nigeria, 1984), p. 31.

13. Falk, *Human Rights and State Sovereignty*, pp. 35–38.

14. Louis Henkin, *The Rights of Man Today* (Boulder, Colo.: Westview Press, 1978).

15. Unesco, *Human Rights, Human Needs and the Establishment of a New International Economic Order*, Doc. 55 78/Conf.

16. Peter Nobel, "The Concept of Peoples and the Right to Development in the African (Banjul) Charter on Human and People's Rights," Paper prepared for the research project, *Refugees and Development in Africa* (Uppsala, Sweden: Scandinavian Institute of African Studies,1984 October), p. 3.

17. Jack Donnelly, "In Search of the Unicorn: The Jurisprudence and Politics of the Right to Development," *California Western International Law Journal* 15, no. 3 (Summer 1985), pp. 473–509. There are also African exponents of this view, see Olusola Ojo and Amadu Sessay, "The OAU and Human Rights: Prospects for the 1980s and Beyond," *Human Rights Quarterly* 8, no. 1 (February 1986), pp. 89–103.

18. Vojin Dimitryevic, "The Right to Development," paper presented at the International Studies Association, 23rd Annual Convention, 1986, p. 2.

19. Walter Rodney, *How Europe Underdeveloped Africa* (London: Zed Press, 1962); Samir Amin, *Unequal Development* (New York: Monthly Review Press, 1976); and Claude Ake, *A Political Economy of Africa* (London: Longman Group, Ltd., 1981).

20. Ann Seidman, *South Africa and Multinational Corporations* (Westport, Conn.: Lawrence Hill and Co., 1977) and *The Roots of the Crisis in South Africa* (Trenton, N.J.: Africa World Press, 1985).

21. Samir Amin, *History of Capitalism in West Africa* (London: Penguin, 1978).

22. Victoria Marmorstein, "World Bank Power to Consider Human Rights Factors in Loan Decisions," *Journal of Law and Economics* 13 (1978).

23. Gwendolyn Carter's recent work, *Continuity and Change in South Africa* (Los Angeles: Crossroads Press, 1986) reveals how little this system has changed in the past twenty years.

24. Cedric de Beer, *The African Disease: Apartheid Health and Health Services* (Trenton: Africa World Press, 1986), provides data on the high infant mortality and tuberculosis among black South Africans.

25. "The Freedom Charter," Congress of the People (Kliptown, South Africa, June 26, 1955).

26. Oboro Ikime, "Towards Understanding the National Question," *Africa Events* (April 1987), pp. 34–45.

27. Shepherd, *The Trampled Grass*, pp. 100–104.

28. Colm Foy, "Crackdown in Kenya," *Afric-Asia*, no. 40 (April 1987), p. 24.

29. *Human Rights in Uganda*, Report from Amnesty International (New York, 1986).

30. "Human Rights Monitor," *Africa Today* 34, nos. 1 & 2 (1987).

31. Eze, *Human Rights in Africa*, p. 97.

32. This union of two quite different ethnic groups has been difficult at

times, but the fact that President Nyerere, a Christian mainlander, has been succeeded by President Mwinyi, a Muslim, is significant.

33. Richard Sherman, *Eritrea: The Unfinished Revolution* (New York: Praeger, 1980) and Tony Hodges, *Western Sahara* (Westport, Conn.: Lawrence Hill and Co., 1983).

34. Moyigahorokoto Nduru, "Sudan: Sharia by Another Name," *Afric-Asia*, no. 40 (April 1987), p. 27.

35. George W. Shepherd, Jr., *Anti-Apartheid: The Struggle for Liberation in South Africa* (Westport, Conn.: Greenwood Press, 1977); see also Richard Kiwanuka, "On the Paucity of Human Rights NGOs in Africa," *Human Rights Internet* 2, no. 4 (November 1986), pp. 10–15.

36. Oliver Tambo, "Certainties and Uncertainties: Strategic Options for International Companies," *Sechaba* (July 1987), p. 3.

37. Michael J. Klare, "The Reagan Doctrine," *Inquiry* (Washington, D.C.: Institute for Policy Studies, March/April 1984).

38. Ved Nanda, "The United States Armed Intervention in Grenada: Impact on World Order," *California Western International Law Journal* 14, no. 3 (Summer 1984).

The long-range impact on world opinion on the U.S.-led invasion of Grenada is not to be measured by popular responses, no matter how enthusiastic, in the United States, Grenada, or, for that matter, anywhere else. When an action of this kind is undertaken by a superpower and the legal basis for this action is at best tenuous, a further weakening of the few existing constraints on the use of force is especially likely to occur (p. 423).

39. Polly Duncan, "A New Generation of Opposition," *Sojourners* (October 1987), pp. 14–19.

40. Art. 28, Universal Declaration of Human Rights, December 10, 1948, GA Res. 217 of A(111), UN Doc A/810 at 71 (1948).

3

Underdevelopment and Human Rights Violations in Africa

Julius O. Ihonvbere

"One man, one vote," is meaningless unless accompanied by the principle of "one man, one bread."[1]

Freedom of speech and expression means nothing to a largely illiterate and ignorant society and similarly, the right to life has no relevance to a man who has no means of livelihood.[2]

The issue of human rights, especially its violation, has become topical in the past decade or so. The debate on the need for an appropriate definition or conceptualization of human rights has been quite intense.[3] In addition, the issue of whether it is necessary, indeed, inevitable, to trade political rights for socioeconomic and cultural rights has been a major aspect of the debate. This chapter does not intend to join the debate, which we see as largely diversionary and superstructural. In fact, without locating such debates within the specificities of particular social formations as well as the dynamics of production and exchange relations, very little, if anything, would be achieved.[4]

This chapter will demonstrate the inextricable linkage between underdevelopment and human rights violations. We argue that the underdeveloped and dependent conditions of the African continent generate contradictions, pressures, and crises that enhance insecurity, conflicts, and the violation of human rights by the state and its custodians. To be sure, our conceptualization of human rights encompasses rights such as freedom of speech, the right to vote and be voted for, and freedom of movement. We contend that a proper analysis and understanding of human rights in any society can only be made by looking at the socioeconomic or material foundations of society.[5] Hence, political institutions and processes, the existence of more than one political party, periodic elections, and constitutionally guaranteed rights mean very little because they all depend on the patterns of production and exchange, the relations among and within social classes, and the location of social formations in the international division of labor.

Furthermore, our understanding of development is holistic.[6] We contend that infrastructural development, increases in GDP, and GNP per capita increases in foreign reserves, and improvements in balance of payments *only* reflect growth. These indicators have meaning only when they are reflected in the qualitative improvement of the living conditions of the majority. Thus, a society can experience tremendous growth but no development as the case of the oil-producing countries demonstrates.[7]

Human rights—economic, social, civil, and political—therefore, cannot be properly understood outside the social equation of specific societies. It is, of course, impossible, in fact undesirable, to generalize on the issue of human rights. At the same time, it is inappropriate to transpose standards of evaluation and determination of human rights from one society to the other. The historical experiences of particular social formations and the consequences of these experiences must be taken into consideration at all levels. Well-worded declarations, charters, covenants, and laws do not guarantee human rights. Human rights are not "things" or "benefits" that benevolent leaderships grant to the people. The rights of people have been won through constant and consistent struggles between those who have reasons to deny these rights to the majority and those who, by their contribution to the growth and development of society, feel they should enjoy such rights. In other words, the level of rights enjoyed in society reflects the intensity, content, and context of class contributions and struggles.

It is quite easy for organizations, individuals, and governments in the Western world to insist as they have done in the past decade or so on the primacy of civil and political rights.[8] In fact, such insistence is sometimes made at the expense of socioeconomic and cultural rights. But, for nations that were never colonized, dominated, and underdeveloped, such insistence makes some sense. Political and civil rights "naturally" emanate from a well-integrated, viable, and productive material base that reproduces itself through the interaction of internal forces using viable and stable political institutions to guarantee a positive atmosphere for the accumulation and domestication of the opposition. However, for countries that have known no peace, stability, or progress since their contact with the forces of Western imperialism, civil and political rights have no meaning, for they are constantly mediated by pressures, expectations, contradictions, and conflicts emanating from the condition of mass poverty, backwardness, dependence, underdevelopment, and peripheralization in the international division of labor.[9] This is not to say that civil and political rights are irrelevant. Our position is that the expectation is wrong that subservient, insincere, and unproductive leaders and dominant forces can or should guarantee human rights in whatever form.

THE AFRICAN CONDITION: UNDERDEVELOPMENT AND CRISIS

The underdevelopment of the African continent is a direct result of the contact between the hitherto underdeveloped social formations and the forces of Western imperialism.[10] This contact culminated in the distortion and underdevelopment of the continent. It also ensured the structured incorporation of the continent into the capitalist-dominated international division of labor. Specifically, the contact with the forces of Western imperialism culminated in the following:

1. The creation of an unhegemonic and unstable state that was incapable after political independence of managing social contradictions and conflicts and thus ensuring the effective reproduction of the respective systemic forces and interests in the continent.[11]

2. The creation of an *unproductive*, corrupt, and subservient dominant class that lacked effective control of its respective economies and was dependent on the productive activities of the bourgeoisie in the metropole for capital accumulation. This dominant class was equally relegated to *unproductive* aspects of their respective economies mostly as "service persons" to foreign interests.[12]

3. The domination of the local economies by profit and hegemony, seeking transnational corporations and the incorporation of the local elites as agents, representatives, shareholders, partners, and so on. This ensured the effective extraction and repatriation of surpluses and a relative congruence of interests between the respective economies and those of the metropolitan states.[13]

4. A general dependence on foreign aid, trade, expertise, and markets which emerged to generate foreign exchange and to promote growth and "development." This more often than not subjugates national interests to external interests, thus promoting vulnerability to external pressure, manipulation, and crisis. The dependence on the production and exportation of a narrow range of cash crops to specific markets in the Western world has deepened the crisis of the continent. Specifically, African nations lack control over determination of the prices of exports and imports, and generally the international economic environment is a hostile one. The continent is plagued by fluctuating prices, declining terms of trade, increasing debts, declining foreign assistance, frequent foreign interference, and the manipulation of international financial institutions against the interests and aspirations of African states.[14]

5. Science and technology which lags behind that of developed nations, engendering not only capital transfer but also a continued inability to harness the forces of nature and protect the environment.

6. Spatial inequalities and rural–urban migration were accentuated by the colonial experience. These inequalities programmed the transition to neocolonial dependence with political independence, particularly with the capture of state power by conservative regimes. Corrupt and unproductive dominant forces eroded the limited legitimacy of the postcolonial state and intensified the contradictions and conflicts which the respective African states inherited. The institutions and structures planted in the colonial period and inherited at political independence were not viable enough to ensure the effective mediation of class contradictions and conflicts, especially in view of the limited hegemony of the state. The distortions of the social formation and the failure of colonialism to completely revolutionize the relations of production grew in Africa along capitalist lines.[15]

In sum, therefore, at political independence the African continent was underdeveloped in all respects. Education was largely dysfunctional, and the institutions and leadership lacked legitimacy, which together with the problems of alienation, instability, mass poverty, and foreign domination, led to near total irrelevance in international relations. Insignificant contributions to world industrial output, illiteracy, rural decay, urban dislocation, and deep-rooted social contradictions characterized African society and politics. Indeed, political independence coupled with the failure of the new elites to carry out an appreciable level of socioeconomic and political transformation generated apathy, opposition, and revolutionary pressures. These pressures in turn compelled African leaders to resort to repression; the manipulation of religion and ethnicity; alliances with powerful foreign interests, particularly for support; ideological containment; and defensive radicalism.[16] As John Hatch has noted:

Events during the 1960s largely destroyed the euphoria aroused by independence, replacing expectancy with cynicism or resignation. A score of regimes, created in the high point of anti-colonial nationalism, were unconstitutionally overthrown. The use of violence, actual or threatened, supplanted political processes over large areas of the continent. The goal of Pan-African unity, for many nationalists a central objective of the anti-colonial campaigns, receded beyond the horizon, a forgotten Utopia. Instead of national prosperity, anticipated from the collective national efforts released by independence, stagnation in the countryside, massive unemployment in the towns and ostentatious luxury for a tiny minority became the general experience.[17]

Furthermore, detention without trial, public executions, inter-communal massacres, commonly succeeded the colonial rule. Freedom to organize trade unions, political parties or co-operatives was curtailed. The right to publish newspapers or to hold public meetings, was widely curtailed. Theft and rapine violence spread through town streets and country paths. Corruption became rampant, graft common-place. Africa seemed to be fast imitating not only the societies of New York, Chicago, Dallas, Hamburg, Marseilles or London, but also those of Johannesburg, Cape Town, Salisbury and Bulawayo.[18]

Compared to the contemporary situation, the African condition which Hatch described in the 1960s can be described as a golden age. The fragility of state structures, the occurrence of coups and countercoups, the vulnerability to external manipulations, and the corrupt and unproductive deposition of the dominant forces have continued to deepen contradictions, insecurity, uncertainty, and conflicts. The industrial, agricultural, and service sectors of the various economies are either stagnating or declining. Import substitution industrialization strategy, religiously embraced in the early period of technology transfer, failed to promote an appreciable level of sectoral integration. Periodic improvements in production levels, trade balances, foreign reserves, GDP, and so on, were not reflected in the timing conditions of the majority of Africa: Poverty, illiteracy, disease, hunger, and marginalization from political and decision-making processes came to characterize life on the continent. As Hugh M. Arnold notes:

Africa is by far the most underdeveloped of the Third World continents. Africa in 1976, with 75 percent of the world's population, accounted for only 1.3 percent of the global GDP. . . . Africa is strikingly behind the other developing continents in literacy. . . . On the very significant Physical Quality of Life Index (PQLI) Africa likewise trails the other developing areas by a wide margin on such development indicators, as life expectancy, infant mortality, health expenditure, energy consumption, and so on.[19]

The squandering of available limited resources on prestige projects, importation of modern and sophisticated military gadgets, and misplaced national priorities prevent African governments from responding concretely to the contradictions and pressures generated by the continent's backwardness. In the attempt to divert attention and contain popular pressures and opposition, the rights of citizens are wantonly violated.[20]

To be sure, the crisis of the continent cannot be understood only from the internal perspective. The harshness of the international environment, rising debt service ratios, frequent increases in the cost of imports, direct military violation of the territorial integrity of African states, Western support for apartheid in South Africa, and declining foreign assistance have contributed significantly to the plight of the continent. The debate on a New International Economic Order, a New World Information Order, United Nations Trade and Development (UNTAD) and General Agreement Trade and Tariffs (GATT) negotiations have done very little to improve the dismal conditions of the majority in the African states. As the Lagos Plan of Action, adopted by African leaders in 1980, laments: "The effect of unfulfilled promises of global development strategies has been more sharply felt in Africa than in the other continents of the world. Indeed, rather than result in an improvement in the economic situation of the continent, successive strategies have made it stagnate."[21]

The adoption of monetarist policies, particularly those recommended by the World Bank and the International Monetary Fund, sharpened these tendencies within the state structures on the continent.[22] The employment freeze, wage cuts, retrenchment of able-bodied workers, elimination of subsidies on essential commodities and services, devaluation of currencies, elimination of control on foreign companies, expansion of security networks, and other monetarist structural adjustment programs have aggravated the underdevelopment of human rights. In addition, the contradictions and conflicts they generate more often than not compel insecure dominant elites to resort to repression. Abebayo Adedeji, the executive secretary of the United Nations Economic Commission for Africa, points to a linkage between mass poverty, underdevelopment, and instability when he observes that "Projections by the ECA indicate that unless the orientation of the African economy changes, there is a danger that poverty and the attendant problems of political and social instability will become considerably worse in Africa in the next two decades."[23] Yet, the current orientation of the African economy is mostly one of attempting to service dependent capitalism, implement harsh monetarist programs and contain popular responses through the use of violence, Draconian decrees, repression, diversionary tactics, and outright violation of personal freedoms and liberties.[24] Clive Thomas has addressed this issue in relation to the Third World generally, but it has great implications for Africa:

One of the many outstanding features of the Third World, one which is of particular concern, is the prevalence of repression, political assassination, disappearances, and other evidence of installed dictatorships. . . . The prevalence of these repressive political forms is the direct counterpart of the absence of internal democratic practices and the virtual outlawing, within these countries, of representative political institutions, multiparty political systems, due process and equality before the law, free and fair elections and so on. Where repression prevails, the possibility of political and social advances for the broad masses . . . , has also lessened.[25]

Under such conditions, as highlighted by Thomas above, it would be (and indeed is) a waste of time to preach human rights or complain about human rights violations without first addressing the historical socioeconomic and political processes and relationships that culminate in the violation of human rights.

DEEPENING ECONOMIC CRISES AND HUMAN RIGHTS VIOLATIONS

Thus far, we have tried to present the harsh realities of Africa's underdevelopment. We have contended that human rights must necessarily be violated within the context of underdevelopment. The condition of underdevelopment in itself constitutes a violation of people's rights. Therefore, under conditions where production and exchange patterns and relationships are under foreign control, and the dominant forces are unhegemonic and largely incapable of mediating the edges of class contradictions and conflicts, human rights for the poor majority cannot be guaranteed. As Julius Nyerere notes: "What freedom has a subsistence farmer? He scratches a bare living from the soil provided the rains do not fail; his children work at his side without schooling, medical care, or even good feeding. Certainly he has the freedom to vote and to speak but these are meaningless."[26]

The above, then, is the crux of the human rights issue in underdeveloped social formations. To be sure, civil and political rights are required to facilitate the successful initiation and implementation of development programs. But equitable distribution of available wealth, the creation of opportunities, the availability of opportunities to participate fully in the initiation of the basic needs of the people cannot be neglected in the process of development.[27] Indeed, unless the majority of the people are mobilized and the rights of the producers of wealth guaranteed, the tendency will be toward deepening alienation and conflicts. The maintenance of political stability, of course, is important to the process of liquidating underdevelopment. Yet, the guarantee of sociocultural rights and economic subsistence of the majority must be a basic right:

Within Africa, however, the right to subsistence is now taken for granted (theoretically) whereas rights to physical security and those civil and political freedoms which are necessary for effective political participation are problematic. Often, the position that subsistence rights must take priority over civil/political rights is taken solely for rhetorical purposes to perpetuate the political monopoly of a self-serving elite. Against such an elite, one needs to consider the meaning of civil and political freedoms for the poor and unfree masses.[28]

But dominant forces whose accumulative *bases* are dependent on the productive activities of foreign interests, the direct and/or indirect looting of public funds, and massive extraction of surpluses from the countryside cannot be expected to guarantee political and civil rights.

The commitment of Africa's ruling classes to the reproduction of the inherited unequal alliance with profit and hegemony seeking transnational interests and their inability (failure?) to embark on a credible process of structural transformation and self-reliance have deepened underdevelopment internally and peripheralization in the world system. Adebayo Adedeji captures very well the consequences of Africa's dependence:

A casual walk through some of our urban centres reveals the existence and worsening situation of the very things which governments have indicated in their statements of development policies and in their development plans as objects of correction and socio-economic change, shanty towns, congested traffic, beggars, the unemployed, both old and young, in desperate search of the means of living, side by side with the manifestations of wealth and high income and conspicuous consumption. . . . Our urban distribution networks continue to be an extension of the marketing system of advanced industrialized countries.[29]

These are very serious issues that have far-reaching political implications for the level of human rights enjoyed by citizens in society. Yet, as we have argued, the ruling elites are not in any way attempting to restructure society in favor of the majority of the people. Those who are deprived, oppressed, and dispossessed should be expected to react, overtly and covertly. To the extent that power elites do not make concessions but respond by repressing nonbourgeois forces, issues of human rights become secondary to an effective resolution of class contradictions and struggles in society. Rather, Africa's dominant classes have initiated:

a highly developed system of terror and repression. Despite poverty and economic crisis, these states finance a large military apparatus. . . . The generalization of terror and repression in these societies is linked to the use of torture, assassination, and other forms of physical violence against opponents, or would be opponents, of the ruling classes.[30]

International declarations, human rights charters, and other well-documented statements on the rights of citizens mean very little to desperate elites who have learned to rely on corruption, repression, and the denial of human rights to reproduce the status quo and maintain their hold on power. To the extent that there is no acceptable "international morality," that the Western powers have no respect for the human rights of others, and that international finance institutions, like the International Monetary Fund (IMF), under the guise of not interfering in the "internal affairs" of other countries, continue to prop up repressive regimes, international declarations can only sensitize some people to the salience of human rights.[31] What would determine the violation or guarantee of human rights, especially in a crisis-ridden and poverty-stricken continent like Africa, is the extent to which socioeconomic contradictions are resolved. Claude Ake, for instance, has argued that in view of the existing socioeconomic crisis in Africa, fascism is perhaps inevitable: "all the more dramatic precisely because of the long drawn-out economic stagnation. . . . One thing that would surely be needed in ever increasing quantities in this situation would be repression. As the economic stagnation persisted, the masses would become more wretched and desperate."[32]

The scenario highlighted by Ake above clearly demonstrates the inextricable relationship between deepening economic crisis and state repression. As repression increases, the oppressed in society will respond, and the ensuing scenario will be one of struggle for survival, not of debate, about whether civil or political rights should take priority over socioeconomic rights:

Wretchedness and desperation would lead peasants to subversion, workers to induce industrial action, and the lumpen proletariat to robbery and violence. Punitive expeditions would then be sent out to liquidate whole villages, armed robbers would be punished by public executions and crimes against property would be dealt with by imposing sanctions of exceptional harshness. Striking workers would be chased by police dogs, locked out, starved out, shot at. Any person or group of persons who looked like being a rallying point against the system would be summarily liquidated. All this is already happening. And things are likely to get worse.[33]

Ake is quite correct. African states have expanded their security networks to deal with opposition. Indeed, the rate at which unions are proscribed, social critics harassed, jailed, or exiled, workers retrenched, security officers given unprecedented powers, and defense expenditures increased has been on an upward trend. Precipitants of the deepening crisis include capitalist production and exchange characterized by inflation, unemployment, a falling rate of profit, bankruptcies, and the like. These crises are reproduced fourfold in Africa, forcing the elites to take panicky and uncertain measures. The trend would definitely continue to the extent that structural transformation is not yet on the agenda in most African states.

CONCLUSIONS

Africa is a backward, foreign-dominated, poor, underdeveloped continent. It is the poorest continent in the world today. This condition is the outcome of the continent's historical contact with the forces of Western imperialism and the postcolonial alignment and realignment of class forces. Therefore, a discussion of the human rights situation in Africa must be located within the context of production and exchange patterns. This is because it is the contradictions and conflicts generated by the dependent and distorted base of production and accumulation that generate tensions, insecurity, and political disposition toward repression and human rights violation. Thus, human rights mean very little within a context of mass poverty, unemployment, illiteracy, hunger, marginalization, and the general lack of basic human needs:

There is no doubt that whatever economic indicator one might like to use, the economic situation of African countries has deteriorated. There are adverse balance of payment problems in general for agriculture, industry, and particularly manufacturing.[34]
There were of course the problems of external debt . . . there were social problems such as un- and under-employment, malnutrition, high infant mortality rates, unequal income distribution and many others. Unfortunately, all these problems have become intensified in the first half of the 1980s.[35]

The problems and contradictions continue to deepen. Continental responses through *The Lagos Plan of Action* (LPA) and *The Final Act* (FAL) of Lagos, as well as *The African Priority Programme for Economic Recovery* (APPER), have remained superstructural and incapable of addressing the strong internal roots of Africa's deepening crisis. At the internal level, national development plans, indigenization, and Africanization programs have only served to further crisis, contradictions, and conflicts. Serious structural changes, mass mobilization and strategies for self-reliant, and self-sustaining growth are not being pursued:

Revolutionary changes in the structure of African economies have clearly not occurred; and even their growth rates have been less than satisfactory. But some very significant changes have occurred—not necessarily for the better—particularly in the relations of production. . . . Efforts to reduce the disarticulation of African economies have had a marginal effect at best.[36]

The above, then, is the root of human rights violations in Africa. Competition for the capture, control, and use of state power in support of private capital accumulation within the context of dependence and underdevelopment militates against the provision of the basic needs of people.

It becomes inappropriate, as many Western scholars tend to do, to discuss human rights as if no class or political dimensions were involved. Can a disparate, dependent, and insecure dominant class guarantee human rights? Can a distorted, disarticulated, dominated, underdeveloped, and dependent economy accommodate demands for basic human needs and human rights? Of what use is a debate as to whether civil and political rights or social and economic rights should take priority when either way marginalized, hungry, exploited, illiterate, and oppressed people would gain very little? Does it make much sense to continue to concentrate on so-called international declarations on human rights, frequently violated by the developed (especially Western) powers when it is obvious that these declarations have meaning and relevance only to the extent that they mediate the powers and interests of local dominant classes? These are crucial questions. Our discussions have provided some answers. To the extent that African societies are class societies, characterized by inequalities in all respects, the struggle for human rights must be seen as part of the struggle for change and progress.

NOTES

1. Amnesty International, "Background Paper on Ghana" (London: Mimeo, 1974), p. 9.

2. Femi Falana, quoted in Babatunde Ojudu, "Nigeria: Morning Yet on Human Rights Day," *African Concord* (June 9, 1987), pp. 6–7.

3. Adebayo Adedeji, "Africa: Permanent Underdog?" *International Perspectives* (March-April 1981), p. 17.

4. For reviews of the various positions on human rights, see R. H. Green, "Basic Human Rights/Needs: Some Problems of Categorical Translation and Unification," *The Review*, 24–27 (1980–1981), and Jack Donnelly, "Recent Trends in UN Human Rights Activity. Description and Polemic," *International Organization* 35, no. 4 (Autumn 1981).

5. For details, see Julius O. Ihonvbere, "Towards a Political Economy of Human Rights in Africa (with Special Reference to Nigeria), Mimeo (Port Harcourt: 1984).

6. See my chapters in Toyin Falola, ed., *Britain and Nigeria: Exploitation or Development?* (London: Zed Press, 1987).

7. For details on Nigeria, see Toyin Falola and Julius Ihonvbere, *The Rise and Fall of Nigeria's Second Republic, 1979–1984* (London: Zed Press, 1985), and ILO, *First Things First: Meeting the Basic Needs of the People of Nigeria* (Addis Ababa: JASPA, 1981).

8. It will be recalled that respect for human rights was a major foreign policy issue for U.S. President Jimmy Carter. Ronald Reagan interpreted this issue to reflect an antisocialist position. Yet, the United States is certainly the greatest violator of human rights in the world. Witness its unrepentant support for apartheid South Africa, its support to rebels in Angola and Mozambique, its unprovoked attack on Libya, its invasion of Granada, its direct interference in the affairs of Latin American states, its attempt to destabilize Unesco and the oppression of Menonites in America.

9. See Claude Ake, *Revolutionary Pressures in Africa* (London: Zed Press, 1978); Neville Brown, "Underdevelopment as a Threat to World Peace," *International Affairs* 47, no. 2 (April 1971); and Claude Ake, *A Political Economy of Africa* (London: Longmans, 1982).

10. See Walter Rodney, *How Europe Underdeveloped Africa* (Enugu: Ikenga, 1981); Franz Fanon, *The Wretched of the Earth* (New York: Grove Press, 1965); E. A. Brett, *Colonialism and Underdevelopment in East Africa* (London: Heinemann, 1972); and Falola, ed., *Britain and Nigeria*.

11. See Julius O. Ihonvbere and Toyin Falola, eds., *Nigeria and the International Capitalist System* (Boulder: Lynne Rienner, 1988) and the works of Hamza Alavi, Colin Leys, Michela Van Freyhold, John Saul, Issa Shivji, Claude Ake, Okwudibia Nnoli, and Paul Nursey Bray on the postcolonial state.

12. See Richard Sandbrook, *The Politics of Basic Needs: Urban Aspects of Assaulting Poverty in Africa* (Toronto: University of Toronto Press, 1982), and Fanon, *The Wretched of the Earth*.

13. See Julius O. Ihonvbere and Amechi Okolo, *Problems of Development in Africa* (Boulder: Lynne Rienner, 1988).

14. See Julius O. Ihonvbere, "The International Environment and Africa's Deepening Crisis: A Critique of the OAU's Lagos Plan of Action and the African Poverty Programme for Economic Recovery," Mimeo, University of Port Harcourt, 1987; and Amadu Sesay, "The Global Economic Squeeze and the Challenges to the Administration of International Organisations: The African Experience," in A. O. Sanda and Olusola Ojo, eds., *Issues in the Administration of Nigeria's Public Sector* (Ile-Ife: Faculty of Administration, 1987).

15. P.C.W. Gutkind and Peter Waterman, eds., *African Social Studies: A Radical Reader* (New York: Monthly Review Press, 1977).

16. See Ake, *Revolutionary Pressures in Africa*; *Briefing Paper on Africa's Economic Crisis*, no. 1, Centre for African Studies, Dalhousie University, Canada, January 1985; and Julius O. Ihonvbere, "Economic Crisis and Militarism in Africa: Responses and Options," Mimeo, University of Port Harcourt, May 1987.

17. John Hatch, *Africa Emergent: Africa's Problems Since Independence* (Chicago: Henry Regnery, 1974), p. 5.

18. Ibid.

19. Hugh M. Arnold, "Africa and the New International Economic Order," *Third World Quarterly* 11, no. 2 (April 1980), p. 295.

20. Ake, *Revolutionary Pressures in Africa*.

21. OAU, *The Lagos Plan of Action for the Economic Development of Africa, 1980–2000* (Geneva: International Institute for Labour Studies, 1981), p. 1.

22. See the World Bank, *Accelerated Development in Sub-Saharan Africa: An Agenda for Action* (Washington, D.C.: 1981). This document, popularly called "The Berg Report," claims to build on the LPA. It recommended the dismantling of controls on foreign investment, the collection of user fees for social services, export promotion (cash crops) to earn foreign exchange, devaluation, and more incentives to private investors.

23. Adedeji, "Africa: Permanent Underdog?" p. 17.

24. The limits of dependent capitalism and dependent development as a strategy of development is clearly discussed in Peter Evans, *Dependent Development: The Alliance of Multinational, State and Local Capital in Brazil* (Princeton, N.J.: Princeton University Press, 1979).

25. Clive Thomas, *The Rise of the Authoritarian State in Peripheral Societies* (New York: Monthly Review Press, 1984), p. xii.

26. Julius Nyerere, "Stability and Change in Africa," Address to the University of Toronto, Canada, 1969 reproduced in *Africa Contemporary Record* 2 (1969–1970), pp. G30–31.

27. Rhoda Howard, *The Full-Belly Thesis: Should Economic Rights Take Priority Over Civil and Political Rights? A Discussion from Sub-Saharan Africa*, University of Toronto, Development Studies Programme, Working Paper No. A1, April 1983.

28. Ibid., p. 3.

29. Adebayo Adedeji, "Perspectives of Development and Economic Growth in Africa Up to the Year 2000," in OAU, *What Kind of Africa by Year 2000?* (Addis Ababa: 1979), p. 61.

30. Thomas, *The Rise of the Authoritarian State*, p. 89.

31. Renate Pratt, "Human Rights and International Lending: The Advocacy Experience of the Task Force on the Churches and Corporate Responsibility" (TCCR), University of Toronto, Development Studies Programme, Working Paper, no. 15, February 1985.

32. Ake, *Revolutionary Pressures*, p. 105.

33. Ibid.

34. See Vhtid Harman, "Theories of the Crisis," *International Socialism*

(1980) and Paul M. Sweezy, "The Present Global Crisis of Capitalism," *Monthly Review* 29, no. 11 (April 1978).

35. Adebayo Adedeji, "The Lagos Plan of Action: Main Features and Some Other Related Issues," Keynote Address to the International Conference on the OAU, ECA, and LPA and the Future of Africa, Ile-Ife, March 1984, p. 7.

36. Ake, *A Political Economy of Africa*, p. 88.

4

Theological Perspectives on Human Rights in the Context of the African Situation

Nienanya Onwu

This chapter focuses on human rights in the context of the African situation from a Biblical perspective. It begins by examining the Biblical perception of the individual which identifies his or her relation to God and responsibility to Him and notes that human rights derive from human responsibility to God. A catalogue of such rights are encapsulated in the concept of righteousness/justice. Both rights and responsibilities are held within a vertical dimension with horizontal implications. Human rights are formulated in the context of peoples' experiences and self-understanding which, in the African context, is characterized by religiosity, vulnerability, and underdevelopment. The chapter identifies some of the constraints on human rights promotion in Africa and suggests some ways of remedying the situation.

The chapter concludes that the neglect of the religious factor produces distortions in human rights promotion and that a recovery of the awareness of our common humanity as the divine image offers us fresh insights into the human rights realization.

INTRODUCTION

The world today is facing a crisis in its understanding of what it means to be "human." The human community, which was once a bulwark of personal security and a source of individual identity, has now become a shifting, changing phenomenon. The individual is no longer integrated as a person by the structure of the society in which he or she lives. There is no longer any doctrine of the individual which can claim universal validity. Human beings are now confronted with a terrifying freedom of choice. The values of humanity, the structures of justice and love, the qualities of true community become tasks to be realized in the give-and-take of human relations rather than the "given" realities on which a person can depend.

This depiction of the human crisis was the primary focus of the Human Rights Declaration by the United Nations in 1948. This declaration imposes an obligation on state members of the international community to ensure a collection of rights to all people. Among these rights are those to life, work, education, and basic human needs like food, shelter, medical care, and social services necessary for health and well-being.

Over forty years have passed since this declaration, but the guarantee of human rights translated into reality has eluded the majority of African states. It is rightly alleged, and not without reason, that there is an elitist approach to the human rights issue and that it is the affluent sections of the society in relation to the state which are the major beneficiaries of the cliche of human rights.[1] In this regard, the majority poor in the African nations are yet to know what human rights mean to them. Perhaps Luis Pasara might have had such a view in mind when he indicated, from a secularist perspective, "that lack of consensus on the definition of development, politicized versions of human rights and the role of lawyers in less developed countries" constitute three difficulties that militate against the realization of human rights.[2]

We admit these positions are part of the larger problem. We would quickly add that a central challenge to our faith and obedience today arising from the many-sided threats to human life and dignity should focus on a recovery of the awareness of our common humanity as made in the image of God, which can offer us fresh insight into our human rights realization and help us to articulate and respond to this challenge. This is because the problems of human rights violations are related to our concept of true humanity and human responsibilities.

In this chapter, we will focus on the Biblical perception of the individual, some of the constituents of human rights in the Bible, indicating the source of human rights and its implication for a humane society. This work presumes that, though we do not have a catalogue of duties called human rights in the Bible, the Bible does reveal the demands of righteousness or justice which function as rights for each member of the community. We will conclude by drawing attention to the problems of human rights in the African context and suggest new directions in the realization of human rights objectives.

THE BIBLICAL PERCEPTION OF THE INDIVIDUAL

The crisis in society as related to human rights becomes critical when we raise the question of who the individual is. This question is related to two other questions: (1) where does a person go for models of true humanity, and (2) what forms of human relations offer themselves for his or her guidance?

Scientific materialism would assert that a person is a machine, no matter how you look at that person. Four areas of study in modern society point toward this conclusion: cybernetics, psychology, sociology, and biology.

Humanism asserts that a person is the standard for everything, responsible for making God, morality, and everything else. Humanism developed during the Renaissance in the fourteenth and fifteenth centuries. The Renaissance was originally Christian but later became a reaction against the excesses of mediaevalism. By the seventeenth and eighteenth centuries, humanism flourished in the period of the Enlightenment. Humanism upholds faith in the individual, faith in science and in reason. There is no room for God or anything beyond the human being. It must be noted that these developments were reactions against Christendom beginning from the Middle Ages through the Renaissance, the Reformation to the Enlightenment, and the period of the Industrial Revolution in Europe. These reactions led to certain distorted views, particularly as related to the individual within the cosmic scheme.

The Bible does not share the views of scientific materialism and humanism. The Christian faith posits a distinctive doctrine of the individual which permeates almost every ethical issue. With profound simplicity the Bible asserts that God created humans in His own image (Gen. 1:27). Here the Bible is presenting us with the fundamental duality of human nature: unique within creation as bearing the divine image. The doctrine of the image of God in humans repels any reductionist view that a person is either a machine or a highly developed animal—whether expressed in biological, psychological, or behavioral terms.

Thus, the Biblical definition of what is "human" has to involve God in respect to human existence and human nature. We are concerned with human nature as a means of arriving at an understanding of humanness in relation to human rights. This dimension raises the question of whether there is something in what it is to be human that entails rights.

Defining what is human is not simply to list those qualities and achievements of human beings that distinguish us from the beasts—rationality, culture, civilization, art, science, and so on. Such things are what our humanity makes possible. Precisely, the essence of our humanity lies in the combination of the fact of our origin in the creative word of God and the fact of our awareness of that origin. In this respect, Emil Brunner was right when he cited Psalms 139 and noted that the Psalmist distinguished between his "beginning" in the historico-physical process of animal reproduction (which he shares with the rest of the animal creation) and his "origin" in the thought, will, and creative act of God.[3] It is the latter which gives rise to the Psalmist's ethical response to God. The essence of his humanity lies not in the process of human birth, not even in the fact of his having been created by God, but in his awareness of the claim of God upon him and of the inescapable demand for a response to that claim.

The Biblical concept of the image of God has been misinterpreted in an individualistic way or misused to justify exploitation of other living beings. For instance, in the Western world, the emphasis of the Reformation on the justification of the individual person has combined with an individualistic view of human life to make the image of God seem a quality belonging to the individual himself or herself.[4] Rather, it must be seen that the individual in the image of God refers to the gift of a relationship to God which brings with it a calling to community and mutual responsibility. The image of God in the individual refers to personal and social community. It speaks of the responsibility involved in cohumanity as living with and for God and each other. It reminds us that human beings are called by God to be mirrors of the love of God to each other. It also reminds us of the proper calling of human beings to be stewards, not abusers, of God's creation. Understood in this way, the affirmation of the image of God radically confronts every kind of exploitation and degradation of human beings, identifying these as a denial and defacement of the divine image.

Accordingly, what essentially masks the human as human includes (1) the individual's relation to God, which is the core of his or her *humanitas* and which this relational perception calls forth and (2) human responsibility to God as the substance of human existence.[5] The fact of responsibility brings us close to the question of rights, duties/obligations, and so forth. Because each human being is aware not only of his or her uniqueness as a creature with a sense of relation to God and a responsibility to God and because other human beings stand on the same plane, each individual instinctively feels that he or she must treat them differently from all else in the cosmos.

But the understanding of human responsibility has become distorted by its directional focus. For instance, humanists and the instinct of most "persons of goodwill" posit primarily our fellow humans for whom we are exhorted to care, for no higher reason or motive than that they are human species as myself. The Biblical concept of responsibility rejects such a position. It does not put human obligation primarily on a horizontal plane, but rather directs it upward to God. Thus, God addresses Cain directly with the question, "Where is your brother Abel?" (Gen. 4:9). Though he might attempt to deny or at least question it, Cain was responsible to God for his brother. This reinforces our understanding of essential humanness as responsibility to God. We are responsible to God for our fellow beings, and this is something we cannot evade on a Biblical understanding of what it means to be human.

We can now talk about human rights as deriving from human responsibility to God. Rights are not to be offered to others on a charity basis; rather, right is a duty to others (Deut. 5:11, 1 Tim. 6:17). There is a vertical dimension to rights, corresponding to what we have emphasized regarding responsibility. To say that *B* has certain rights is simply the entailment of saying that God holds *A* responsible to do certain things in respect of *B*. *B* has rights under God, because God is as concerned with how *B* is treated as with how *A* acts. To introduce the idea of "merit" confuses the issue. It is not because *B* has rights that I must act in some way because *B* deserves it; rather, it means that God requires it of me and I owe it to God to fulfill the responsibility.[6]

Accordingly, both responsibility and rights are located in God. The Cain and Abel incident focuses this point too. Having faced Cain with his inescapable responsibility, God points to Cain's right: "Your brother's blood cries out to me from the ground" (Gen. 4:10). In a similar vein, God ordered Elijah to confront King Ahab with the question, "Have you killed and also taken possession?" (I Kings 21:19). Characteristic of all strands of Israel's traditions is God's concern for the rights of the defenseless in society.[7] The implication of the above indicates that the language of rights was originally a religious language but has today become a political language. What is noteworthy is that these situations portray conflict situations. Thus, the language of "right" appears to be most used where there is a breakdown of relationship, a conflict of interest, or a dispute over what is fair. This suggests prima facie that the whole conflict over human rights is a consequence of human fallenness in the divine economy.

We must disagree with A. Bloom's view that the Bible knows nothing of an inherent worth or of "inalienable rights" within a person apart from that person's decision to do God's will.[8] Rights do not emerge from doing God's will; they are solely the correlative of the responsibility of one human to another. It is the individual's duty to obey the demand of God that justice be done that is the primary and objective factor. Thus, a Biblical and theological discussion of human rights begins with a definition of the human that requires God. This will inevitably differentiate it from any secular humanist view which omits this divine dimension.

HUMAN RIGHTS IN THE BIBLE

The Biblical concept of human rights derives from God. It is encapsulated in the demand for righteousness or justice[9] which functions as rights for each member of the community. Some translations perceptively translate the justice terminology as "rights" (Jer. 5:28 RSV). The later practice in modern society of specifying rights in a catalogue or bill is an important development, for it more clearly identifies the agreed-upon minimum in social relations. Since it is not possible to present a comprehensive list from a Biblical point of view, we will only highlight some of them.

Before we do so, it is important to recognize that the conception of what is "right" or "just" antedates both Old and New Testament times. The Law of Hummurabic Text was about human rights.[10] But this was not clearly appreciated until God revealed Himself in the Old Testament times but fully and finally in Christ Jesus in the New Testament period.

The Hebraic concept of righteousness or justice represents a fidelity to the demands of a relationship, whether the relationship is with God or man.[10] As in the traditional African society, the Israelite is in a world where "to live" is to be united with other fellow human beings in a socio-religious context. This web of relationships—king with the people, judge with complainants, family with tribe and kinfolk, the community with the resident alien, and the poor in their midst and all with the covenant of God—constitutes the world in which life is played out.[11] The demands of these various relationships are seen in the different settings of Israel's history.

In the Old Testament, human rights are viewed in the context of human suffering due to oppression in all its forms. If there had been a Biblical list of human rights, it would begin with the right to life. Quite early in Biblical history, God confronted Cain who had murdered his brother with violating his brother's right to life. Likewise, God hears the living cry of the sinned against. The whole train of events in this direction is set in motion by the outcry of Israel against their Egyptian oppressors (Ex. 2:23). Their rights to freedom, to the fruit of their own hand, to worship the God of their fathers, and even to normal family reproduction and life were all being violated. The Exodus was the restoration and confirmation of their rights, and a judgment on their oppressors. This new experience of freedom was consolidated on a covenant basis at Sinai with the Decalogue as a foundational charter (Ex. 20).

But the Decalogue is prefaced by a clear statement of the new freedom won for the nation by the redemptive power of God (Ex. 20:2). For the two are inseparable—the freedom that redemption achieves and the responsibility it entails. In the Exodus, God conferred rights and freedoms on the people. But for the purpose of preserving them, these were immediately translated into responsibilities. Accordingly, as the Decalogue states them, those who were now free to worship God must worship Him alone without idolatry (Ex. 20:3–7). Those who now had the right to work as free people and the freedom to rest were given the responsibility to preserve and grant Sabbath rest to others including beasts (Ex. 20:8–11). Those who were now free from oppressive violations of their family life were responsible for preserving parental authority and the sexual integrity of marriage (Ex. 20:12, 14). Freed from violence and terror, they must uphold the sanctity of life by avoiding murder (Ex. 20:13). With the prospect of property ownership, they were not to steal or covet what belonged to their neighbor (Ex. 20:15, 17; I Kings 21:17). Freed from injustice themselves, they were to protect a neighbor under suspicion or trial associated with the stipulations of the Decalogue. The list would include the rights of dependent persons—women, children, slaves, widows, orphans, the poor, prisoners, and aliens (Ex. 21).[12]

Read thus, the Decalogue manifests two distinctive features: (1) the rights are expressed in terms of responsibilities, and (2) the rights and responsibilities are held within a vertical dimension. It was God's initiative of grace that provided the framework of freedom within which the rights and responsibilities could be exercised, and it was to God and under God that such exercise would take place. The rest of the social laws and institutions of the Old Testament can be seen as designed to maintain the demands of righteousness on which the nation was founded. Accordingly, rights presume deliverance within a redeemed community.

Other rights may be found outside the Ten Commandments. For instance, the right to property ownership was typified in the granting of the people the land of Canaan as an inheritance, a right that rested not on their merits but on God's love and faithfulness to His covenant with Abraham. Deuteronomy 7:7 spells this out. It is also confirmed in God's denouncement of Ahab over Naboth's land.

But the awareness of some of these rights did become perverted into arrogant assumption at the hands of the powerful few in the community. Neglecting the demands of righteousness in the covenant for reciprocal loyalty, they treated their God as a celestial insurance policy for their own convenience and protection. Naboth was killed and dispossessed of his land by King Ahab (I Kings. 21). In Nehemiah Chapter 5, there arose a great outcry of the people because they had been denied the right to eat; they were forced to mortgage their land and eventually to sell their sons and daughters as slaves to pay off excessive interest to the rich. Nehemiah criticized the rich and the officials for their neglect of their obligation to God. In Nehemiah 5:9, the rich are questioned as to why they did not walk in fear of God. Verse 13 puts the response of the rich firmly in a vertical mode.

The prophets of the eighth century B.C. expounded on the violation of human rights. The rich and powerful sell the "righteous" for silver and the needy for a pair of shoes and trample the head of the poor into the dust of the earth (Amos 2:7, 5:11). Amos culminates his judgment against the rich and exploiters of his day by proclaiming that their injustice negates their worship of God (Amos 5:21, 24). Likewise, Ezekiel recalled the judgment of God which fell on Sodom and Gomorrah as a result of the "outcry against them that has reached me" (Gen. 18:20ff). According to Ezekiel 16:49, the sin of Sodom was that she and her daughters were arrogant, overfed, and unconcerned; they did not help the poor and needy. A graphic description of the failure of the rich and powerful to promote and protect human rights is found in Isaiah 58:6–7.

Admittedly, the marginal groups in society become the scale on which the justice of the whole society is weighed. When they are exploited or forgotten, neither worship of God nor knowledge of Him can result in true religion. This concern for the rights of the defenseless in society is central to the understanding of the righteousness of God who is the provider and defender of the rights of the oppressed. Yet the poor and the oppressed can establish their own rights on the firm ground of God's responsibility to them to be just/righteous, since to dwell under the protection of God is the highest human right. To possess that is to have cause for praise when secondary human rights are denied (Ps. 56:11). Even when people do their worst, the redeemed person of faith can commit his or her right to God in hope.

When we come to the New Testament, some of the Old Testament stipulations are echoed in the concept of "righteousness" in a deeper way. When we put the Cross and Resurrection at the heart of the matter, we see that the primary issue of human rights relates to salvation.

The New Testament is absorbed with the question of "how a man has the right to enter the kingdom of God, and how wide that right extends." This question is the New Testament reformulation of the Old Testament aspiration of being in a continuous relationship with God in a covenant context. It is in this light that the Biblical writers placed the demands of righteousness or justice in the context of the Kingdom. Matthew gave it the clearest expression when he stated Jesus' words as follows: "Except your righteousness exceeds that of the Scribes and Pharisees, you will never enter the Kingdom of God" (Matt. 5:20). The demands of righteousness function as rights for each member of the community. Consequently, the Sermon on the Mount (Matt. 5–7), the parables, and most other teachings of Jesus contain different aspects of human rights. In Matt. 5:21–26, the injunction of "no anger" which posits the use of "abusive language" on another as the greatest of the sins in this category guarantees the right to life and respect for human dignity. The injunctions of "no lustful desire" and "no divorce" (5:27–30, 31–32) guarantee the sanctity of marriage and family life. The rights to freedom from discrimination and freedom of movement are enshrined in the teaching of love of enemies (5:43–48).

According to the New Testament teaching, the love of one's neighbor found in a parochial sense in the Old Testament has gained a wider dimension in that it now includes "the love of enemies." The only reason for the recognition of the "enemy" as a "person" is based on God's providential love for all (Matt. 5:45, 48). The neighbor may be encountered both directly as an individual and indirectly in a group. In all these relationships, the individual's welfare and dignity are at stake. The parable of the Good Samaritan raises the question of who the neighbor is. When applied to our concern with human rights, the lawyer was actually asking, "who can be said to have rights upon my love?" But Jesus recognized that the question was wrong because preoccupation with defining other people's rights will always end up by limiting one's responsibility. It is not an accident that Jesus summarized the entire law of God in love first to God and then to neighbor. The Biblical perception of love therefore begins with an orientation of the self toward God and one's neighbor's needs.[13] Love is a motivating factor in human rights.

In other teachings of Jesus we find some other constituents of human rights. For instance, the parable of the laborers in the vineyard (Matt. 20:1–16) indicates the right to employment. In the encounter between Jesus and the rich man (Matt. 19:1–22), we find the demand for redistribution as the right of the poor to a fair share in the resources of the community. The right of equality before the law is a basic presumption of the Biblical teaching. The right of children of God not to be the servants of anyone else or Mammon and the right to be protected from the arbitrary exercise of power are also indicated (Matt. 22:15–22; 20:25–28). The right to basic human needs like food, shelter, clothing, medical care, and other social facilities is depicted in the parable of the last judgment in Matthew 25:31–46. This parable affirms in a most surprising way the ultimate significance of love demonstrated in response to the poor, the needy, and the oppressed.

On the whole, the implications of some of these tenets which we have noted in both the New Testament and the Old Testament go beyond even the rights provided in modern secular states.

According to the theology of love and human dignity which we noted earlier,[14] human rights are not claims against the sovereignty of God, but rather, respect for human rights is an implication of recognizing God's supremacy and His Fatherhood.

Our entire Biblical focus indicates that the concept of "righteousness" reflects three aspects that capture "human rights" understanding in a Biblical and theological context—namely, "equality" in that everyone possesses rights, "respect" in that rights help to preserve human dignity, and "perception of common need" in that rights work to protect the minimal conditions for life together.[15]

When "rights" are viewed as secular in origin, emphasis is placed on "humanity" over God and on "freedom" over responsibility. But our perspectives make clear that human rights derive from God and that He reacts whenever they are violated.[16] They are designed for the common good of people and the community under God. They imply new patterns of human socioreligious relationships without which life is less human. Whenever and wherever they are violated, human beings are placed under the necessity to recover the awareness of their common humanity as made in the image of God; for the denial of human rights is a defacing of the divine image in the individual. A person's relationship with God and Christ in the anticipation of perpetual union with Him in the coming Kingdom and the love of God for each person are the motivating factors in human rights realization in Biblical perspectives.

HUMAN RIGHTS AND THE AFRICAN SITUATION

In the context of the Biblical perception of human rights encapsulated in the concept of "righteousness or justice," how does Africa fit into the picture? We admit that in modern times human rights has ceased to be a religious theme. It has now become the language of political criticism (which, of course, reflects its religious root). However, we note that a social program can be built on rights but not on a vague concept of the worth of the individual alone. The motto of the United States of America, "In God We Trust," is a collective affirmation of God as the center of human existence, even if this can be reluctantly acknowledged today. Nor would it be denied that the American Revolution in the eighteenth century drew its ideology from the times and stated its cause to the world in terms of human rights from their collective affirmation of religious faith.[17] The same is also true of Great Britain which in the past has been a Christian nation.

It is doubtful whether Africa would deny the religious factor in the formulation of "human rights" in the constitutions of the different nations that make up the continent. For instance, in spite of Nigeria's acclaimed "secular status," its Human Rights Declarations in the 1979 Constitution are formulated on the basis of a belief in God. The preamble to the Constitution reads: "We the people of . . . Nigeria . . . resolved to live in unity and harmony as one indivisible and indissoluble sovereign nation under God . . . "[18]

Human rights are formulated in the context of people's experiences. The world of the Biblical times is like the African world, distinguished by religiosity, vulnerability, and underdevelopment.[19] Added to these characteristics are the problems of a precarious world-view, tribalism, insensitivity, caste systems, organized violence, religious discrimination, and colonialism. The human rights formulations in most postindependent Africa were aimed at dealing with such issues in order to uphold human worth and human dignity.

It is perhaps becoming obvious to some people today that the concentration of rights on a few individuals over against the common good of the community has revealed the risk that lies within freedom. The present degeneration of the African condition in most African countries is clear testimony of the failures of their leaders to uphold human dignity and worth. In most African countries, the influence of the state on the people is felt in mass unemployment, overtaxation, retrenchment, privatization as in Nigeria, and the Structural Adjustment Policy (SAP). In such a situation, obviously the people have been denied their rights and freedom even to exist. The only well-known freedom in most African countries today is the freedom to anticipate when the right to breathe air is denied. Consequently, for the majority of the impoverished masses, human rights remain a platitudinous Utopia.

Scholarly attempts have been made to explain the failure of human rights promotion and protection in Africa. The three views of Luis Pasara which we have identified earlier should be noted.[20] R. N. Trivedi has identified poor economy as a major obstacle, since human rights make continuous demands on the economic system.[21] His Marxist view becomes apparent in his claim that "the story of human rights is the story of human aspirations linked with the stages of economic progress." His comment on the economic factor is important, but it is too materialistic.

Professor Osita Eze, in his recent book, *Human Rights in Africa*, has provided more reasons for the laxity of human rights promotion and protection. Among others they include colonialist influence, economic and political power, concentration in few hands, low level of education and politicization of the majority of the Africans, the nature of leadership, and laws that are anachronistic and alien to the African condition.[22]

Here we will comment on some crucial facts that have not yet been brought out. The nature of leadership in Africa has been widely acknowledged.[23] It is our belief that related to this dimension is the hypocrisy of the majority of African leaders, who at one point may play the role of mediator of human rights, while at the same time, being the oppressor. This hypocrisy is carried down to the grassroots level precisely because anyone who seeks to be a mediator of human rights is always repressed by those in power. African countries have often had the misfortune of having impostors as their leaders.

Similarly, although the educational factor is widely acknowledged to be important, it is often ignored that the educational system in Africa is not geared to making people either sensitive or aware of their rights. The danger in overlooking this aspect of education as related to the majority poor in Africa is lack of response. In other words, the response of the victim (the oppressed) to the impostor (authority) and the real mediator (human rights advocate) is a great hindrance to human rights promotion. Our Biblical perspectives indicate that the battle for human rights begins with the reaction of the "victim" to the impostor. This reaction is spoken of in terms of "crying out" or "complaining."[24] The majority of the African population do not denounce their leaders because of their helplessness, compounded by fear and want. As victims, they lack the power to be recognized or supported. The person who criticizes the regime can end up dying a painful death with all the victims (the oppressed population) watching or even supporting the authority without any positive response to the victim. The case of Jesus in the Bible is the clearest example of how the victims to whom He had devoted His life, work, and ministry joined those in power to bring about His crucifixion and death. Human rights from the "top" is a fallacy.

At this point, let us point out a crucial factor that has escaped the critical eye of scholars—namely, the cosmological factor or the religious factor which has to do with people's perceptions of their experiences and self-understanding. The cosmological factor shapes the people's culture, which is the totality of that perception. Two facts are noteworthy here. First, the cult of hero-worship involving respect for authority, physical strength, rites, and material success, but not for solid human values is related to the cult of strength which takes diverse expressions in Africa. Among the Igbo of Nigeria, for instance, the cult of strength is perceived as the personal Chi or guardian angel, and in this it assumes a mystical expression. In traditional Africa, the cult of strength refers to mere hard work or art acquired by a person which enables a person to attain a measure of success in all undertakings.

Because Africans generally glorify material success, this concept has become bastardized to include corruption, murder, and any other wickedness to attain recognition by the society. In this context, therefore, most African nations do not uphold the worth and dignity of the human being. The dynamics of traditional social organizations emerge from a cosmology that is precarious, competitive, oppressive, and exploitative. Success in economic and political life is glorified. In the pursuit of economic and political ambitions, human beings lose their centeredness and sacredness. They become pawns, agents, ladders, numbers to be used but not persons any more. In most parts of Africa, personhood does not exist.[25] The humanity of the other is diminished by social injustice, which includes African colonialism. Clearly, the majority of African leaders are still at the lowest level of their human spiritual development. They are ruled by "passion," and "passion" manifests itself in lust, pride, anger, greed, materialism, and vanity. Since human rights are associated with goodness, they are based on spiritual values.

This takes us to a discussion of "morality." It is a well acknowledged fact in traditional Africa that morality derives from religion. Consequently, the dominant African world-view is incurably religious.[26] Africans understand God in the names they bear, in folktales and myths as the source and provider of the earth. They believe there is a constant interaction between the world of people and the world of the spirit. The eighteenth-century idea of a *deus abscoinditus* in Western cosmology is foreign to Africa. God is an existential dynamism. Africans recognize moral laws and norms as divinely given for living in a moral community, and they believe that any violation of such moral norms would attract a blessing or a curse

from God or the "gods." Given this conviction, the excesses of traditional Africans are minimized.

After Europe invaded the continent, Africans' traditional religious
attachment to their experiences and self-understanding was eroded
by the introduction of modernity and a secularist world-view. The
new African elites, by declaring themselves free from God and the
"gods," have been the worst victims. In "power positions" they do
not see themselves as being responsible either to God or to the people. The naked exercise of power in most African nations is an indicator of the neglect of the religious factor. The consequences of
their actions, even if not acknowledged, will confirm their evil, for
human rights are spiritually based. The question, then, arises, Is
there any hope for human rights in Africa?

THE DYNAMICS OF HUMAN RIGHTS REALIZATION: SUGGESTIONS

1. African countries should minimize their urge to establish international
   recognition in international politics and focus inwards to develop their
   skills and agriculture. The inherent danger is the antagonism of the
   superpowers. For instance, Nigeria spends a great deal of money aiding
   freedom fighters in South Africa, which is good. At the same time, the
   country has created many enemies and has spent huge sums of money
   on military hardware to deal with imagined external enemies, while the
   majority of its citizens suffer.

2. Africa should begin to create the type of leadership it requires to initiate
   a creative change, since "power" is "creative" when wielded by those who
   identify themselves with the hardships of the common people. This view
   has Biblical support especially in the person of Jesus Christ.

3. The "mediator group" in any African nation should be accorded support
   and recognition by the people. In Biblical times, God designated some
   individuals and prophets as the mediators or champions of human
   rights, and they were acknowledged as such by their society. This entails
   the positive response of the victims (the oppressed masses) to them for
   their encouragement and security. Even if the mediators paid the highest
   sacrifice, they would at least be satisfied that their effort had not been
   in vain.

4. The victims of oppression, which in our context are the majority of the
   Africans, should express public resentment of government policies that
   undermine their rights. The impact of this method is well known in our
   Biblical perspective. It is a tragedy when the masses of people are silenced
   by a few. It is true that the victims of oppression are so mesmerized by
   their leaders' power and their own deprivation that it appears they are
   powerless to act. This situation calls for courage of mind and mass
   mobilization through labor unions, age grades, and religious groups.

5. The religious factor is the most critical in this respect: The people's recovery of the divine image in themselves is needed. Africans are religious by nature, and the religious factor should not be divorced from other aspects of their lives. It has social, political, and economic implications. To operate on the basis of ideology without God cannot be creative. Leviticus 19 calls for a practical holiness that is a reflection of God's holiness. It is because human responsibility to God is primary and because social breakdown results from failure in that primary direction that God raised prophets and not social reformers (cf. Hosea 4:1). The whole conflict over human rights is a consequence of the individual's separation from God. Rights and responsibilities are held in a vertical and horizontal dimension motivated by love and our relation to God.

In sum, recovery of the awareness of our common humanity as beings made in the image of God offers us fresh insights into human rights realization. Because human social institutions pervert the love within them, repentance and forgiveness (cf. Neh. 5:9–13) are needed for structural changes to be made which manifest more love and protect human rights, as God's righteousness demands.

NOTES

1. R. N. Trivedi, "Human Rights, Rights to Development and the New International Economic Order: Perspectives and Proposals," in *Development, Human Rights, and the Rule of Law, Report of a Conference Held in the Hague,* April 27–May 1, 1981 (Oxford: Pergamon Press, 1981), pp. 131–41.

2. Luis Pasara, "Human Rights and Development: A Difficult Relationship," in *Development, Human Rights, and the Rule of Law,* pp. 181–85.

3. Emil Brunner, *Man in Revolt: A Christian Anthropology,* English trans. O. Wyon (Cambridge, Eng.: Lutterworth, 1939), p. 89.

4. Marsha Wilfong, ed., "Towards a Common Testimony," *The Reformed World* 39, no. 5 (1987), pp. 645–60.

5. Brunner, *Man in Revolt,* pp. 50, 94. We may modify this slightly and say that responsibility is the normal, mature expression of the human relationship with God. Otherwise one might be in danger of denying human status to those of defective or nil rationality and responsibility such as infants or imbeciles. But an infant has a relational awareness of its parents long before it can rationalize or act responsibly on it. The same must be allowed for the relationship between God and persons for whom we cannot use normal means and measures of judgment but whom we still regard as human.

6. I am indebted to Dr. C.J.H. Wright in this perspective in his *Human Rights: A Study on Biblical Themes* (Bramcote: Grove Books, 1979), pp. 8–28.

7. Ex. 22:21–22; Deut. 14:29; Ps. 82:3–4; Wx. 3:7–8; Amos 2:7; 5:11, 21, 24; Is. 58:6–7; Neh. 5; Ezk. 16:49; Matt. 25:30–46. See Jose Miranda,

Marx and the Bible, English trans. John Engelson (Maryknoll, N.Y.: Orbis Books, 1974), pp. 77–106.

8. A. Bloom, "Human Rights In Israel's Thought: A Study of Old Testament Doctrine," *Interpretation* 8 (1954), pp. 422–32 (p. 425).

9. This concept has received full testament in N. Onwu, "The Social Implications of Dikaiosune in Saint Matthew's Gospel" (Ph.D. thesis, University of Nigeria, Nsukka, 1983).

10. John C. Haughey, ed., *Faith That Does Justice* (New York: Paulist Press, 1977), pp. 68–109.

11. E. Achtemeier, "Righteousness in the Old Testament," in *Interpreter's Dictionary of the Bible*, vol. 4 (Nashville, Tenn.: Abingdon Press, 1962), p. 80.

12. Cf. Haying Simha Nahmani, *Human Rights in the Old Testament* (Tel Aviv: Chachik, 1964), pp. 30–31, 53, 65, 71, 78.

13. Onwu, "The Social Implications of Dikaiosune."

14. A little comment is needed to clarify what we mean when we use the word "dignity." Several authors have made a distinction between dignity that is "appraised" and dignity that is "bestowed." Bestowed dignity is imparted to the individual by God. Human value or worth based on the love of God for all people is bestowed dignity. Human worth may seem to be appraised dignity since the human race, created in God's image, possesses certain qualities that enable it to carry out its mandate to have dominion over the rest of creation (Gen. 1:28). But as the concept functions in the ethical texts so far referred to, the value accruing to humanity through its creation in God's image is in fact bestowed by God. All people are honored because their common creator and loving protector is God. This is further established in the fact of the love of God for all people in the offering of Christ. See Stephen Mott, *Biblical Ethics and Social Change* (New York:Oxford University Press, 1982), pp. 41ff.

15. Ibid., pp. 48–58.

16. God hears the cries of the poor and oppressed whenever their rights have been violated; see Gen. 4:10; Ex. 2:23, 22:22–23, I Kings, 21:17–19; Neh. 5:1, 9–13.

17. Mott, *Biblical Ethics and Social Change*, p. 53.

18. *The Constitution of the Federal Republic of Nigeria, 1979* (Department of Information, Lagos).

19. N. Onwu, "The Current of Biblical Studies in Africa," *Journal of Religious Thought* 41, no. 2 (Fall/Winter 1984–1985), pp. 35–46.

20. Pasara, "Human Rights and Development," pp. 181–85.

21. Trivedi, "Human Rights," pp. 131–41.

22. Osita Eze, *Human Rights in Africa* (Lagos: Nigerian Institute of International Affairs, 1984), pp. 62–64.

23. Cf. Chinua Achebe, *The Trouble with Nigeria* (Enugu, Nigeria: Fourth Dimension Publ., 1983).

24. Mott, *Biblical Ethics and Social Change*, p. 53.

25. N. Onwu, "The Distorted Vision: Reinterpretation of Mark 8:22–26 in the Context of Social Justice," *West African Religion* 29, nos. 1/2 (1980), pp. 46–52.

26. John S. Mbiti, *African Religions and Philosophy* (London: Heine-mann, 1970), p. 1.

5

Human Rights Issues and Violations: The African Experience

Osita Eze

In general discourse, human rights present problems of definition, scope, emphasis, limitations, access to impartial tribunals, and their jurisdictional scope. In Africa these issues are compounded in varying degrees by the basic condition of underdevelopment; by ideological orientations, whether capitalist or socialist; and by and large, by factors of religion and cultural traditions. The fact that most of Africa was subjugated by colonialism raises the problem of the appropriateness of imposed Judaeo-Graeco jurisprudence and institutions which emphasize litigation rather than conciliatory methods of settlement of disputes prevalent in African "traditional" societies. More critical, however, is the factor of underdevelopment which since the late 1970s has been characterized by stagnation, regression, and the increasing impoverishment, in absolute terms, of the majority of African peoples, an underdeveloped productive capacity and science and technology base, and the consequent inability to deal with problems of ecology and natural disasters. These factors are more evident in the rural sector where about 90 percent of the population lives—marginalized and alienated from the national and international movements in the field of human rights. They have also progressively led to the loss of national sovereignty and capacity for autonomous national decision making and a parallel development of foreign penetration and domination.

With regard to violations of human rights, to a large extent, the traditional approach is invariably limited to actual breaches of rights guaranteed or imminently threatened, and invariably requires that a complaint must show interest (*locus standi*)[1] in the matter. It does not matter that partial emphasis on human rights that are protected (civil and political rights and the right of private property) and the exclusion of socioeconomic rights may constitute concrete material breaches that may not be justifiable; that the ruling class using the instrumentality of the state—parliament, the judiciary, and the executive—promote and reinforce these breaches; that the nature of the socioeconomic system which perpetuates minority domination represents instances of violence and permanent breach; and that emphasis on individual rights neglects the validity of group rights.

The question that then arises is, is it sufficient to emphasize, in the technistic of technojuristic tradition, that violations arise only when formally guaranteed rights are breached? Should we not transcend pure formalism to the exposition of substance that underpins the basic contradictions between what is formally guaranteed and its concrete attainment?[2] In sum, is it not more appropriate to examine, what for want of a better expression, could be categorized as institutionalized permanent nonjustifiable breaches which in the end determine and shape the contents and essence of human rights protected?[3] Does this approach, which does not ignore the limited value of "legal" rights guaranteed, not show up their limitations and point in the direction of dynamic transformation of the philosophical basis and material foundations of human rights in a continent that has for centuries experienced, and continues to experience, basic derogations of human rights?

We intend to examine these issues in this chapter. In so doing we will emphasize the role of the state in its interaction with political and economic factors; the partial choice of rights guaranteed; the role of social groups and the interconnectedness and interdependent character of the various facets of our material existence—economic order, politics, culture, literature, art, psychic human conditions, and so on. We will show that these facets are better understood and influenced if they are visualized as part of the comprehensive totality, not as disjointed morsels of the historical process.[4] We also maintain that the Marxist dialectical method which proceeds from thesis, antithesis, and synthesis; that rejects unobservable phenomena; that emphasizes social reality; and that analyses contradictory elements—liberty and oppression, abundance and misery, class contradictions, and so on—represents the most scientific methodology for penetrating the essence of social phenomena, of which law and human rights are a part.[5] While we will emphasize conditions in independent African states, we will also examine, even in a limited manner, the impact of the global system on human rights performance in Africa.

MEANING AND SCOPE OF HUMAN RIGHTS

The meaning of law and the perception of human rights and their scope have varied depending on an area's stage of development, the structure of society, and the character of social relations of production. In Africa as elsewhere, law and human rights took root with the emergence of private property and various stages of state formations.[6] In the early phases, particularly before the Renaissance in Europe and the colonial imposition, the source of law and the basis of its ultimate validity were metaphysical, being either religious or naturalist or a combination of the two. Even though the concept of human rights appeared much later, the idea of justice or fairness which existed in various forms in all societies had already laid the foundations of what are now known as human rights. The African notion of human rights must therefore be examined in the context of its material experiences through the various phases of socioeconomic formations—primitive communalism, slavery, feudalism, and imposed capitalist structures.[7]

THE PRIMITIVE COMMUNAL PERIOD, OR THE SO-CALLED AFRICAN SOCIALISM, TO INDEPENDENCE

If, as it has been argued, the chief functions of law in any society are to preserve personal freedom and to protect private property, then by implication this twin role of law could not have applied during the period of primitive communalism. In this period, because of the low level of development or productive forces, the basic economic law was that of subsistence obliging individuals to live together, to jointly own the instruments and objects of labor (land, etc.), to work together and to share together. Therefore, the possibility of surplus and its private accumulation was precluded, leading to exploitation and inequality. Property relations as they exist in modern socialist states differ markedly from the communal ownership prevalent in primitive communalism for several reasons. (1) They are based on developed productive forces capable of generating surpluses that are appropriated by the state to serve general social welfare; (2) they are based on highly centrally organized and developed institutional structures, which nevertheless permit mass participation in the decision process and control of the same. Only a technological and scientific society is capable of rapid mobilization and development of human and material resources to serve well-defined goals rather than essentially that of simple economic activities of gathering, hunting, and, in the later years, animal husbandry, farming, and rudimentary handicrafts.

Once we appreciate these material differences, it becomes difficult to accept Keba M'Baye's romanticism about traditional African societies being socialist and humanist.[8] That precolonial African societies knew of a system of human rights adapted to the political and social and (one may add economic) situations prevalent at that time is not in doubt. But could this have been the case under primitive communalism when law could not have existed and when societal relations were governed by norms, customs, and moral standards that lacked the character and force of law? When M'Baye argues that the right to life, to work, to freely express oneself, and to practice religion existed, could he not be referring to subsequent developments that heralded societies differentiated on the basis of class—slave and feudal societies?

Most African societies did not experience classical slavery as it occurred in Europe and Asia. Nevertheless, there were institutions of slavery, pockets of slave-owning communities, not to mention the slave trade, which contributed immensely to the development of Europe and the New World. What human rights did these slaves possess?[9] The social ostracism of Africans parented by "freed" slaves still persists in many African countries today, and slave institutions may well exist in some of them. Yet these are part of Africa's precolonial heritage. The working of iron and metals; and the gradual development of technologies in the field of agriculture, transport, and textiles created the basis for the gradual implantation of feudalism both in its classical pattern as in Ethiopia and in a different form in some parts (such as Nigeria) where a feudal nexus was created by the allegiance owed to rulers, homage paid to them, and taxes and labor extracted from them.

In the more hierarchical societies, rulership was hereditary and governance—lawmaking, administration, and execution—was left in the hands of selected ruling families who also led the army in the apparent desire to protect their domains against foreign invasion.[10] Even in the so-called atomized and republican societies (Igbos), the heads of families and clans who were entitled to the labor of the family or the clan, as the case may be, used this to accumulate wealth and assume leadership roles, thus leading to class differentiation.[11] The predominant agricultural and underdeveloped economy therefore determines the limits of human rights. The rights and freedoms, to the extent that they existed, could only be exercised by the majority within this framework, and their application to the rulers and the ruled could not have been equal.

Colonialism had a decisive impact on this state of affairs. It deprived the African ruling classes of the right to make and enforce laws for their own people.[12] They lost the initiative to determine their economic, political, social, and cultural organization. Their total existence became subordinated to the imperatives of the colonialists. Imperialist laws, the sense of justice and equity, and the idea of what was civilized were effectively put in place. Local customs and laws which the colonialists considered abhorrent to their sense of justice—such as the caste system, trial by ordeal, witchcraft, and the killing of twins—were abolished.[13] In the ensuing decades the capitalist philosophy was gradually enthroned, together with the corresponding legal superstructure, thus creating new classes and new problems of human rights protection. Yet side by side with the imposed system there existed what was left of customary and Islamic conceptions of law and human rights, even when this vestige provided the motive for the evolution of African jurisprudence.

In summary, precolonial Africa, except for the primitive communal period, knew of human rights, and derogations. Each period was conditioned by its material historical experience, the level of its socioeconomic development, and its total belief system. At each epoch the ruling classes determined what these rights should be, their material scope, and who should enjoy them. Its inegalitarian nature ensured not only technical, but also institutional violation.

INDEPENDENT AFRICA: THE PHILOSOPHICAL UNDERPINNING OF LAW AND HUMAN RIGHTS

African jurisprudence, or what is left of it, continues to be fundamentally shaped by the common law and civil law experiences of Europe and to some extent the New World. The critical points of this legal movement include the Magna Carta of 1215, the Bill of Rights of 1688, the French Declaration of the Rights of Man and Citizen of 1789 which in turn was influenced by the American Declaration of Independence of 1776—all of which built on the gains made in the field of human rights by the Jews, the Greeks, and the Romans.[14]

In the earlier phase, these developments were marked by the near exclusiveness of the natural law theory connoting that laws derived from God and were discernible by human reason or that they derived from human nature. The natural law theory was thus not only a response to these conflictual relations, but also an attempt to rationalize them, which proved inadequate particularly with the fall of the

Holy Roman Empire, and with the decline of religion as a source of law, as a result of the secularization of state affairs and the Renaissance which emphasized the scientific method and rejected unverifiable phenomena.[15]

The positivist school of law which followed the Renaissance saw law as a product of human efforts, and thus the school rejected the idea of natural law and metaphysics. In its extreme form, the school was concerned only with pure law and excluded the metalegal factors that shape and ultimately give law its essence. By characterizing the source of law as the will of the sovereign[16] or a command of the sovereign, it not only implied the character of law as based on unequal relations, but also negated the utopian naturalist concept of social contract according to which the people transferred the power of governance to the rulers and reserved the residual right to reclaim it when the conduct of rulers became unconscionable.[17] Yet the purity of the positivistic school could not explain the basic inequalities inherent in the capitalist system that gave birth to it.

The sociological school, which is a variation of the positivist school, accepted the impact of metalegal factors and insisted that society should be so organized that law and its implementation should take into account social factors. According to one viewpoint, this involved the notion of social engineering, which implied the building of as efficient structure as possible which should satisfy the maximum wants with minimum friction.[18] However, the sociological school failed to address the state's critical role in its interaction with economic and political structures in a capitalist society.[19] It failed to see that the interests were not merely competing but also contradictory and that even when some of these interests might not be antagonistic, antagonistic relations dominate. In effect, the sociological movement failed to address itself to the class character of state power and the law that is its creation.[20]

Increasingly, the basic law of constitution and the derivative laws have come to be influenced and shaped by socialist jurisprudence in some African countries. These countries include mostly those that waged liberation wars against the colonialists—Algeria, Mozambique, Angola, and Zimbabwe as well as Ethiopia under Mengistu, Tanzania, and Congo Brazzaville. The emphasis of the United Nations' Charter on respect for fundamental human rights and human dignity without any form of discrimination, even though originally intended for the Western powers who suffered from Nazi racism, created the foundation for universalization of a broad scope of human rights. The United Nations' effort in this area continued with the epoch-making Universal Declaration of Human Rights of 1948 which was concretized in the two covenants of 1966.[21] The works carried on by various international organizations such as the International Labor Organization, the United Nations Committee for Trade and Development, the World Health Organization, and Unesco continue to influence human rights concepts in various African states as well as the world community at large.

Side by side with the dominant role of Judaeo-Graeco jurisprudence there still exist, particularly in the field of family law and property ownership, such concepts deriving from customary and Islamic traditions as were saved by the imperial powers. Increasing efforts are being made to upgrade and integrate these two systems into the imposed systems in order to accord with concrete material and philosophical conditions, as is reflected in many local laws and an African Charter on Human and Peoples' Rights adopted in Nairobi in 1981. The Charter in its preamble takes into consideration "the values of their historical tradition and the values of African civilization which should inspire and characterize their reflections of the conception of human rights."[22]

It is not surprising, therefore, that fundamental provisions on human rights in African countries, where they exist, may combine principles derived from the various inherited schools of jurisprudence and the traditional precepts.[23] Ultimately, the degree to which human rights are violated or protected will depend on the nature of the socioeconomic system in place in each African country, their varied levels of development, and the character of the ruling class and the state. The ruling class plays a dominant role, whether in socialist- or capitalist-oriented states in influencing the degree of popular participation and democratization in all African states.

The legal significance of preambles could have some impact on the extent to which the substantive provisions of human rights are observed since if they have no legal value they will remain essentially moral imperatives. African countries with a common law tradition tend to accord provisions of the preamble some role in the interpretation of the substantive rules in certain circumstances. The Tanzanian case of *Adamji v. E.A.P. & T.*[24] ruled that "the preamble to the constitution does in law constitute part of the constitution and so does not form part of the law." In the Nigerian case of *Attorney General of Ogun State and others* v. *The Attorney General of the Federation*, the Supreme Court enunciated that in the interpretation and application of the constitution the preamble to the constitution must always be borne in mind.[25] The High Court of Abeokuta had earlier ruled that "the preamble is part of the constitution and may be used in order to ascertain the meaning but only when the preamble is clear and definite in comparison with obscure and indefinite enacting words. The preamble serves to portray the intention of its framers and the mischief to be remedied but as a general rule the preamble is to be resorted to only in cases of ambiguity in the constitution."[26] Could the provisions in the preamble also influence the interpretation of enacting provisions where there "is a compelling reason"?[27]

The reason for examining the legal significance of the preamble is that it often incorporates such basic principles of government as justice, equality, and democracy which have direct relevance to human rights provisions guaranteed in the constitution. To the extent that there are no clear provisions in the substantive part of the constitution, such principles may and should be conducive to greater and wider concretization of human rights guaranteed in the constitution. Whether they influence interpretation in the positive or negative sense will in the end depend on the character of the ruling class which interest the judiciary invariably serves.

A more acute problem arises when reasonably clear provisions dealing with economic, social, and cultural rights are embodied in the Fundamental Objectives and Directives of State Policy, which are then declared nonjusticiable. This is the case when there is an apparent contradiction between these and substantive provisions of the constitution. The 1979 Nigerian Constitution directs the government to eradicate illiteracy, to promote science and technology, and, when practicable, to provide compulsory and universal free secondary, university, and adult education. The Directives also provide for the right to private property which is confirmed in the substantive provisions of the constitution, while at the same time guaranteeing the freedom to hold opinions and receive information through the medium of private property and private schools. On the one hand, the Objective Principles and Directives of State Policy envisage that the government should provide equal and adequate educational opportunities at all educational levels. On the other hand, educational institutions are seen as economic activities capable of private ownership. Despite the courts' usually liberal interpretation of the constitution and the basic contradiction between general provision of education which should be equal and adequate, the court held in *Archbishop A. O. Okojie v. A. G. Lagos State* that the intended act was unconstitutional since it ran contrary to Section 36 of the constitution, which they cannot infringe and to which they must conform and be subsidiary to.[28]

Yet Section 13 of the Objectives and Directives stipulates that "it shall be the duty and responsibility of all organs of government, and of all authorities and persons, exercising legislative, executive or judicial powers to conform to, observe and apply the provisions of this Chapter of the constitution."

Since the responsibility to ensure compliance rests with the legislature and the electorate, its utility in terms of influencing judicial decisions has by and large been emasculated. Technically, the interpretation may be sound, but it simply confirms the partial choice made by the ruling class as to what rights are enforceable, and the marginalization of socioeconomic rights on which all else depends. It is consistent with the principle of preeminence given to private property over social goals.

The practice of francophone African countries with respect to the legal significance of the preamble is not as unequivocal as that in countries with a common law tradition. In some of these countries the preamble is regarded as having some constitutional value, especially when it is clearly and expressly formulated. In other countries, the preamble is seen as representing general principles of law that should inspire legislative and administrative action, and it is not seen as a prescription of either a constitutional or legislative nature. The impact of the preamble on judicial interpretations of fundamental human rights provisions will in the end depend on the practice prevalent in each country.[29]

AFRICAN EXPERIENCES: TECHNICAL AND INSTITUTIONAL VIOLATIONS

Most African constitutions embody provisions on human rights which may be justiciable or nonjusticiable. Some of the preambular provisions refer to the French Declaration of Rights of Man and Citizen, and other provisions are similar to those elaborated in the Universal Declaration of Human Rights. Since all independent African states are members of the United Nations and other relevant institutions, it is assumed that they accept the foundations for human rights promotion and protection elaborated therein.

But there is selective emphasis on protected human rights, depending on whether the underlying philosophical value system is capitalist or socialist or even Islamic. The secular capitalist states emphasize civil and political rights along with the right to private property. Civil and political rights include the right to life; prohibition of torture or inhuman and degrading treatment or punishment, slavery or the slave trade; the right to liberty and security of persons to freedom of movement, to equality before the law, privacy, and freedom of thought; the right to opinions, peaceful assembly, and freedom of association; and the right to take part in the conduct of public affairs and to vote and be elected at genuine periodic elections.

Invariably, all are entitled to enjoy these rights without distinction as to race, sex, color, language, religion, political or other opinion, national or social origin, birth or other status. Yet the role of the dominance of private property, even in the developed welfare states, in perpetuating inequality and injustice is often glossed over on the basis of the primacy of individual freedom to pursue goals in a free enterprise system with minimal state intervention and control. Nearly everywhere, whether in secular Christian or in Islamic states, discrimination exists based on sex, religion, and political opinion. Racism and ethnic-based discrimination persist. Chad, Sudan, Kenya, Uganda, and to some extent Nigeria represent instances of ethno-based or racial discrimination.[30]

If we consider certain categories of human rights, the situation is nearly the same. In most cultural and religious traditions the right to life is accepted as fundamental and sacrosanct. Yet the manner in which it is guaranteed empties it of its substance. The right is conceived primarily in a technistic manner. Everyone has the right to life, and life may not be taken except in certain specified circumstances according to due process, in self-defense or defense of property, or in the course of lawful arrest, even when the force used may be reasonable. Hardly any distinction is made between loss of life where only private property is the object of defense. Somehow primacy is given to private property over life, thereby confirming the thesis that the major task of the capitalist state is to protect private property by force or war if necessary.[31]

More fundamentally at the institutional level, no provision is made for the socioeconomic and cultural rights needed to sustain life: the right to work, to obtain social security, fair wages, and equal remuneration for work of equal value without distinction of any kind, to enjoy an adequate standard of living, freedom from hunger, to get an education, to form trade unions, to enjoy the highest attainable standard of mental and physical health, to take part in cultural life, and to enjoy the benefits of scientific progress and its application. In nearly all African countries, at most 20 percent of the population can claim to enjoy in varying degrees these privileges without which the right to life is reduced to a mere palliative. Without life there can be no society and no rights. Yet the manner in which that right is conceptualized and applied raises serious doubts as to the commitment of most ruling classes to human rights generally.

The inability to guarantee socioeconomic rights is a factor of underdevelopment, resulting from neocolonial development strategies. Nearly everywhere this inability has led not only to stagnation but also to regression and the increasing impoverishment of a growing majority of African peoples. Even though the principle of self-determination which encompasses both civil and political as well as social and economic rights has been progressively accepted by African countries, its implementation in various countries has varied immensely. The right implies that all peoples have the right to self-determination by virtue of which they freely determine their political status and pursue their economic, social, and cultural development. It also implies that all peoples may for their own ends freely dispose of their natural wealth and resources without prejudice to any obligations arising out of international economic cooperation based on the principle of mutual benefit and international law.[32] Subject to these reservations, the African Charter on Human and Peoples' Rights also stipulates that this right shall be exercised in the exclusive interest of the peoples and that in no case shall a people be deprived of it. In case of expropriation, the dispossessed people shall have the right to the lawful recovery of its property as well as to an adequate compensation.[33] Not only shall all peoples have the right to development, but all states have the duty, separately or in cooperation with others to ensure they exercise the right of development.[34]

The rights to self-determination and development represent the core of the problem and a point of departure for African performance in the field of human rights. This is not to deny the value of civil and political rights which under certain circumstances provide limited opportunities for reform. In most countries of Africa these rights have remained mainly illusory. "Self" in the right of self-determination approximates to the incumbent ruling class which determines what and for whom "development" means or is meant for. With increasing economic crises, these ruling classes have progressively been subjugated by imperialism, the IMF, and the World Bank which serve primarily the interests of imperialists, just as the neocolonial arrangements typified by the Africa, Caribbean and the Pacific (ACP) arrangement have imposed conditions that promote the interests of local and foreign capital to the detriment of the African masses. The African countries have become great debtor nations and overwhelmingly depend on foreign capital, technology, and expertise. They have increasingly lost their sovereign right to make autonomous decisions in matters of national development. Under the circumstances, the right of self-determination and development has ceased to be taken seriously. This tendency is reflected internally by increasing poverty and inequality. In this context one is better able to appreciate the limited efficacy of the civil and political rights guaranteed in most African constitutions.

To begin with, despite pretensions to the contrary, the basic laws (constitutions) are invariably made not by the people but by vested interests, lawyers, bankers, industrialists, merchants, and other elite, and in some cases traditional rulers as well. Consequently, these rights reflect a bias favorable to these groups. The right to life has already been examined.[35]

What can be said about the democratic right to participate in public affairs, which should not only ensure that the majority participate in shaping the political economy but also that they are in a position to effectively control the rulers? Most constitutions invariably provide for periodic elections whether under multi- or uniparty systems. There is invariably general franchise and adult suffrage. The elections are expected to be free and fair. How does an ignorant population with a low level of consciousness achieve these objectives, when they do not understand the issues involved? When they are alienated from the mainstream of governance and are manipulated, intimidated, or blackmailed into voting, and in many cases both the electoral register and the voting are rigged and votes and offices bought and sold, with the result that the same class is elected into office to continue oppressing and exploiting the masses? It does not make much sense, therefore, to wave the constitutions and declare that African constitutions guarantee the right of citizens to participate in governance.[36]

What about the notion of equality before the law and equal protection of the law? Access to the law implies knowledge of the law even when bourgeois law insists that ignorance of law is no excuse. Most of the population is indeed ignorant of the law. They see the legal institutions and the law which they apply as alien and do not have the economic means to pursue claims before the courts, even when they are aware that their rights have been infringed. In many African states the legal aid scheme is not extensive enough to cover a larger section of the population that may not be in a position to pay high legal fees.[37] Invariably, the right to counsel is negated because the quality of legal service available will in the end depend on the economic means, social status, and so on, of the litigants. It is in this context that the constitutional requirement for a fair hearing is better understood as primarily benefiting the privileged.

What about the principle of separation of powers—between the legislature, the executive, and the judiciary—which should minimize arbitrariness and be conducive to the impartiality and independence of the judiciary?[38] Does it make much sense when the same class enacts the laws, interprets them, and enforces them? Is it not logical that the laws and their implementation should promote and sustain productive relations favorable to this class? The law itself is arbitrary with respect to the majority, and its interpretation and execution are not likely to be different. When you add to this the principle of the rule of law implying respect for fundamental human rights, democracy, and the imperative of obedience to the law, it becomes clear what end it is intended to serve. In the circumstances, disobedience to unjust laws amounts to breach and the imposition of sanctions that are enforced with all the instruments of coercion a state possesses. In the end it serves to preempt a radical transformation of the inequitable socioeconomic system in place. Any attempt in this direction might amount to a crime against the state and may lead to the death penalty and harassment by security officers. What then for the right to life, freedom of expression, and so on?[39] Even when judges have taken the oath to uphold the constitution, both the executive and the legislative may interfere when the ruling class feels threatened or angered by judicial decisions. President Kaunda of Zambia once declared, with regard to the independence of the judiciary, that such independence would be maintained "on the condition that its criticisms were constructive."[40] In the Ethiopian case of *Tewfic v. Public Security Department,*[41] the representative of the Public Security Department failed to appear before the court, despite a court order to that effect. The Nigerian military, reacting to the Supreme Court's decision in *E. O. Lakanmi and Anor v. Attorney General (West) and Others,*[42] nullified not only the decision but also all judicial decisions, and so forth, affecting the decrees made by the federal military government. In Uganda under Idi Amin, the judiciary was so terrorized that it ceased to act as an arbiter.[43]

In some instances the courts have insisted on their guaranteed independence.[44] But there is always the danger that in the prevalent fluid situation that exists in most African countries, the independence of the judiciary could be threatened, since it emphasizes the interpretation and application of the law, whether just or unjust.

If the right to work remains a luxury, the right of workers to organize and promote their interests is still precarious. In many cases, not only are trade union rights circumscribed, but also the leadership is often coopted into the ranks of the ruling classes.[45] Strikes may be banned in certain sectors, and radical trade unionists may be proscribed. Industrial peace is promoted to create an environment for appropriation by local and foreign capital, the state playing the role of broker between them. Minimum wages, where they exist, are mostly inadequate to meet the basic needs of workers. Therefore, the right of workers to strike or to prosecute claims before the courts or tribunals can only have marginal effects. What then for the right to an adequate standard of living, to freedom from hunger, and to the enjoyment of the highest attainable standard of mental and physical health as well as the right to take part in cultural life and to enjoy the benefits of scientific progress and its application?

What about the freedom of expression which includes freedom of the press as well as the right to receive information? To begin with, the practice of hoarding information by most African governments makes it difficult for the ruled to assess and inform government decisions. Routine information is often clearly marked "secret," and publications reactivate the secrecy laws found in the statute books of most African states. Publication of material embarrassing to government may lead to sanctions. No doubt there is need to protect certain information, the exposition of which might threaten national security or lead to disaffection or imminent breach of the peace. But who decides on these sanctions, the courts or the government? Whereas in many cases the courts of law have the last say, there might be some respite. They might be subject to prior restriction in which the granting of licenses might be used discriminately or they might be censored. But these derogations must be seen in their proper context. In capitalist-oriented states the media are invariably owned or controlled by the bourgeoisie, both public and private, and censorship exists (1) to ensure conformity with the government policies generally accepted by the ruling classes or (2) to prevent the exposure of government or political leadership malpractices. In some of the countries the media might even be controlled by foreign capital, and in nearly all countries they are influenced by foreign media.[46]

We could go on and on, not because one is necessarily cynical or pessimistic, but because our concrete material and psychic conditions are what they are. They have become more precarious.

What about the socialist-oriented states? They too are plagued by the problems of underdevelopment, and as a consequence they too have increasingly come within the grip of imperialism. There are some differences, however. They proffer an anti-imperialist posture. They have attempted in varying degrees to abolish private property and to extend the participation of the masses in the decision-making process. For instance, the 1969 constitution of the Peoples Republic of the Congo provides for a workers' party. Article 30 of the constitution provides that all means of production be constituted in the communal properties of the people which are in the hands of the state, properties belonging to people's cooperative organizations as well as personal property. Even though private property is guaranteed, subject to its not being used to the detriment of another, it is provided that in the interests of the general public restrictions may be imposed on the right to property. The state can take certain economic measures to encourage the working masses to unite themselves against exploitation. In addition, the constitution makes provisions for the right to work and envisages the promotion of health care and education.[47]

The constitution of the Republic of Benin confirms the adoption of an anti-imperialist program of national construction and a national socialist orientation based on Marxist Leninism. The ultimate objective is to liquidate the imperialist economic base and to enable the public sector to play a leading role in the economy. Both nationals and foreigners may own the means of production, subject to their being used in conformity with set objectives. The Revolutionary National Assembly is to be composed of elected commissaries of the people, although what qualifies one for election is not stated, as in the case of the Algerian Constitution of 1976. Finally, the constitution makes provision for progressive attainment of full employment, health care, and education which are within the purview of socioeconomic and cultural rights.[48]

The Algerian constitution reaffirms the adoption of the "irreversible option of socialism," although it is not quite clear to what extent recent reforms in that country have affected that option. Freedom of expression guaranteed under the constitution cannot be used to undermine the basis of the Algerian socialist revolution. Not only has the government taken over the major means of production, but also it has been specifically stated that wealth or ownership of business is incompatible with the representation of the people. Accordingly, the constitution provides that the majority within the Elected Peoples' Assemblies be made up of workers and peasants. Party and state institutions are charged with the duty of realizing socialist goals and socializing the means of production, which constitute the fundamental basis of socialism. In addition to civil and political rights, the constitution also provides for social, economic, and cultural rights, such as the rights to work, health, and education.[49]

The amendment to the interim constitution of 1967 confirmed the socialist option enshrined in the Arusha Declaration. Other African countries—Burkina Faso, Ethiopia since Mengistu, Mozambique, and Angola—have adopted the socialist option, and their laws and human rights regimes are expected to follow a similar pattern. While the adoption of a socialist option does not signify the enthronement of socialism, it does by and large point to the rejection of exploitation inherent in a free enterprise system. Realizing that private property stands in the way of effective human rights promotion and protection, every effort is being made to enthrone the social ownership of the means of production. There are invariably gains in the process of mass mobilization and participation at various levels of government, and the dichotomy between the urban and rural centers is more directly addressed. There is hardly any pretension with respect to the concept of separation of powers since all organs of government, even though entrusted with their respective functions of lawmaking, adjudication, and execution, are nevertheless expected to work in unison to promote and secure socialist goals. The judges are no doubt independent, in the sense that they are obliged to apply the law, but in so doing they are expected to be guided by the principles of socialism which inform the laws. Just as with the three arms of government, the press is expected to inform the people of socialist goals and to promote and defend the goals of socialist revolution. Freedom of expression is thus limited by the imperatives of building a socialist state.

These objectives might not have been achieved in many instances because measures taken have not been sufficiently deep rooted; because the leadership is not fully committed to socialist goals; and because various forces, both internal and external, collude to subvert the building of socialism. Failures to achieve these objectives have nothing to do with the merits of socialism which has the potential for establishing a more rational human social order. The failure to make much progress should not be equated with the failure of socialism per se, but rather should be regarded as resulting from a lack of clarity in the goals sought and the adoption of wrong tactics and strategies to overthrow nascent local capitalism and imperialism.

From a certain perspective, the difference between the capitalist and socialist concept of law and human rights is that in the capitalist view basic contradictions exist between declaration and objective conditions to achieve them. In the socialist view, private property and imperialism are seen as the main causes of underdevelopment and as obstacles to the enjoyment of human rights.

CONCLUSIONS

If we have emphasized institutionalized nonjusticiable violations of human rights, it is because we are convinced that they are at the root of the problem. Human rights, particularly civil and political rights, cannot make much sense unless the material economic and social conditions lie at their base. The illiterate, the poor, the sick, and the exploited have little access to these rights. To the extent that socioeconomic rights are not guaranteed, then to that extent will civil and political rights remain palliatives for the masses of Africans whose rights are thereby in reality violated.

This is not to deny the limited opportunities which such rights offer. They can (within limits) provide opportunities for challenging the exploitative systems in place and show up the contradictions between what is postulated and actual reality. In the end these limited rights serve primarily to moderate intraruling class conflicts.

The record of violations of human rights in Africa remains very discouraging. Some progress might have been made since independence, but the increasing impoverishment of the African peoples, together with the growing reach of imperialism in the African countries with the active collaboration of the local ruling classes which has increasingly undermined the capacity of these classes to take the initiative and to make autonomous decisions in matters of national development, leaves little room for consolation. If the African masses are to gain from the national and world movements in the field of human rights they must be at the center of development. They must participate in that process on the basis of self-reliance. They must also be in the forefront of national liberation which can only be achieved on the basis of anti-imperialist struggle. In effect, what is needed is a socialist transformation of African countries which alone will ensure that the majority decree laws are protective and promotional of their human rights and not violative of them. This, in our view, is the central problem of human rights protection or violation.

NOTES

1. *Olawoyin* v. *Attorney General, Northern Nigeria* (1966) ALL NLR 296, *Chibee Tyough* v. *Attorney General, Benue State and 4 others* (1982), 3 NCLR, p. 734.

2. I. Shivji, "From the Analysis of Forms to the Exposition of Substance: The Tasks of a Lawyer Intellectual," *Eastern African Law Review* 5, nos. 1 and 2 (1972), pp. 6–7. Osita C. Eze, "Human Rights, Legal Rights or Social Rights," *Human Rights Education in Nigeria*, in L. A. Jinadu and U.M.O. Ivowi, eds. (Lagos, Nigeria: Nigeria National Commission for Unesco, 1982), pp. 96–99.

3. Ibid.

4. F. Baran, "The Commitment of the Intellectual," in F. Baran, ed., *The Longer View* (New York: Monthly Review Press, 1966), p. 8; Osita C. Eze, "Human Rights, Legal Rights or Social Rights."

5. T. E. McCarthy, J. B. Marie, S. P. Marks, and L. Sirois, *Human Rights Studies in Universities*, under the supervision of Karel Vasak (Paris: Unesco, 1978), p. 82.

6. "The Origin of the Family, Private Property and the State," in Marx/ Engels, *Selected Works* (Moscow: Progress Publishers, 1982), pp. 461–556; Lenin, "The State and Revolution," *Collected Works*, vol. 25; Patrick F. Wilmot, *Sociology, a New Introduction* (London: Collins International Text Books, 1985), Chapter 4; Osita C. Eze, ed., *Society and the Rule of Law* (Owerri, Nigeria: Totan Publishers, 1987), p. 21.

7. Osita C. Eze, *Human Rights in Africa: Some Selected Problems* (Lagos: Nigerian Institute of International Affairs, in cooperation with Macmillan Nigerian Publishers, Ltd., 1984), p. 14.

8. Keba M'Baye, "Organisation de L'unite Africaine," in *Les Dimensions Internationales Des Droits De L'Homme*, Chapter 4.

9. W. Rodney, *How Europe Underdeveloped Africa* (London: Zed Press, 1962).

10. J. F. Ade Ajayi and Ian Espie, *A Thousand Years of West African History* (Ibadan: Ibadan University Press, 1965); E. O. Esiomokhai, *The Colonial Legal Heritage in Nigeria* (Akure: Fagbamibe, Publishers, 1986), pp. 2, 11–17.

11. A. Afigbo, *Ropes of Sand: Studies in Igbo History and Culture* (Oxford: Oxford University Press, 1981).

12. P. Gonidec, *Les Droits Africains: Evolution et Source* (Paris: R. R. Pichon and R. Durand Auzias, 1978), p. 18; E. O. Esimokhai, *The Colonial Legal Heritage*, Chapter 2.

13. See *Oke Lanipekun and Others* v. *Amao Ojetunde* (1944), AC 170; *Eshaugby: Eleko/Nigerian Government* (1931), AC 662, 673; M. B. Hooker, *Legal Pluralism: An Introduction to Colonial and Neo-Colonial Laws* (Oxford: Clarendon Press, 1975), p. 129; T. O. Elias, *British Colonial Laws* (London: Stevens and Sons, 1982), pp. 93–95.

14. H. S. Commanger, ed., *Documents of American History* (New York: Appleton-Century Crofts, 1948), p. 103; U. O. Umezurike, *Self-Determination in International Law* (Hamden, Conn.: Archon Books, 1972), pp. 7–8; L. Henkin, "Rights Here and There," *Columbia Law Review* 81, no. 8 (December 1981); Eze, *Human Rights in Africa*, p. 69.

15. Reginald W. M. Dias, *Jurisprudence* (London: Butterworths, 1976), p. 75 et seq; Leo Straus, *Natural Right and History* (Chicago: University of Chicago Press, 1971); Osita C. Eze, "Toward a Positive Conception of Human Rights," Paper presented at the International Conference on Human Rights Education in Rural Environments, organized by the Department of Jurisprudence.

16. D. Lloyd, *Introduction to Jurisprudence* (London: Butterworths, 1978), pp. 291, 292; Dias, *Jurisprudence*, Chapter 15.

17. *The Social Contract* (1762 Everyman Library), pp. 13–15; Henkin, "Rights Here and There," p. 1591.

18. Alan Hunt, *The Sociological Movement in Law* (London: Macmillan, 1978), pp. 11–30.

19. Ibid., p. 151.

20. Osita C. Eze, "Theoretical Perspectives and Problematics," in Osita C. Eze, ed., *Society and the Rule of Law*, p. 30.

21. International Covenant on Economic, Social, and Cultural Rights and International Covenant on Civil and Political Rights, both of which have since come into force.

22. African Charter on Human and Peoples' Rights, CAB/LEG/67/14 Rev. 3 1981, para. 5.

23. C. Ameluxen, "Marriage and Women in Islamic Countries," *Human Rights Case Studies* 2 (1975), p. 89.

24. LRT No. 6, p. 10.

25. (1982) 3 NCLR, vol. 3, p. 166.

26. *Chief Victor Olabisi Onabangjo* v. *Concord Press Nigeria, Ltd.* (1981), 2 NCLR, p. 399.

27. *A. G.* v. *Prince Earnest August Hanover* (1957) AC 436 and 463. See also H. Chand, *Nigerian Constitutional Law* (Modinager, India: Santosh Publishing House, 1982), p. 15.

28. (1981) 3 NCLR, vol. 3, p. 166.

29. See Conseil d'Etat, January 25, 1957, "Syndicat Federal des fonctionaires malagaches et assimile," cited in T. G. Verhelst and Zugmunt B. Plater, eds., *Constitutional Guarantees of the Individual*; T. G. Verhelst, ed., *Legal Process and the Individual: African Source Materials* (Addis Ababa: Centre for African Legal Development, Faculty of Law, Haile Selassi I University, 1965), pp. 31–32, preamble to Togolose Constitution of 1963.

30. Eze, *Human Rights in Africa*, Chapters 4, 5, and 6.

31. Adam Smith, *An Inquiry into the Nature and Causes of the Wealth of Nations* (Chicago: Encyclopaedia Britannica, 1952), pp. 308–15; H. J. Laski, *A Grammar of Politics* (London: George Allen and Unwin, 1967), pp. iii–v.

32. Ibid., Article 21 (2).

33. Ibid.

34. Ibid.

35. Ibid.

36. See B. O. Nwabueze, *Constitutionalism in Emergent States* (London: C. Hurst and Co., 1973).

37. Legal aid is often limited to specified criminal cases, and the property qualifications are generally low. See A. M. Akiwumi and H. G. Eshetu, "Legal Aid in French-Speaking Countries," both in *Legal Process and the Individual*.

38. B. O. Nwabueze, *The Presidential Constitution of Nigeria* (London: C. Hurst and Company in association with Enugu: Nwamife Publishers, 1982), pp. 30–35; Chand, *Nigerian Constitutional Law*, p. 9.

39. Osita C. Eze, ed., *Society and the Rule of Law*, Chapters 1 and 6.

40. See *African Research Bulletin* 6, no. 7 (July 1–31, 1969—August 15, 1969), p. 1479 et seq.

41. (1965), unreported Ethiopian High Court case.

42. SC 58/1069. See also *The Supremacy and Enforcement of Powers of Decree* 1970. Subsequent military governments in Nigeria have enacted similar legislation. See also the Somalian case of *Abdulrezak Ahmed* v. *The State* (1970 Habeas Corpus Petition 31/70) and *A. Ahmed Amin Moallin* v. *The State* (1970 Criminal App. no. 15) precluding the Supreme Court from entertaining proceedings in habeas corpus in matters that fall within the jurisdiction of the National Security court. See Somalie Law No. 12 of March 3, 1970.

43. H. Kyemba, *State of Blood* (London: Corgi Book, 1977), p. 116; *Uganda and Human Rights Report of the International Commission on Jurists* (Geneva: United Nations, 1977), pp. 23–24.

44. Brun-Otto Bryde, *The Politics and Sociology of African Legal De-*

velopment (Frankfurt am Main: Alfred Metzner Verlang, 1976) p. 68.

45. U. G. Damachi, "The Role of Trade Unions in the Development Process, with a Case Study of Ghana" (New York: Praeger Publishers, 1974); *Daily News*, Tanzania, January 5, 1973, p. 1, reporting the manner in which a strike by the Democratic Movement of Tanzania (DMT) workers was quelled. See Patrick E. Ollawa, *Participatory Democracy in Zambia: The Political Economy of National Development* (Elms Court, Devon: Arthur H. Stockwell Ltd., 1979), pp. 157–60.

46. See "Index on Censorship," 16, no. 2 (February 1987) and 16, no. 3 (March 1987). See also Osita C. Eze, "The Quest for Communication Freedom and Consequences for National Development," Paper presented at the National Communications Policies Conference, Topo Badagry, Nigeria, February 2–7, 1982.

47. The Constitution of the Peoples Republic of the Congo, December 31, 1969, Articles 33 and 34.

48. The Fundamental Law of the Republic of Benin of 1977 Preamble and Articles 13, 19, 23, 24, 32, 127, 131, and 147.

49. The Algerian Constitution of 1976. See also Osita C. Eze, "Right to Health as a Human Right in Africa," in Rene-Jean Dupy, ed., *Right to Health as Human* (The Hague: Sigthoff and Nordhoff, 1979).

PART II

ISSUES AND VIOLATIONS

6

Revolutionary Violence, Development, Equality, and Justice in South Africa

Okwudibia Nnoli

Revolutionary violence is associated with a political program designed to effect a change in the social order. It usually occurs in the form of resistance against obvious social evils. Its goals are greater equality, justice, and freedom for the majority. It seeks the safety and freedom of both individual and group from threats to life and property and their protection from fear and doubt of all forms of danger.

Violence is often the result of the domination by the ruling class over the underprivileged classes, initially by force but sustained later by propaganda, intimidation, blackmail, bribery, and corruption. Usually visited by a dominant minority on a powerless majority, it is commonly based on a combination of exploitation, repression, and fragmentation of the majority which places them below a minimum level of existence and always at a disadvantage. Inevitably, confrontations ensue between spokespersons of the poor majority and those of the ruling class, including revolts, uprisings, and civil wars.

The objective of revolutionary violence is to pull the majority of the population above the minimum level of existence and to eliminate their disadvantage. When successful, it tends to move the socioeconomic and cultural system toward an ever larger measure of power to the people for conscious participation in building their own

future; higher production for societal needs; nonexploitative relations of production and equitable principles of distribution; production that is oriented toward the reality, needs, and aspirations
of the masses; and the maximum possible enjoyment of culture by
the masses, as well as an aesthetically and ecologically sound environment.

Only pacifist liberals will deprecate such a humanizing violence.
This is because they absolutize the concept of violence by avoiding
the necessary distinction between aggressor and victim, predator
and prey, exploiter and exploited. Such a view loses all practical
meaning as well as all moral force. No contribution to peace and
progress is likely to emanate from a lofty "even-handed" condemnation of all violence. It can only give aid and comfort to the subject
of an aggressive war without deluding the victim of aggression. To
eliminate war is essentially to eliminate aggressive war. To suggest
that it can be done by eliminating wars of liberation conducted with
revolutionary violence subverts both human logic and human values.

Violence that is used to hold a person down in poverty, ignorance,
disease, prejudice, hate, and exploitation must be distinguished
from violence used to free a person from these obstacles to human
progress. The latter violence serves to remove impediments from the
path of a person's realization of his or her potentialities as a morally
autonomous agent. It implies the removal of a whole arsenal of restrictions on an oppressed person that had limited his or her area
of choices and opportunities. In the process it removes the major
obstacles to human creativity such as lack of self-confidence and
self-respect, generates a new social and political consciousness that
is regenerative, and frees the individual from despair, powerlessness, helplessness, and inaction. The individual becomes fearless,
and in addition, acquires the consciousness of a common case, national identity, and collective esprit de corps. Such a consciousness
is vitally necessary for building a new society at a higher level of
human creativity. It is a prerequisite for an assault on all forms of
labor alienation, including those that arise from the odious system
of apartheid.

APARTHEID, INEQUALITY, AND INJUSTICE

Apartheid in South Africa is a monstrous system of structural
violence that is sanctioned by law and protected by a conscious policy
of militarization of the country's domestic life, as well as military
aggression against the neighboring black states. It is a particularly
vicious and dangerous form of human domination, whose central

tenet is racism. Based on a doctrine of white supremacy and racial discrimination, it not only separates by law the white, coloured, Indian, and black peoples from one another, but also emphasizes the division of the black population into different peoples. It then organizes a system of discrimination based on this separation. This is done by a complex and detailed system of legislation that literally covers all aspects of the life of the nonwhite population, and is symbolized by the Pass Laws which provide for complete control over the movements of the black majority.[1]

Like all ideologies, apartheid serves material interests. Its main function is to create such an inferiority complex among the blacks as to enable their maximum exploitation by white private capital and the capital of imperialism. Indeed, apartheid expresses the tenacious clinging of private capital to the methods and practices of primitive accumulation. As under slave labor, it promotes profit maximization by keeping that portion of the national wealth that accrues to the black people, as consumers, to the barest minimum. Consequently, the real wages of the African miners are lower today than they were in 1911.[2] The denial of the humanity of the slave is repeated under apartheid. In order to mobilize broad support for the process of accumulation, private capital has bribed the other classes of the white community. White workers receive monthly cash grants and reserved jobs, and white farmers receive huge subsidies and loans, as well as free black labor, including especially prison labor directed to the farms.[3]

Economic exploitation of the black majority by the white minority is at the heart of apartheid. South Africa is a unique capitalist society to the extent that profit maximization is the overt, principal objective of state policy.[4] It operates as a perfect model of a naked capitalist social formation that brooks no interference whatsoever with the profit motive. This value in turn has become the motivating force of apartheid. All state policies and institutions in South Africa have been built on the profit motive and derive their meaning and life force from it.

Under the governance of this profit motive the black majority occupies a most unenviable position as mere toilers. Although they are the major producers of the social wealth, they produce it not for their own benefit but for its appropriation by the white minority. When they are permitted to consume part of this wealth, their share is manipulated to coincide with that proportion which will produce in them the maximum amount of work on a continuing basis.[5] In other words, the black African is not regarded fully as an individual like his white counterpart; rather, the black is perceived as a commodity that can be quantified in profit and loss terms. As mere labor power, blacks belong to the same category as gold, diamonds, and other commodities. In essence, the apartheid system denies their humanity and consequently exploits them beyond the limits morally permissible for humanity. The Bantustan policy of separate black townships is an eloquent testimony to this inhuman exploitation. The Bantustans (homelands) convert the black population into pools of cheap labor for white enterprises.

Under these circumstances, labor alienation of the black majority is a pervasive aspect of the South African production process. Not only are they assigned to menial, marginal, and uncreative roles; but also, their wages are extremely low. For example, the black migrant worker is paid wages sufficient to maintain only one person, on the grounds that his or her real home is in the countryside and as such there is no need for the wage to support a family. Similarly, black workers do not enjoy any social security on the grounds that they can return to their villages to be cared for. Such labor alienation cannot promote the creativity which is so vital to development; in fact it frustrates it. Therefore, apartheid is antidevelopment.

At the psychological level, apartheid is equally alienating. Apart from the alienation which it creates by confining the black workforce to noncreative and nonsupervisory roles, it is a constantly reiterated insult to all black people individually and collectively. Therefore, it not only violates their psychic existence, but it also brings shame and humiliation on their persons collectively. Consequently, it is a source of anger among the blacks. Acquiescence to it undermines self-respect, self-confidence, self-actualization, and creates fear, anxiety, frustration, helplessness, and despondency. Apartheid reduces the blacks in South Africa to an inferior status, alienating them from themselves through a system of humiliating racist discrimination, brutalization, repression, and popularization of the image of the black's inferior status. It creates the rejection of self, or, at least, a profoundly disturbed ambivalence on the part of the black.

Furthermore, the apartheid society has erected a comprehensive and highly repressive framework of legislation designed to deny blacks any meaningful political rights. Among these laws are the Native Administration Proclamation, the Natives (Urban Areas) Proclamation, the Masters and Servants Proclamation, the Suppression of Communism Act (1950)—renamed and reinforced as the Internal Security Act (1976), the Riotous Assemblies Act (1956), the Sabotage Act (1962), the Terrorism Act (1967), and the Groups Areas Act. At the labor front this legislation denies workers the right to leave their jobs against the wishes of their employers, enforces very harsh labor discipline, gives the state complete control over the recruitment and distribution of black labor, and drives all black nonworkers without permanent residence to the Bantustans. Politically, these laws have been made irreversible by the denial of the franchise to blacks, numerous bans on black leaders as well as social and political organizations, various treason trials, withdrawal of passports, and indefinite detention without trial of political dissenters, during which time they are held incommunicado and the authorities have no obligation to inform relatives. Many blacks have simply disappeared without a trace behind this wall of silence. Others have died in detention as a result of police brutality.

The majority of the African masses are abandoned in the pit of ignorance, poverty, disease, and squalor. They are crushed, degraded, disenchanted, blinded, and divided by the inexorable power of apartheid. The gap between economic and welfare indicators for South Africa reflects the extreme inequality in the distribution of income and production capacity within the country.[6] With a Gini coefficient of inequality which in 1975 stood at 0.68 percent (0 being perfect equality), South Africa has the most unequal distribution of income for any economy for which data are currently available.[7] In 1980, the per capita white income was 12 times higher than African income generally, 5.3 times higher than that of coloureds, and 3.9 times higher than Indian income.[8] Wealth distribution is similarly unequal. With the top 5 percent of the wealth holders accumulating 88 percent of personally owned wealth; six groups of business companies control 84 percent of the assets on the stock exchange; and a mere 704 persons hold some 60 percent of the directorships of all public companies in the country.[9]

About 30 percent of black African households in metropolitan areas of the country live below the poverty line, with the figure rising to 70 percent in the rural areas and Bantustans where most of the blacks live.[10] The situation is very severe in particular areas. For example, a study of the Mahlabitini district of Kwa Zulu in 1981 shows that the mean household income was R114 per month, with 43 percent of it coming from remittances of migrant laborers and 16 percent from pensions. The national subsistence income was R184 per month.[11]

This income inequality is reinforced by inequality in the distribution of services, including access to fuel, transportation, food, water supplies, and health care delivery. For example, in the Mhala rural African community, 706 people share one water tap; 16 percent of the school children have bilharzia; 39 percent have no breakfast prior to coming to school; and 46 percent suffer from active tuberculosis.[12] In the Transkei, an average family spends 187 minutes a day fetching water; and in the Manguzi area of the Kwa Zulu homeland more than 60 percent of the households have more than a one hour round trip to water, which otherwise costs thirty-three times more than running tap water in the urban areas.[13] Similarly, in the black township of Alexandria on the outskirts of the affluent suburbs of northern Johannesburg, sewage flows in the streets because the existing bucket system is overloaded. And in the small town of Clarens in the Orange Free State, the 800 residents of the black township have only twelve pit latrines to use, an average of sixty-six persons to each toilet.[14] In addition, in the forest regions of Kwa Zula inhabitants walk about 3.6 kilometers to fetch firewood and spend 2.5 hours collecting it, while in the grassland area the distance is 8.3 kilometers and the time 4.5 hours. In Cape Town fuel for cooking, lighting, and heating costs more per unit for the poor blacks than for the whites—R65 and R25 per household, respectively.[15]

The pervasive migrant labor system imposes unjust hardship on the black population. Overall, 20 percent of these migrants spend 3.5 to 7 hours a day traveling to and from work; the other 80 percent spend about 2.5 hours a day.[16] Some spend more time commuting than they do sleeping. In addition, the system generates grossly distorted patterns of population settlement; undermines stable family and community life; militates against adequate wages and social security; and hampers adequate housing for workers, worker organizations, and health care delivery for workers. The Abolition of Influx Control Act of 1986 has not remedied the situation substantially. It only affects a very small proportion of blacks living in "white South Africa." The rest are still governed by the Aliens and Immigration Laws Amendment Act of 1984 which requires that they obtain permission to live or work in "white South Africa." Administrative measures that manipulate black access to land, housing and jobs in the urban areas, as well as a firm implementation of the Trespass Act, have preserved the essence of the Pass Laws.

Another consequence, as well as reflection, of inequality and injustice in apartheid South Africa is the high rate of black unemployment. About 37 percent or 4.5 million blacks of working age are either unemployed or underemployed. In the rural areas (Bantustans) the figure is 50 percent.[17] There unemployment and poverty are so endemic that a recent nationwide Surplus People Project stated that their living conditions were so bad that they "must be seen to be believed." More than half the households survive on R80 per month, with 90 percent of this money being sent by migrant workers residing in the urban centers.[18]

Housing and nutritional conditions in South Africa are similarly inequitable. In March 1985 there was a surplus of 37,000 houses for whites, while shortages for the other social groups were as follows: coloured 52,000; Indians 44,000; and blacks 538,000.[19] Even then the black townships were designed as dormitory suburbs for black workers and were "simply uni-functional sleeping areas with little or no sense of place." With regard to nutrition, about one-third of all black children under fourteen years of age are underweight and stunted for their age because they suffer from malnutrition.[20] Consequently, in 1982 the infant mortality for the various groups was: blacks, 80 per 1,000 live births; coloured 59 per 1,000, and whites 13 per 1,000.[21] It reached as high as 282 per 1,000 in the Bantustans.[22]

Political repression and state terrorism have traditionally been used to check the South African blacks' deepseated revulsion and resentment of this system of inequality and injustice. The daily brutalization of the black majority by the South African police is a commonplace of the South African political scene. Africans were shot and killed during the 1919 Anti-Pass Campaign, as well as during the strike by 80,000 Rand African miners and the Port Elizabeth African workers strike in 1920. In 1921 the notorious Bulheck Massacre left 163 Africans killed and 130 wounded. The Bondelswart Massacre of 1922 saw 100 people shot dead and hundreds more wounded. Similarly, blacks were killed during the Durban beer boycott of 1929, at Potchefstroom and Durban during the 1930 Anti-Pass Campaign, at Worcaster in 1930, at Vereenigning in 1938, and during the Rand miners strike in 1946. More than eighteen Africans were shot down during May Day demonstrations in Johannesburg on May 1, 1950, following the introduction of the Unlawful Organisations Bill (the predecessor of the Suppression of Communism Act).[23] Heavy jail sentences were imposed in 1952 on African National Congress (ANC) and South African Indian Congress members who galvanized the masses into defiance of apartheid legislation from June 26 to December 1952. A spate of Draconian legislation was introduced by the white racist government as another response. Moreover, following the adoption of the ANC Freedom Charter on June 26, 1956, some of the 156 black leaders arrested were tried for high treason for five years, and a number of them were jailed.[24]

Following the Sharpeville massacre of 1960 and the associated proscription of the ANC and the Pan-Africanist Congress (PAC), African political expression has been vented in workers' strikes and demonstrations as well as spontaneous uprisings of the black population at large. These activities have also provoked fierce and violent police confrontation, brutality, and repression. In September 1973 the police in Carletonville killed eleven striking miners. In the summer of 1980 some striking municipal workers in Johannesburg were dismissed, 2,000 being sent to the Bantustans. During the same year, the Good Year Company dismissed 1,000 of its workers for going on strike, and 60 trade unionists were arrested and tried for various strike-related activities. In 1981 several hundred trade union activists were arrested in Ciskei. In February 1982, a white trade unionist, Neil Aggett, was killed in prison for his support of black resistance.

The repression of the spontaneous Soweto uprising of 1976 is especially illuminating of apartheid political repression. On June 16 the South African Students Movement (SASM) organized a demonstration in Soweto, only to be confronted by vicious police which mowed down hundreds of people. More than 300 people were killed. A general uprising of the students and workers followed this massacre. The racist regime responded with more bullets. Over 1,000 blacks were killed, many of them children and teenagers. Several thousand others were arrested. In the wake of the Soweto uprising, Steve Biko, leader of the Black Peoples Convention (BPC), was arrested, tortured while in prison, and eventually killed by his prison guards. On October 19, 1977, the racist regime banned eighteen organizations within the black consciousness movement that Biko led.

The daily police killings and massacres of the black population since 1984 represent a desperate attempt by the South African racist state to contain the widespread and spontaneous uprisings against apartheid which have continued unabated. The racists have admitted seizing and detaining more than 8,500 leaders of the black movement in a period of two months since they proclaimed a state of emergency on June 12, 1986. Apart from understating these figures, they are silent on the thousands arrested before the imposition of the emergency. Ever since, thousands more have been arrested and detained, including children and teenagers. Through a strict press censorship, the state tries to hide these gross brutalities as well as the torture of prisoners. During 1987–1988 the apartheid regime killed over 3,000 people and injured or maimed for life many thousands more. Some were slaughtered and their bodies mutilated by the secret murder squads of the Pretoria regime.[25]

At the same time, the racists have recruited the most degenerate members of the oppressed blacks such as thieves, murderers, pimps and drug peddlers, armed them, licensed them to kill as they wish, and set them against freedom fighters. These criminals are presented as conservatives fighting against radicals in the so-called black-on-black violence. Similarly, the apartheid regime has encouraged its puppet leaders in the Bantustans to kill and persecute activists of the black struggle. The situation has become particularly serious in Bophuthatswana, Lebowa, and Kwa Zulu. They are part of the white minority's arsenal for the political repression of the blacks. Therefore, whether in the mass shootings at Langa, Mamelodi, Alexandria, and Soweto, or in the notorious and criminal activities of Inkatha hoodlums and the repression in the Bantustans, the apartheid regime expresses its unflinching commitment to inequality and injustice in South Africa.

INEQUALITY, INJUSTICE, AND DEVELOPMENT

The inequality and injustice that pervade apartheid South Africa is inimical to the country's development. Although it enjoys a highly sophisticated industrial economy reputed to be the strongest in Africa, the nation's level of development falls far short of its potential. It is maintained by the unbridled exploitation of the black majority and their exclusion from the benefits of that economy. Under these conditions such a level of development cannot be sustained. Even if it could be sustained, its potential could not be maximized. The human rights implied by equality and justice are critical to a people's progress.

In fact, development is not possible without the full liberation of the creative energies of the individual in society. But such a liberation presupposes the enjoyment of certain rights implied by equality and justice such as the right to work, food, education, and health services; and freedom of speech, assembly, movement, privacy, and participation in the decision processes affecting one's life. In the absence of these rights, the people cannot be fully committed to the creation of new values and products, and the ability of the society to take care of its ever-increasing population is severely limited. Even when the society can cater to the social and economic needs of the population, the enjoyment of these rights is still necessary for full flowering of the people.

That conception of development in South Africa which equates development with economic growth and social welfare is faulty. It disregards such factors as inequality, injustice, exploitation, and oppression from the realm of analysis. In addition, it focuses on economic growth as reflected by increases in the GDP, industrialization, food, and capital formation, as well as welfare services addressed to basic needs, increased economic efficiency, and the construction of the infrastructure such as roads, railways, and electricity. Hence, a high premium is placed on capital formation and on the rate of growth of GDP and industrialization, and hardly any premium is placed on whether these are the result of foreign or indigenous creativity, the creativity of the minority or majority of the population; who benefits from this growth—foreigners, the rich or poor; and the consequences of this pattern of distribution for further development. The most dramatic form of human intervention in the development process, notably revolutions, cannot be entertained by analysis. The individual becomes mired in a mass of data. A person's role in the process and its consequences for that person as a human being are completely ignored. Under the circumstances reality cannot even be understood, let alone be transformed.

Development is first and foremost a phenomenon associated with changes in a person's humanity and creative energies, not in things. It is a dialectical phenomenon in which the individual and society interact with their physical, biological, and interhuman environments, transforming them for their own betterment and that of humanity at large, and being transformed in the process. The lesson learned and experiences acquired in this process are passed on to future generations, enabling them to improve their capacities to make further valuable changes in interhuman relations and their ability to transform nature. It is the unending improvement in the capacity of the individual and society to control and manipulate the forces of nature as well as themselves and other individuals and societies for their own benefit and that of humanity at large. As a process of actualizing the individual's inherent capacity to live a better life, development implies increasing skill and capacity to do things, greater freedom, self-confidence, creativity, self-discipline, responsibility, and material well-being.

Every society, whether developed or underdeveloped, forever struggles to realize fully its potential creativity. Development is a progressive process that probably has no end. Its goal at any particular time and place is circumscribed by the obstacles to realizing this potential. These obstacles vary from society to society, depending on their inherited level of production, the nature of their productive forces, the relations of production, patterns of social and cultural relations, the quality and creativity of the ruling circles, and the hostility or benignness of the physical environment and the neighboring societies. As old challenges are overcome, new and sometimes more intractable ones take their place. Therefore, development connotes training in the art of using local resources, including creative human energy, in the problem-solving rather than a wholesale imitation of the path to a good life that some societies have achieved. From this viewpoint it is possible for a people to accept the fact that they are not all that they ought to be without feeling inferior to other peoples.

Thus, development refers to the individual's progressive and qualitative self-improvement. This is brought about primarily by the cooperative use of his or her labor. In this way human beings have been able to tame the wild, build very complex structures, organize large populations, and extend their lifespan. Therefore, development occurs when labor conditions improve. Such an improvement varies directly with the elimination of all human and nonhuman impediments to the creative application of human labor. The most significant impediments are those that cause labor alienation.

In general there are two aspects to the alienation of labor, the one being psychological and the other, material. Psychologically, labor alienation is the consequence of the consignment of the individual to a low-level, menial, noncreative, and marginalized role in production. In this role people cannot take the initiative, are unable to comprehend the necessary interdependence of roles in the work process, and are the victims of a structural relationship of command and obedience. As human beings they are denied the opportunity to acquire self-confidence in the creative process. Workers lose all sense of initiative and creativity because their productive activities are in no way meaningfully connected in their minds with the general results of production or their basic needs. For them work is only a source of wages, not the extension of their social selves.

Materially, the alienation of labor arises when individuals are denied an adequate material compensation for their contribution to production. The same alienation results from poor health, ignorance, and in general the hostility of the physical and biological environment which reduces workers' productivity and consequently their material rewards. Therefore, the workers are also exploited and alienated from their labor when the funds that could be used in the public interest to provide them with social, health, and other welfare services are diverted to luxury consumption of a privileged minority of the population.

Although development thus centers on the individual, it has a social content. A particular state dominated by a particular ruling class always directs a particular form of development. In the process it may use direct violence or structural violence. Whether, when, and which types of violence will be used usually depends on whether it is unnecessary or impossible to use force to change or restore the balance between competing vital class interests. Therefore, violence is fundamental to the process of development. The form of development in a particular country is the product of a definite correlation of domestic class forces and international social forces. Structural violence represents a form of development organized by the dominant minority in the service of its psychological and material interests, and maintained in the final analysis by an intimidating system of armaments. It directly contradicts an alternative form of development meant to pull the majority above the minimum existence and eliminate their disadvantages. Thus, the link between violence and development may be reformulated in terms of the struggle to establish or sustain a particular form of development. In normative terms revolutionary violence is justifiable with respect to a concept of development formulated as the movement of the whole socioeconomic and cultural system toward greater progress on the basis of increased equality and justice in social relations.

REVOLUTIONARY VIOLENCE AND THE STRUGGLE AGAINST APARTHEID

South Africa has constructed a formidable shield of armor around apartheid. It has succeeded in doing so by employing its considerable foreign exchange earnings to purchase arms, luring the Western powers to support its armament policy by its anti-Communist propaganda and by advertising its strategic location at the Cape of Good Hope. It has also been assisted by its easy access to external capitalist sources of technology for the expansion and modernization of its armed forces. The strong industrial base with which it manufactures modern arms and ammunition, and its devotion to give top priority to military expansion.

Thus, South Africa spent $2,510, $3,491, $2,971, and $2,982 million on arms in 1975, 1977, 1979, and 1982, respectively.[26] This expenditure is more than twice that of all the frontline states combined.[27] Even this does not properly reflect the military position of the racist regime. It does not include the cost of maintaining the enormous trained reserve, the citizen force, and the paramilitary forces such as the Commando, Boss personnel, and the quasi-military police force. In addition, it excludes the expenditure on the forces deployed in Namibia. The truth is that white South Africa is a highly militarized society, and that militarization is not motivated by any present military threat from within or without the borders of the country. Instead, it is built around a single-minded pursuit of the antidevelopment policy of apartheid. The intention is to intimidate black South Africans and the frontline states into some accommodation with that odious policy and to lure the Western powers into a similar accommodation.

This overbearing arms posture of racist South Africa destroys the will of the white regime to compromise on apartheid. First, it creates the illusion that victory is around the corner. Consequently, the military establishment is more confident and arrogant. More emphasis is then placed on arms and more arms. This illusion is heightened by such events as the Nkomati Accords with Mozambique as well as the relatively unchallenged South African incursions into

Angola, Lesotho, and Botswana. Nevertheless, the internal struggle against apartheid has intensified. People have exploded on an ever-increasing scale. The policy of scapegoating represented by the cross border raids and invasion has become less and less credible. It has become clear that the dynamics of the opposition to racism lie within South Africa itself.

Second, armaments have encouraged the racists to launch a policy of intimidating their opponents into making most of the concessions in any bargaining situation. Thus, in negotiating with the frontline states, it agrees to give up nothing that is related to apartheid in return for concessions by these states on such fundamentals as support for the liberation movements. Even then, as the aftermath of the Nkomati Accords has shown, the racists have not lived up to their own side of the bargain.

Third, the will to compromise is often associated with cultural, economic, and social interests. In this way it is possible to separate it from the armaments system. As these interests are satisfied, the will is reinforced and the militarization is scaled down. In South Africa, however, there is a very close link between the sociocultural and the military. They are so intimately tied together by apartheid that the will to compromise is tied to the military and its armaments system. Apartheid thrives on violence, economic exploitation, socio-political discrimination, and racial segregation. All these are held together by an escalating armaments system. Therefore, only a significant dent in this shield of armor will loosen these ties and provide the opportunities for the will to compromise to emerge from the socioeconomic and cultural level. Only revolutionary violence of all peoples and states oppressed by apartheid can do this.

Fourth, the history of the struggle against racism and colonialism in Southern Africa from Angola and Mozambique to Zimbabwe and now South Africa has shown that the racist's will to compromise has always been encouraged by the black majority's use of revolutionary violence against the structures of white racism. In the process, of course, the African states and peoples concerned have inevitably incurred some costs. But such sacrifices have often paled into insignificance with the achievement of their goal of freedom, equality, and justice.

Fifth, the arrogance associated with an overwhelming superiority in armaments has encouraged the racists to foreclose all avenues for peaceful change within South Africa. Consequently, the use of violence by the liberation movements and their moral and material support by the frontline states is inevitable. As noted earlier in this chapter, following the proscription of the African National Congress and the Pan-Africanist Congress, African political expression was manifested in workers' strikes and the spontaneous demonstrations and uprisings of the population at large. Each action has been met by violent police confrontation, brutality, and repression. The racists have even rebuffed their desire for a nonviolent solution by the front-line states as contained in such documents as the Lusaka Manifesto.

The implementation of apartheid is creating a serious financial burden for South Africa. President Botha admitted that the financial burden of the country's military presence in Namibia alone amounts to L800 million annually.[28] A number of countries have imposed economic sanctions following South Africa's declaration of a state of emergency in 1985. Economic boycott of white-owned businesses in black townships has created severe economic hardship for some white businesspeople. Apartheid is also to blame for the loss of markets for South African goods in many countries of Africa, Asia, and Latin America. And the racist regime is no longer able to disguise the severe economic crisis which its intransigence on apartheid is imposing on the country. "Inflation is on the march, unemployment is growing, the balance of payments is in disorder and there is no growth."[29] The cost of the Bantustanization of South Africa has become increasingly prohibitive. "Separate development was the most expensive economic method which could be used to solve South Africa's problems."[30]

Much property has been destroyed or damaged, and many lives have been lost as a result of apartheid. The number of people killed in political violence and sabotage in South Africa was six times greater in 1983 than in 1980. During the same period, the number of cases of violence increased sixfold.[31] While in 1983 about 214 people were killed in 395 cases of political violence, in 1984 over 1,000 were killed. The figure was much higher for 1985. In fact, 1984 and especially 1985 and 1986 have seen a general, massive, and widespread uprising of the black population against apartheid. The white racist reaction has been to increase violence and brutality. As a result, the number of dead and wounded has escalated.

White South Africa remains intransigent over its policy of apartheid, even though the world community has repeatedly condemned it. The country has faced isolation by many members of that community, especially in cultural relations, though not in economic matters until 1986. Many countries and organizations now provide the ANC and PAC with moral and material support, thereby underlining their opposition to apartheid. The Lusaka Manifesto as well as many other African professions of good intentions toward the white community have been formulated to reassure the white community, but to no avail. All avenues for peaceful change have been closed.

During his later presidency, even Ronald Reagan abandoned his friendly posture of constructive engagement, and the American Congress imposed wide-ranging economic sanctions, threatening more if apartheid were not quickly dismantled. In the face of this increased hostility from the world community, the apartheid regime has become more adamant and hardened in its attitudes. In the face of the people's increased resistance, it has intensified state violence.

All efforts to use nonviolent means to overcome this South African intransigence have failed. Until very recently, the use of worldwide economic sanctions as a pressure on Pretoria has met with the disapproval of the Western powers. Limited sanctions were imposed following the state of emergency declared by the racists. It was designed to cause as little damage to the South African economy as possible. Until recently the West refused to disinvest in the racist enclave.

As a nonviolent pressure the arms embargo imposed on South Africa by the world community has remained ineffective. Today, in spite of the 1963 and 1977 embargoes, the racists have increased their armaments over the pre–1963 level in geometric proportion. Since then the country has emerged as a significant world power. All this has been made possible by Western shipments of arms to the country. South Africa now probably has nuclear weapons which it developed during the period of this embargo.

In the face of this South African intransigence over apartheid, revolutionary violence in the form of guerrilla war has become inevitable. Violence is being used to resolve the contradiction between apartheid and the development of the black community in South Africa. That violence is based on the idea that the people are the motivating force of all successful enterprises. It encourages not only their mobilization, but also reliance on them as the top priority in all national endeavors. Durable peace and success in development require the support of the population. In the absence of this support, ruling classes rely on arms or foreign assistance. In other words, they declare war on their own people or bypass them in the process of development.

The oppressed blacks have responded with revolutionary violence in the factories, in their communities, schools, and in the struggle against the South African Defense Force (SADF) occupying the black townships. They have seized the strategic initiative, with the state resorting to force and more force without being able to subdue them.[32] The emergence of street committees, people's courts, popular forms of defense, and other grass-roots forms of democracy have rendered the apartheid system ungovernable, eroded the conventional methods of administration, and compelled the military to use more force.[33]

REVOLUTIONARY VIOLENCE AND DEVELOPMENT IN SOUTH AFRICA

The current black resistance to apartheid using revolutionary violence has scored some success. This resistance has taken the form of increasing and more damaging attacks by the Umkhonto we Sizwe, industrial strikes, unionization of the workforce, formation of the Confederation of South Africa Trade Unions (COSATU) and its anti-apartheid demands, waves of school boycotts involving millions of students, attacks on those blacks who collaborate with the apartheid regime, and a successful consumer boycott of white-owned stores in black residential areas. These evident successes attest to the fact that even without arms an oppressed people will inevitably find a way of throwing off oppression.

The significance of Soweto and the current wave of struggles is that a disarmed people, with nothing but their will to be free, harboring no illusion about the military and economic power of their adversary, nor about his intentions and resolve to kill as many as he could to subdue their will, have decided to fight, and if necessary die, rather than continue to live as slaves.[34]

Revolutionary violence against apartheid serves the cause of development not only because it removes the major obstacles to the progress of the black majority in South Africa. It also generates a new social and political consciousness among them that is regenerative. It frees them from their inferiority complex by destroying the myth of white superiority and invincibility, and from their despair and powerlessness. It makes the black man fearless, restoring his self-respect and self-confidence, values that are important for qualitative self-improvement or development. It promotes the mobilization of the masses, which introduces the ideas of a common cause, common struggle, and national identity. Such a consciousness is vitally necessary for building a new society at a higher level of human creativity. It is a prerequisite for an assault on all forms of the alienation of labor that arises from the odious system of apartheid.

Such mobilization of the popular forces enables the people to take the initiative economically and politically and to gain the necessary experiences in these areas of national life. In the process they acquire the capacity to make decisions about what is produced, how and why: and how the products are distributed. Similarly, they are able to assume responsibility for making the decisions which affect their lives. They are no longer the object but the subject of politics. And only the pressure of the vast number of the toiling black masses of South Africa applied through their mobilization and native participation in the organization and supervision of agricultural, commercial, industrial and political enterprises and supported by their organized power is capable of maximizing the development potential of the country.

The unorganized efforts of the people can only be a temporary dynamic in the development process. Neither stubborn courage nor fine slogans can be a substitute for organization. Revolutionary violence against apartheid enables the black masses to achieve organization. Through mobilization for violence against official racism, they have formed organizations that are seizing the initiative in politics and waging a relentless war against apartheid.

Finally, revolutionary violence also stimulates an increased technological capacity to transform and adapt the economy to changing demands and conditions. The struggle against apartheid provides a favorable condition for developing such a technological perspective. During times of war, the basic needs of the people come to the fore, especially the need for physical survival. When such needs are threatened, the creative energies of the people are galvanized and mobilized behind the survival effort. The population is often forced to improvise, to rely on local resources and initiatives, and to be innovative while maintaining the initiative. These factors are crucial to the development process.

CONCLUSIONS

The link between violence and development is often posed as the link between the armament system and development.[35] It appears in another form as the relationship between disarmament and development. The phenomenon of disarmament is the process of deflating the armaments dynamics, dismantling the stockpile of armaments, and eliminating the role of the armaments industry, including its research and development, in conflict resolution. Thus, it is significant in reducing violence, and disarmament is dialectically linked with direct violence.

The link between violence, armaments, or disarmament and development is often seen in terms of the relationship between expenditures on the armament system and increased productivity of the economy, with productivity tied to project construction. In this regard two schools of thought exist. One school believes that the link is positive because of the technological spinoffs of the armaments industry and nationalism of the armed forces, especially in the poor countries of the world.[36] The other school adopts a more moral posture. It decries the excessive expenditure on arms relative to that on the basic needs of the population. Therefore, it views the link as negative. Its assumption is that reduced spending on armaments would release more funds to be spent on development projects.[37] Both condemn violence from a pacifist liberal viewpoint and regard development in infrastructural terms.

Empirically, both schools have failed to justify their positions. The modernization of the Third World countries through the intervention of the arms industry in the economy, and the armed forces in politics, has not materialized. Instead, the resultant political instability has compounded the difficulties of improving the population's quality of life. The economy has also declined. Similarly, there is no evidence that resources released from cutbacks in arms spending would necessarily go into expenditure on development projects rather than to other forms of "waste" or unproductive spending.[38]

When a human-centered conception of development is linked to resistance against structural violence by means of revolutionary violence, then the positive impact of violence may be observed. The key lies in the impact of that means of action on self-confidence. Self-esteem is crucial for overcoming challenges. It prevents one from being subjectively overwhelmed by the magnitude of the problem, demoralized, or sapped of the will to succeed. Such self-confidence is incompatible with the state of acute and pervasive alienation of the South African black that is generated by apartheid. That policy is presently the major obstacle in the path of South Africa to a self-sustained creative transformation of the labor of the vast majority of its population and consequently the society's quality of life.

At the same time, a moral argument is sustainable because revolutionary violence and development are linked by the struggle for human rights without which the creative energies for development will be stunted and peace rendered ephemeral. Apartheid denies the black majority of South Africa the fundamental human rights, and it denies them easy access to employment, education, health care, and social welfare services generally. But these rights are crucial for a full moral existence of a society, and for the development process. Their realization improves the capacity of man to liberate himself from all forces that constrain his social self reproduction, self extension and the maximum release of his creative energy. A society that denies these rights to its majority has no moral claim to existence. And so the struggle continues.

NOTES

1. SIPRI, *Southern Africa: The Escalation of a Conflict* (New York: Praeger, 1976), p. 26. In 1986 the Botha regime made a belated attempt to reform

the Pass Laws. Nevertheless, their substance has remained, as has apartheid.

2. Thabo Mbeki, "South Africa: The Historical Injustice," in Douglas G. Auglin, Timothy M. Shaw, and Carl G. Widstrand, eds., *Conflict and Change in Southern Africa* (Washington, D.C.: University Press of America, 1978), p. 136; Francis Wilson, *Labour in South African Gold Mines* (Cambridge: Cambridge University Press, 1972).

3. Mbeki, "South Africa," p. 141.

4. Ibid., p. 139.

5. Ibid., pp. 139–40.

6. Cf. Jill Nattrass, "South Africa's Status in the International Development Stakes," *Indicator SA* 1, no. 1 (1983), pp. 3–9.

7. Michael Savage, "The Cost of Apartheid," *Third World Quarterly* 9, no. 2 (April 1987), p. 603.

8. Ibid.

9. Cf. Charles Simkins, "How Much Socialism Will Be Needed to End Poverty in South Africa?" Paper presented at the Conference on Apartheid in South Africa, held at University of York, October 1986; Jan Limbard, "Power in the Market Economy," *Focus on Key Economic Issues*, no. 34 (Johannesburg: Mercabank, 1984).

10. Mike McGrath, "Global Poverty in South Africa," *Social Dynamics* 10, no. 2 (1984), pp. 38–48.

11. M. Gandar and N. Bromberger, "Economic and Demographic Functioning of Rural Households in the Mahlabatini District," *Social Dynamics* 10, no. 2 (1984), pp. 61–69.

12. Cf. Francis Wilson, "South African Poverty Major Issues," *Social Dynamics* 10, no. 2 (1984), pp. 61–69.

13. Savage, "The Cost of Apartheid," p. 605.

14. Ibid.

15. Ibid., p. 606.

16. Ibid., p. 607.

17. Cf. Jill Nattrass, "The year 2000 from the 1986 Viewpoint," *Energos*, no. 13 (1986), p. 17; Herman Gilomee, "Afrikaner Nationalism and the Fable of the Sultan's Horse," *Energos*, no. 13 (1986), p. 38; D. Gilmour and A. Roux, "Urban Black Unemployment and Education in the Eastern Cape," Carnegie Conference on Poverty, Paper 120, University of Cape Town, 1984.

18. Cf. *Housing Research Review*, no. 8 of the National Building Research Institute (Cape Town, 1986).

19. David Dewar, "Urban Poverty and City Development: Some Perspectives," Carnegie Conference Paper No. 163, Saidru, University of Cape Town, quoted in Savage, "The Cost of Apartheid," p. 616.

20. Cf. J.D.L. Hansen, "The Child Malnutrition Problem in South Africa," Carnegie Conference Paper No. 208, Saidru, University of Cape Town.

21. Savage, "The Cost of Apartheid," p. 618.

22. Ibid.

23. O. R. Tambo, "South Africa Freedom Day" in the ANC, ed., *Selected Writings on the Freedom Charter 1955–1985* (London: ANC, 1985), pp. 32–33.

24. Ibid., p. 34.

25. O. R. Tambo, *Forward to Peoples' Power* (Harare: Ministry of Information and Broadcasting, 1986), p. 5.

26. Sources: Sean Gervasi, "Breakdown of the United States Arms Embargo" in Western Massachusetts Association of Concerned African Scholars, ed., *U.S. Military Involvement in South Africa* (Boston: South End Press, 1978), p. 140; U.S. Arms Control and Disarmament Agency, *World Military Expenditures and Arms Transfers 1972–82* (Washington, D.C.: ACADA Publication, 1984), p. 44.

27. Ibid.

28. Colin Legum, *African Contemporary Record* (New York and London: Africana, 1986), p. A9.

29. Quoted in Bernard Magubane, "South Africa: A Luta Continua," Paper presented at the biennial conference of the African Association of Political Science held in Addis Ababa, Ethiopia, May 13–15, 1985, p. 34.

30. This quote in Magubane, "South Africa" is credited to Dr. Otto Count Lambsdorff who until 1986 was West Germany's minister for Economic Affairs.

31. Legum, *African Contemporary Record*, p. A5.

32. Horace Campbell, "The Dismantling of the Apartheid War Machine," *Third World Quarterly* 9, no. 2 (April 1987), p. 482.

33. Ibid., p. 488.

34. Magubane, "South Africa," p. 48.

35. Cf. United Nations General Assembly, *Study on the Relationship Between Disarmament and Development* (New York: United Nations, 1982); Peter Lock, "Armaments Dynamics: An Issue in Development Strategies," *Alternatives* 6, no. 2 (July 1980), pp. 157–78; Nicole Ball and Milton Leitenberg, *Disarmament, Development and Their Interrelationship* (Los Angeles: Center for the Study of Armament and Disarmament, California State University, 1980).

36. Cf. Emile Benoit, *Defense and Economic Growth in Developing Countries* (Lexington, Mass.: Lexington Books, 1963); Emile Benoit, Max F. Millikan, and Everett E. Hagen, *Effect of Defense on Developing Economies*, Main Report, Vol. 2, ACDA/E–136 (Cambridge, Mass.: MIT Press, 1971).

37. Cf. Ruth L. Sivard, *World Military and Social Expenditures, 1977* (Leesburg, Va.: WNSE Publications, 1977); Nicole Ball, "Defense and Development: A Critique of the Benoit Study," *Economic Development and Social Change*, no. 31 (April 1983); Nicole Ball, "Military Expenditure, Economic Growth and Socio-Economic Development in the Third World," Conference paper no. 3, of the Swedish Institute of International Peace Research.

38. R. B. Duboff, "Converting Military Spending to Social Welfare: The Real Obstacles," *Quarterly Review of Economics and Business* 12 (Spring 1972), pp. 7–22.

7

The Effect of Militarization on Human Rights in Africa

Zdenek Cervenka

THE MILITARIZATION OF AFRICA

Introduction

The issue of militarization is very important in Africa: out of 52 independent African states in 1987 only 12 to date have been spared the turmoil of military coups and conspiracies to overthrow civilian governments. They are Botswana, Ivory Coast, Senegal, Egypt (the overthrow of the Egyptian monarchy by the young colonels Neguib and Nasser has been widely regarded as part of decolonization), Morocco, Swaziland, Zambia, Zimbabwe, Malawi, Tunisia, Mauritius, and Djibouti.

The term *militarization* does not refer only to rule by the gun or to military conflicts and the arms suppliers that keep them going. Military rule has become a style of government and a way of life, imposed on the general populace without their consent. The term can be used broadly to describe the following situations in Africa:

1. The process of usurpation of political power by soldiers through military coups

2. The armed conflicts in Africa and the importation of arms, by which African wars are perpetuated

3. The arms buildup and military expenditures

In many respects the civilian one-party state, in which the will of the party, often synonymous with the head of state, is enforced by a powerful security apparatus, bears a striking resemblance to that of military regimes.

The Military Coup d'Etats

On reflection it is remarkable that the massive involvement of the military in the political life of Africa, at the time of the postwar wave of independence, was both unforeseen and unthinkable. The euphoria of freedom, optimistic concepts of nation-building and economic development, the revival of traditional culture and values, symbolized by "the African personality," were all generated by African rejoicing over the collapse of the colonial empires. Armies were regarded as a legacy belonging to the colonial past. In December 1961, on the eve of Tanzanian independence (then Tanganyika), Julius Nyerere told an audience at the London Africa Bureau that his country would not need an army after independence. At that time his view was shared by many analysts of African affairs, all of whom were impressed by the charisma of the new African leaders and their vision of a new era of peace, prosperity, and unity in Africa. For example, all the contributors to one of the first books about the African military (*The Role of the Military in Underdeveloped Countries*, published in 1962) agreed that the postcolonial states in Africa "are not threatened by military usurpation because they have scarcely any military forces."[1] Indeed, it was easy to forget the existence of African armies, because they were small in size and were believed to be "nonpolitical." They were then viewed only as a variation of civil servants, except for the fact that they used guns, rather than pens, in their line of work.

The high expectations of the general African populace about the betterment of their lives, raised by their elected governments, proved to be short-lived. The colonial structure, inherited by the new administrators of the independent states, was not conducive to new directions in economic policies—which were now designed to reduce the dependence on ex-colonial powers. Their budgets could not cope with the demands for an expansion of education, health care, and social services, and the pressures to create new jobs. Nor could they sustain the ambitious projects of industrialization, which were then seen as the only way of dispensing with Africa's humiliating role as a supplier of raw materials for the European markets.

The growing disappointments over unfulfilled promises were exacerbated by the flare-up of "tribalism," as government priorities and the allocation of funds were increasingly questioned by groups who felt they had been discriminated against by the people in positions of political power. This mood of discontentment was quickly seized upon by opposition groups, who now began to organize public resentment into a political challenge to the legitimacy of the civilian government.

It was at this point that the governments chose not to risk testing their popularity by elections. Instead, they resorted to silencing their critics. This political repression has been recognized as having paved the way for military intervention. It is a sad historic fact that Ghana, the first black African state to win independence and whose president Dr. Kwame Nkrumah had inspired the quest for African unity, was also the first African country to introduce a Preventive Detention Act—which today is now part of the legal inventory of many African countries.

Concurrently, with domestic political tensions, dark ideological clouds were gathering over the African continent. The Cold War divide between the West and the East, further complicated by the Soviet-China dispute, was also paralleled in Africa. It found expression in the formation of "radical" and "moderate" political groupings of states, classified in accordance to their policies at home and their relations with Western or Communist powers. Such African alliances were variously called the Casablanca Powers, the Brazzaville Group, and the Monrovia Group.

The first military intervention occurred in Sudan in 1958. The instigator was General Ibrahim Abboud, who took over power without armed conflict at a time when the newly independent country was facing severe economic difficulties. The next coup was in Togo in January 1963, when President Sylvanus Olympio was shot dead by rebelling soldiers. The event gave rise to great indignation throughout Africa, and it almost wrecked the preparations for the Summit of African Heads of State and Government, subsequently held in May 1963, at which time the Organization of African Unity was established. Ghana was suspected of having initiated the Togolese coup because of its strained relations with the Olympio government, over the issue of harboring Ghanaian political dissenters. The author of this chapter, who was then a member of the staff of the Ghanaian president, can testify that the Togolese coup was as much of a surprise to President Nkrumah as it was to the then Nigerian foreign minister, Jaja Wachuku, who pointed an accusing finger at Nkrumah.

The "unreserved condemnation of political assassination" was embodied in the Principles of the OAU Charter (Article III) at Nigeria's insistence. The overthrow of the Algerian president, Ben Bella, by his trusted colleague Hoari Boumedinne in 1965 was still a shock, but it was viewed as an act of treachery rather than as a coup, because it was bloodless. The military coup in Nigeria in January 1966 changed Africa's attitude to military seizures of power. It began to be recognized that a coup d'etat was a means of changing an unpopular government, that is, unpopular with the soldiers rather than with the people—who had little to say about their own fate. After the Nigerian civil war (1967–1970), Africa was never the same; many countries experienced a whole series of coups and counter-coups and a succession of military rulers.

The experience of the coup d'etat, which swept through the continent, exposed the fragility of Africa's new political institutions. Those who greeted the advent of soldiers into politics, as a new modernizing force that was disciplined and capable of promoting progress, were to be terribly disappointed. The military's constant intervention into politics and the ease with which they killed their opponents and harassed their fellow citizens gave rise to a new mood, expressed by the Nigerian writer and publisher Peter Enahoro in the following passage:

Except in those countries where armed struggle led to independence, our post-colonial history shows a record of State bloodletting worse than the imperialists ever permitted. Once upon a time we welcomed the intervention of the soldiers in politics because in our frustration with politicians, we thought the soldiers might provide a disciplined alternative. But military rule has become a fashion and we have come to a stage whereby any handful of conspiratorial soldiers with reckless ambition in their hearts and a demoniac insomnia raging in their heads were free to seize power at will. We discovered also that power violently seized has led to power violently lost, with the people as ultimate losers.[2]

Wars of Liberation and Wars of Attrition

The commitment by the leaders of independent African states, such as Dr. Kwame Nkrumah of Ghana and Abdul Gamal Nasser of Egypt, to the "freedom fighters" (as the nationalist guerrillas were called) led to armed struggle. In the Portuguese African colonies, Rhodesia, South Africa, and the Congo insurgents began to receive funds and arms, at first from individual countries and, since 1963, from the Liberation Committee of the OAU. But arms began to flow to other corners of Africa, where the liberation struggle was taking place within the boundaries of independent African states: Secession was a goal for movements in Eritrea and in the Southern Sudan.

The establishment of the OAU did not bring peace to the continent. In defiance of the solemn undertaking of the founding fathers of the OAU: "Inspired by a common determination to promote understanding among our peoples and co-operation among our States in response to the aspirations of our people for brotherhood and solidarity, in a larger unity transcending ethnic and national differences";[3] armed conflict flared up between Algeria and Morocco in October 1964, four months after both had signed the OAU Charter. In 1965 border wars erupted between Somalia and Kenya, and between Somalia and Ethiopia. The latter conflict culminated in the war in the Ogaden in 1975.

Apart from the Congo, the most disastrous conflict, in terms of victims, was the Nigerian civil war of 1967–1970 in which more than a million people died. The protracted war in the Portuguese African colonies was also costly, and in Angola the new Popular Movement for the Liberation of Angola (MPLA) regime came under attack from a rival movement, the National Union for the Total Independence of Angola (UNITA), supported by South African soldiers, who were themselves repelled by a massive military operation orchestrated by Cuba and the Soviet Union.

In 1987 there were ten major and minor armed conflicts in Africa— Western Sahara, Southern Sudan, Eritrea, Angola, Mozambique, Namibia, and South Africa—which, as a special case of militarization, are discussed in the next section. Unrest remains, and occasionally it erupts in violence as in Uganda and in the Zairean provinces of Shaba and Kivi.

The Situation in South Africa

By far the most frightening conflict is that in South Africa, where 20 million blacks are resisting the oppression perpetrated by the 4.5 million white minority. In the summer of 1985 this conflict escalated into open and large-scale violence. Since then, the struggle has claimed more than 2,000 lives, and the figure is rising despite the imposition of emergency laws by the Pretoria regime.

At an international symposium entitled "The Militarization of Africa," organized by the author of this chapter in Stockholm in November 1986, Dr. Simon Baynham described the situation:

A total strategy is being co-ordinated at the national level by a national security management system, at the apex of which rests the State Security

Council. There can be no doubt whatever that the evolution and radicalization of the national security management system has greatly enhanced not only the public profile, but also the political influence of the security establishment at the highest levels of government.

The strength of Pretoria's security apparatus is not in doubt. To appreciate the magnitude of the coercive instruments available to Pretoria, one has to look much wider than the full service South African Defence Force (SADF) which is 95,000 men strong. Together with the citizen force and the commando element of the standing force, South Africa has a potential military force of about one million white males between the age of 18 and 45, and there are about 1.8 million firearms held in private white homes. On top of this is the paramilitary South African Police (SAP), which is being rapidly expanded. It is probably 56,000 at the moment, including its reserves. Then come the special railway police, the prison guards, and the administrative board police. In the last few months special constabularies were recruited and have been put into operation in the black townships.

It is no exaggeration to say that the South African security establishment is one of the strongest, toughest and most brutal in the non-communist world. What is more, these forces have had almost continuous counter-insurgency operation experience over the last 25 years. They gained tremendous experience in Angola, Zimbabwe and other neighboring states before these gained independence. The regime also has an overwhelming advantage in terms of military equipment from basic weapons to heavy armor.[4]

Military Expenditures

The militarization of Africa has been brought about by military coups, armed conflicts, and the suppression of internal dissent by the police and paramilitary forces. This state of affairs has led to a formidable expansion in the strength of African armies and the state security apparatus, and in turn has produced a dramatic rise in Africa's military expenditure. Because no African country has an arms industry (with the exception of South Africa and to a certain degree Egypt), it follows that all African conflicts are fought with imported arms. There are about 1.6 million men in African military forces and, in addition, about 1.4 million in the police and paramilitary forces.

In 1961, Tanzania did not believe it would have need for any military strength (at independence its army was only 2,000 men strong), but today it has over 45,000 men in arms. Zambia, whose president Kenneth Kaunda has been a leading proponent of peace and humanity, has found it necessary to increase its army from 3,000 in 1964 to almost 20,000 in 1987. In the aftermath of the civil war, in the early 1970s, Nigeria had an army of over 252,000 men. Although this number has been reduced to its present size of 160,000 men, the country still has one of the largest armies in Africa.

The armed forces in Ethiopia grew from 50,000 in 1975 to 251,000 in 1980, a fivefold increase, and today that number is in excess of 300,000. If one also considers police and other paramilitary units, this figure rises to 320,000, and together with the security intelligence forces, it becomes more than 400,000. Thus, Ethiopia has the largest standing army in black Africa, second only to Egypt in the whole of Africa. With a total population of 42 million people and a gross national product (GNP) per capita of less than $100, Ethiopia is one of the most militarized states in the world.[5]

With its oil wealth, Angola has been able to acquire the weaponry to build up a fairly powerful and sophisticated army and air force, with almost 50,000 troops in the armed forces. It has the largest army in southern Africa, in terms of personnel, apart from South Africa. Angola has more than 150 combat aircraft including MIG–23s and SU22s, and it also has extensive missile systems. In addition, by virtue of its strategic alliance with the Soviet bloc, which was forged at the time of independence in 1975, until 1989 there were 30,000 Cuban troops in the country.[6]

But the arms race has not been confined to the large countries and to those countries directly involved in armed conflict such as Ethiopia and Angola. Even tiny Rwanda has increased its armed forces from 2,000 to 5,000 men, and Burkina Faso, one of the poorest countries in the world, has doubled its army from 2,000 to 4,000 men.

The full burden of the recurrent annual costs of this buildup of military forces becomes even clearer when one considers the cost of paying and maintaining armies under modern conditions. This is especially so as African soldiers now regard themselves (in monetary terms) as belonging to the higher and middle strata of society. It has been estimated that to maintain a single battalion of infantry requires 400,000 pounds a year in pay alone. Putting such a battalion in the field costs another 200,000 pounds a year, making the annual cost of a single infantry battalion roughly 600,000 pounds. The costs of maintaining artillery and mechanized battalians are much higher, possibly almost twice as much; for the air force it is obviously even greater.[7]

Today Africa spends about $15 billion per annum on arms, which is almost double the amount the sub-Saharan countries are receiving in development aid. Figure 7.1, based on SIPRI (Stockholm International Peace Research Institute) sources, illustrates the trend, but it is far from complete. Information about purchases of arms and other military expenditures are difficult and sometimes quite

Figure 7.1
African Military Expenditures, 1974–1986

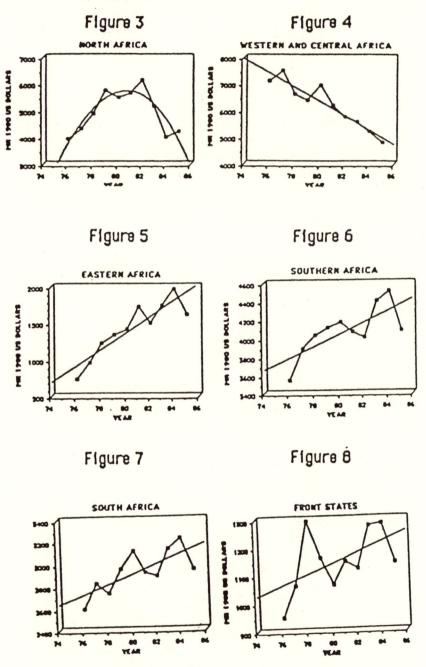

Source: SIPRI Military expenditure database.

impossible to obtain. Besides, many governments devise elaborate systems to cover up military expenses in their budgets or do not include them at all in their financial estimates. This is both for internal and external reasons. Publicity about the allocation of large amounts of foreign exchange funds, for military purposes, is dangerous at a time when the general populations are bearing the brunt of tough austerity measures, imposed by the same military people who are placing the orders for arms. Exposure of military expenditures might easily spark violent protests, which not even the soldiers would be able to contain. Similarly, the military governments are aware of the criticisms leveled against them by the international community, which questions their import priorities. Hence, they prefer to keep the information about arms purchases secret.

Barter deals, such as Ethiopian coffee for Soviet arms, do not enter the official trade statistics of the countries concerned. It is impossible to establish either the volume of the transaction or the price. Besides, arms are a unique commodity, the price of which is determined by the buyer's degree of need. Another method is to keep the proceeds, from the sale of various commodities, outside the country in a special account used for arms purchases. Weapons are also bought on credit, which is again difficult to trace. Nicole Ball, a well-known international analyst of arms expenditure, has shown that for many African countries internal security, and above all the security of the regime, are far more important than external security considerations. The priority attached to arms purchases made at the expense of economic development stems from the fact that armed forces occupy an important, if not central, role in most countries. Thus, they are given what they want. For example, in Liberia after the 1980 coup the salaries of the armed forces generally doubled.

In an absolute sense, the military and security expenditures of African countries are relatively low. However, when they are related to a country's resources they can be very high, even excessively high. Nicole Ball has explained that it is wrong to regard security expenditures in African countries as synonymous with arms transfers. The popular belief is that arms expenditures are related to accumulation in the stock of weapons. In fact, security expenditures are divided into several categories. The first consists of operational costs, such as salaries and maintenance expenditures. Second is the capital expenditure, which includes the procurement of weapons as well as the construction of military facilities.[8]

Finally, military expenditures are closely linked to foreign intervention. Arms suppliers forge strong ties between the buyer and seller, and even more so if arms are part of foreign aid. The dependency of the recipients of arms supplies, known as "the spare parts policy," provides foreign powers with considerable influence on both the domestic and foreign policies of their clients.

THE CONSEQUENCES OF THE MILITARIZATION OF AFRICA FOR HUMAN RIGHTS

Militarization in Africa has had the following consequences:

1. It has caused the brutalization of African societies.
2. It has been largely responsible for the refugee problem in Africa.
3. It has brought about the degradation of human rights manifested by the misery and suffering of millions of Africans.

The Brutalization of African Societies

One of the most alarming consequences of militarization in Africa has been the change in attitudes toward traditional values. Whereas respect for human life formerly occupied a central place, today life has become very cheap and in some countries the summary execution of political opponents has become a common practice. The heinous crimes against humanity committed by the regimes of Idi Amin, Bokassa, and Nguema are all well known, and there is no reason to dwell on the details. One would like to believe that such crimes had ceased with the removal of the people who perpetrated them. However, "lesser crimes" still go on. For example, torture has become a part of the routine of interrogation by the police, not only in South Africa, but also in a number of African countries. But soldiers and the police are not alone in using violence.

Many of the arms sold throughout sub-Saharan Africa are peddled by deserters and demobilized soldiers, and they fall into the hands of bandits and robbers—some of whom are former soldiers. This situation has led to a tremendous increase in armed robberies and holdups, in which the victims often lose both their possessions and their lives. Public executions of these criminals has become a regular spectacle. Although this punishment is meant to deter other bandits, it only induces them to make sure there are no live witnesses. These are, of course, extreme examples. Less cruel but much more common has been the harassment of ordinary people by their military overlords. The cool arrogance with which the Acheampong soldiers used to whip the market women in Ghana, or simply steal their goods, was a sight that will continue to haunt those who witnessed it.

Military rule, besides destroying the basic rights of individuals, has also destroyed the concept of government legality. The soldiers assume the role of judges who pass judgment on the government's performance. They are also executioners who mercilessly punish the members of the government they overthrew. Charges of corruption, mismanagement, incompetence, and tribalism are the usual reasons by which the military justify the coup. The right of soldiers to overthrow the government and dispose of its members in any way they see fit is reinforced by the speed and smoothness with which they are accorded international recognition. Nobody any longer questions whether the new government fulfills the basic conditions of legality as prescribed by international law, one of the conditions of which is the support of the majority of the population.

This new concept of "military legality" has been further complicated by those instances in which the soldiers in power are overthrown by other soldiers, seeking access to the same power. Needless to say, they justify their actions by almost the same identical reasons that motivated the, by now, deposed solders to usurp power in the first place. The coup becomes legitimate whenever it succeeds. The winners are the judges and executioners; the losers are sent before the firing squad. The experience of the African generation of the past twenty-five years has been aptly summarized up by Peter Enahoro:

The experience of the last 25 years has browbeaten us into a largely meek and submissive civilian populace. Detention without trial, instability of tenure of office, unpredictable university shut-downs and the waging of vengeance, all these have taken their toll. Nothing better illustrates the throes we are in than the plight of the young African who was born in 1960. He has seen many of his generation driven to the ground by the changes in government brought about by way of the gun. He is surrounded by controls and restrictions. His local newspapers tell him that his leader is infallible, but foreign newspapers are almost hysterical in claiming that African leaders are inevitably corrupt. The young African has been brought up to believe that civilians become politicians only because they want to steal public funds.

Furthermore, it is a generation that has been bathed in an orgy of bloodletting. A typical young person of the generation has never known an absolute period of peace. Public executions, military coups, political show trials have featured through most young people's lives.[9]

The Refugee Problem

The refugee population of Africa grew according to UN figures from about 800,000 in 1960 to between 4 and 5 million in 1987. No other continent comes close to this figure. The very fact that we do not even know how many refugees there really are in Africa indicates how little we know about conditions in which they live.

Most speeches, articles, or books on the African refugee problem start with a statement that slavery, colonialism, and tribalism are the root causes of the refugee exodus. But most refugees in the Sudan (the country with the largest number of refugees) have come from Ethiopia, whose heartland was never under colonial rule. In fact, the Sudan, Djibouti, Somalia, Kenya, and other countries in Africa, the United States, Asia, and Europe have received more refugees from Ethiopia than has been generated by any other country in recent times.

Neither is it easy to see slavery, colonialism, or tribalism as dominating causes behind the presence in the Sudan of refugees from Uganda, Zaire, and Chad. In these cases, as in Ethiopia, it is an internal conflict or revolutionary struggle in disrespect of human rights and humanitarian values, which have set entire populations on the move to escape political persecution or civil disturbances, making life at home unbearable or too dangerous to be suffered any more.[10]

To examine the problem of refugees in Africa is beyond the scope of this chapter. It suffices to mention that refugees are largely the product of armed conflict or persecution in their home countries, with the second reason often being ecological disaster. Apart from the above-mentioned exodus from Ethiopia, there are thousands of Saharouis who fled from the Western Sahara to Algeria, Ugandans who fled to Kenya and the Southern Sudan, and South Africans who took refuge in the frontline states. There are also large numbers of refugees who fled from areas of conflict within the same country, such as in Angola, Mozambique, and Namibia.

The Degradation of Human Rights

The breakdown of democracy in Africa, for which both military regimes and authoritarian one-party states bear an equal responsibility, has given rise to a kind of "double morality" about human rights. The argument goes as follows, as we once heard from one OAU secretary-general himself, that the Western concept of human rights is not really suited to African conditions. These "specific African conditions" have been well described by the well-known commentator, Pini Jason:

So human rights in Africa becomes hostage to the struggle for power, self-perpetuation and the liquidation of the opposition. Virtually all post-independence heads of state have become life presidents. The democratic process has been assaulted. Changes of government have not been through the ballot, but the bullets of impatient military dictators. Where one despot has been removed, it is through the agency of another tyrant who eventually behaves like one who, having rescued a helpless woman from the ravages of a rapist, proceeds to rape her.[11]

The point is that the UN Declaration on Universal Human Rights (the emphasis is on Universal) does not make any distinction between races, continents, or countries. Africans are entitled to the same human rights as any other human beings in the world. The introduction of the concept of people's rights into the African Charter on Human and Peoples' Rights, specified in Articles 15 as the "right to work"; Article 16, the "right to medical treatment"; and Article 17, the "right to education," has often been used as an argument by those who put material welfare before personal freedom.[12] It is not by coincidence that Romania, the most unbending Communist dictatorship in Europe equaled only by Albania, is known for the eloquency of its representatives at the United Nations and other world forums, about people's rights to shelter, clothing, food, work, and medical care. Freedom of individuals and their right to decide about their own lives; to freely express their views; to practice their chosen religion; and to have the right of protection against the abuse of power by the agents of the state—these are dismissed by the advocates of the material content of human rights as irrelevant and decadent.

If the Romanian view is to be taken seriously, then the South African black mine workers, who are better fed and housed when compared to other miners in independent African countries, should not have too much to complain about. Yet, the black South African Trade Unions are the backbone of the political resistance against apartheid, and they fight for their civil rights as hard as they do for their pay. The example of South Africa is also relevant to the general issue of human rights in Africa. In the words of Pini Jason:

I do strongly believe that the struggle against apartheid must be backed up with a demonstrated commitment in the rest of Africa to the principle of human rights, not just to prove to the West that we have the credentials to ask for equality and human rights in South Africa, but to show that we are convinced of the moral necessity to respect the rights of all African citizens.

In the present world, we cannot afford to isolate ourselves morally. Either we claim our rightful place in the community of nations and subscribe to its universal moral code or we unwittingly determine our own place on the fringes of civilisation.[13]

The degradation of human rights is also closely connected with economic development. Economic progress cannot occur without the active participation of people in the development process. The lay public, as well as experts, must be involved in shaping the direction of development, deciding on priorities of various projects and taking part in the evaluation process. Since military rule, and for that matter one-party rule, is the antithesis of democratic government, it is hardly surprising that the soldiers have failed in their numerous attempts to remedy the defects in the national economy—which they promised when they seized power.

The myth that military training provides a country with skills that can be used in the civilian sector has long been exposed. Getting trained to run the best army in the world does not normally equip a person to run a country. Basic military training tends to make soldiers in a hurry all the time. The reality is that, while a lot can be said for doing things in a hurry, the results are often disastrous. By the time a military government consolidates itself in power, how to hold on to that power becomes its main and sometimes its sole aim, and this necessarily leads to increased security expenditure. Thus, even if it were inclined or equipped to tackle development, it would not have the funds to support any such program.[14]

THE LEGALITY OF INTERNATIONAL CONCERN ABOUT THE VIOLATION OF HUMAN RIGHTS IN AFRICA

Measures have been adopted by the international community of states against South Africa—by the United Nations, the British Commonwealth, the European Community, as well as by individual states, including the United States. These responses stem from the recognition that apartheid constitutes the most serious breach of human rights in our time, and that it is a threat to peace and security in the southern African region—and indeed to the world at large.

There is also a direct link to the right of development. Apartheid is, after all, a policy of development in South Africa—a "separate development." If development is to be understood as a process of nation-building and also the reduction of state power in order to provide a broader base for the development of civil liberties and human rights, then South Africa really constitutes a test case of the final stage of decolonization. Apartheid is a culmination of colonialism by virtue of its racialism and by its policy of separate development from above without the participation of the people. The current crisis in South Africa is also a crisis of legitimacy because even the South African government has recognized that it does not represent all South African people.[15]

Human rights are indivisible from world peace. Any government in Africa, Europe, or any other part of the world, which rejects basic principles of human rights, including personal freedom, and which rules without the express consent of its people is potentially unstable: There is a real connection between human rights and peace and security. The rights to "freedom, equality, justice and dignity," described by the Charter of the OAU as "essential objectives for the achievement of the legitimate aspirations of the African people," are identical with the aspirations of all peoples throughout the world. There are no "major and minor" human rights, general observance of which should not be given "greater or lesser" attention—hence, the legitimacy of international concern for the violation of human rights in all parts of the world.

The work of international bodies that monitor the infringement of human rights in Africa, such as Amnesty International, the International Commission of Jurists, the European Commission of Human Rights, and the churches, is to be commended. But unless the same degree of concern is displayed by African institutions, movements, and individuals, it will have little effect on the responsible governments.

Democracy, unlike revolution, cannot be exported. The change must come from within African society, not from outside. Herein lies the task of the African intellectual at universities and other educational institutions, the press, the trade unions, the churches, and other institutions: to use every opportunity for drawing the general public into a debate about human rights and thus seek to influence their governments.

The situation is not as hopeless as it seems. In Sudan the military regime was deposed by a civilian (!) uprising. Nigeria, the host country of the Port Harcourt Conference, has taken the bold step of declaring respect for human rights the cornerstone of its domestic policies.

The African Charter on Human and Peoples' Rights, despite its imperfections, is an important achievement. It represents the admission on the part of the signatory states that "fundamental human rights stem from the attributes of human beings, which justifies their rights for an international protection." The Charter will make it increasingly difficult and uncomfortable for African leaders to preach observance of human rights abroad, while disregarding them at home.

The process of demilitarization of Africa will be a long and complex one, for it does not just mean a simple transfer of power from a military to a civilian government. It means, above all, a demilitarization of minds. The disillusionment and cynicism that have been bred by the succession of armed redeemers, promising things they never delivered during the past thirty years, may take another thirty years to heal.

NOTES

1. E. Shils, "The Military in the Political Development of the New States," in J. Johnson, ed., *The Role of the Military in Underdeveloped Countries* (Princeton, N.J.: Princeton University Press, 1962).

2. *Africa Now*, no. 7 (1985).

3. The Organization of African Unity's Charter: Preamble Report.

4. Simon Baynham at the International Symposium on The Militarization of Africa, held at SIPRI, Stockholm, November 10–12, 1986. The Scandinavian Institute of African Studies, 1986, p. 13.

5. Major-General Ibrahim Ali, at the International Symposium. See note 4 above; for the exact reference in the report, see page 14.

6. Tony Hodges, at the International Symposium. See note 4 above; Hodges is also the author of *Angola to the 1990s* (London: Economic Intelligence Unit, 1987).

7. Colin Legum, "The Impact of Militarization on the Natural Resources of Africa," *African Contemporary Record* (New York and London: Africana, 1986).

8. Nicole Ball, "Security Expenditure and Economic Growth in Developing Countries," *Pugwash Annals, 1985* (London: Macmillan, 1986).

9. Peter Enahoro, "The Legacy of 25 Years of Freedom," *Africa Now* (January 1986).

10. Peter Nobel, *Refugee Law in the Sudan*, Research Report No. 64, 1982. Scandinavian Institute of African Studies, Uppsala.

11. Pini Jason, "Human Rights for Africa," *New African* (November 1986).

12. The African Charter of Human and Peoples' Rights was adopted by the OAU at its eighteenth ordinary session in Nairobi, June 24–27, 1981. Only twenty-one of the fifty member states have ratified it. At the same time, twenty OAU member states were listed by Amnesty International as violators of human rights.

13. Jason, "Human Rights for Africa."

14. Elizabeth Ohene, at the International Symposium; see note 4.

15. Konrad Ginther, at the International Symposium; see note 4.

8

A Continent in Crisis: Migrants and Refugees in Africa

Michael J. Schultheis

Africa is sometimes called a continent on the move. But Africans have always been "on the move," long before they had any contact with Europe. In a vast and sparsely populated continent, people and communities migrated to maintain ecological balance, to seek a more secure environment, and to achieve better living conditions. Almost every region of Africa has witnessed various streams of population distribution and redistribution, although it is impossible to define them precisely and to delineate their frontiers.

Population displacements and human migrations are neither unique to Africa nor confined to the twentieth century. They are the inevitable companions of war, civil conflict, and prolonged economic deprivation. They also accompany rapid economic and social change. However, present migration patterns in Africa have several alarming dimensions. An estimated 10 million or more Africans are uprooted from their homes. Nearly half are refugees; the rest have left their homes in search of food. They reflect the widespread famine, political conflict, and declining standards of living, especially in rural areas.

The purpose of this chapter is to identify some generally unexamined dimensions of migration in Africa. It views refugees as one category of migrants, often no more vulnerable and at no greater risk than other migrants. Alternatively, it views most Africans "on the move" as refugees, in the sense that they are reluctant migrants, compelled to move by forces beyond their control. Consequently, this chapter makes no sharp distinction between the two.

The methodology employed is to view migrants not simply as individuals and families who move to survive, but as symptomatic of deeper problems in the institutions and structures of the African countries and in the world systems of which they are a part. This chapter proposes and develops the general thesis that migration in Africa today can be understood only in the context of poverty and underdevelopment. It necessarily summarizes many aspects of the issues involved, because of limitations of space.

The chapter is developed in three sections. The first gives a general overview of present conditions in Africa and places migration within that context. The second section looks more specifically at the subgroups of migrants termed *refugees*. It reviews the major areas of refugees and the limitations of the term in the African context. The third and concluding section explores the roles of nongovernmental organizations (NGOs), especially church and other religious organizations, both in alleviating the plight of migrants and refugees and in addressing the underlying causes.

POPULATION MOVEMENTS IN AFRICA

The General Context

The Demographic Setting

The population of Africa totals about 500 million. It is a young population—half is under fifteen years of age—and growing by 3 percent or more annually. The large proportion of young people places a heavy burden on the resource base and on the present working population, who, for the most part, are illiterate and have limited skills. At the present rate of growth, the population will double within twenty-five years and by the end of the century will exceed 750 million.

Nearly 80 percent of the population live in rural areas. As economies become more diversified, this proportion will decline, even though the rural population continues to grow in number. A healthy rural economy provides both food for the growing total population and income to support the economic diversification process. In other words, the rural production sectors must grow faster than the population to meet the food needs and to enable this diversification to occur. The relatively small nonagricultural sectors of the economy and the urban areas have a limited capacity to absorb the growing population.

The present crisis in Africa is a result of the general economic decline and the breakdown in the agricultural production sectors, a process that has been cumulative over the past decade and is evident in the widespread famine of the mid–1980s. UN agencies estimate that in 1985 famine in Africa placed between 30 and 35 million people in twenty countries seriously at risk. Almost 10 million people had to abandon their homes and lands in search of food and water.[1] Hundreds of thousands of people in sub-Saharan Africa are leaving the countryside; they face a bleak future in shanty towns of already crowded cities. A recent UN report projects that an additional 200 million people will relocate to African cities by the year 2000.[2] Much of this relocation can be traced to a breakdown in the rural areas, rather than healthy growth in the nonagricultural economic sectors.

The Economic Setting

Twenty-three of the world's poorest countries are in sub-Saharan Africa. Their annual per capita income is below U.S. $200, and the economic situation is not encouraging. Per capita output declined by more than 11 percent from 1980 to 1983. In 1970 Africa was producing enough food to feed itself; in 1982 the equivalent of the entire urban population was being fed on food imports.[3] These statistics translate into four highly visible realities:

1. Expanding hunger and increased infant mortality
2. Deterioration of the economic infrastructure
3. Shortages of consumer goods and high rates of inflation
4. Increased corruption and internal social conflict

Several factors lie behind the economic crises in Africa. There are interrelated causes, some arising from the internal structures of the economies and others from their relationship to the international system. The economies of the sub-Saharan African countries are largely agricultural; many rely on one or two export crops for foreign exchange earnings. Much of sub-Saharan Africa lies in marginal rainfall areas, and drought is a recurrent factor of life. The Sahel countries have experienced continue a rainfall shortages over the past fifteen years. Rainfall in 1983 and 1984 was the lowest in a century. Drought immediately affects agricultural production and sharpens the competition between export and food crops for land, family labor inputs, and other available resources. Prolonged drought undermines normal coping mechanisms, accelerates the deterioration of the land in a process called desertification, and leads to famine.[4]

The nature of Africa's linkages to the world economy has also contributed to the present economic difficulties. The 1980s have been characterized by higher prices of basic imports, especially petroleum products and manufactured goods, and by lower prices for exports (mainly agricultural products and minerals). This translates into a balance-of-payments crisis for most countries. Foreign exchange reserves are depleted, and suppliers' credits are dried up. Those domestic sectors that depended on imports are badly affected. The entire transportation infrastructure in many countries has deteriorated, with multiplier effects on agricultural production and marketing.

Poorer countries attempted to minimize the impact of rising petroleum prices and the global recession of the late 1970s and early 1980s by borrowing and by deferring payments on capital investment programs, with the expectation that their economies would return to the growth rates of the 1960s and early 1970s. Continued recession further complicated the problems they faced. In 1985 the total debt held by African countries was approximately U.S. $150 billion. The sub-Saharan countries hold U.S. $90 billion, which represents approximately 55 percent of their gross national product. Their debt-service ratio (payments on interest and principal) for 1985–1987 is expected to be 35 percent of export earnings (up from 13 percent in 1982).

Instead of providing additional assistance to ease the impact of this crisis, major international donors imposed stringent adjustment policies on many poor countries as a condition for bilateral aid and International Monetary Fund (IMF) and World Bank credits and loans. The effect was to contract further their already depressed economies. Governments were forced to cut back social service and developmental programs. In some instances, this contributed to bureaucratic rigidities, corruption, economic decline, and military coups.

The present economic difficulties that affect African countries are a combination of misdirected development programs, shifts in the international economy and their inability to adjust properly to those shifts, entrenched bureaucracies, and the vagaries of the climate. Whatever the causal interactions and relative importance of these several factors, the results are evident in several areas: (1) hunger and economic hardship for most people and communities, which do not have access to other sources of food; (2) increased corruption among government officials and bureaucrats; (3) growing unrest across the population; and (4) the increased militarization evident in many countries. This is the context in which migration and refugees are being generated in Africa today.

General Migration Patterns

Internal Migration

Migration involves both movements of population over time and space and generally changes of residence. It can be described in terms of duration, distance, the nature of movements, and whether they occur within a country (internal) or between countries (international). Population censuses, administrative records, population registers, and border check records, often supplemented by sample surveys, provide data to describe these movements. In Africa regular reliable data on population movements are rarely available.

Internal migration is often described by four streams, based on rural and/or urban areas of origin and of destination. In normal times, the relative importance of these streams depends to a great extent on the diversification of the economy, the rural-urban distribution of the population, and the political-economic policies of the country. In times of upheaval and stress, the streams may be independent of such factors.

In most of Africa data are not available to disaggregate the migration streams into these forms. It may be useful, however, to note the elements of this typology and the general nature of each stream:

1. Rural to rural: This form remains important in some areas, in terms of both numbers and impact on origin and destination region. Migrants in this stream tend to originate in areas of high population density and land shortage, which often was created by colonial land alienation and the demands of capitalist economies. Historically, this form was short term and often seasonal, as in the case of agricultural and other wage workers. It placed pressure on family structures and communities when workers were away from their home areas for extended and critical periods.[5] Over time such migrants tend to become permanent wage earners and to be joined by their families.

   The famine situation in many areas introduces a new dimension to this stream, as families and entire communities are forced to migrate in search of food. Although these begin as temporary moves, depending on the agricultural recovery in the post-famine years, they may become permanent. Government may also promote resettlement, from famine areas to higher potential areas, as presently in Ethiopia.

2. Rural to urban: This stream is often viewed as natural and inevitable in Africa, given rural population growth, land shortages, and the prospect of better economic opportunities in urban areas. In many countries, education encourages this movement. School leavers tend to move stepwise, from villages to towns and cities. A growing number of rural-to-urban migrants are now permanent urban residents. Many are second-

generation, and their children are urban-oriented, with little appreciation of country living.

The present economic decline introduces new elements in this movement. Urban economies are contracting, with declining urban employment and economic opportunities in the urban areas. At the same time, famine and breakdown in the rural areas force people toward towns and urban areas where imported food supplies are available.

3. Urban to urban: This stream is found in countries with a broad urban base, such as Nigeria, where employment opportunities are dispersed. Migrants usually move within the urban systems and stepwise, toward the more advanced areas.

4. Urban to rural: This stream takes two forms. The first is circular, where migrants begin and end their movements in their home community. The rural areas provide a social security cushion for workers released from the urban and industrialized sectors of the commercialized economy. The second involves a colonization movement, with the intent to exploit underdeveloped rural areas or to change their population configurations, sometimes for political reasons.

International Migration

This type of migration involves movement across national borders, usually to neighboring countries. In an earlier period, such borders did not exist. The colonial demarcation of frontiers was arbitrary and undertaken with little regard for local considerations or needs. The consequences are well known, but African governments show no inclination to redraw national boundaries. Many aggressively protect the borders and intercept what once were natural movements of pastoral and other border peoples.

In many areas of Africa today, people cross national borders in significant numbers because of economic and political factors. For example, there are an estimated 2 million immigrants from neighboring states in the Ivory Coast, driven by famine in the Sahel and attracted by the better opportunities there. Professional and skilled people move more freely across the continent, largely from one urban center to another. But many international migrants are refugees in the strict definition of the term (see below). This stream is largely rural to rural, although people often move either to refugee camps for security reasons or to food distribution points near town and urban centers.

Toward an Explanation of Population Movements

Migration theory tends to look on migrants as individuals, who make migration choices according to a calculus of personal economic gain. Equilibrium theory generates models and attempts to ascribe determining characteristics to the migrants and causal factors to their choices, with probability parameters for projected changes in the various streams.[6] This theory has little relevance to the situation in Africa today.

The thesis set forth here is that most population movements in Africa today are the result of poverty and economic deterioration, particularly in the rural areas. Famine and political conflict are manifestations of these conditions. The causes are both internal and external. They have historical roots, which frequently are used as excuses to justify inaction. They are often the result of political decisions and economic policies and practices. They are vastly complicated by interdependencies in the global economy and by the Cold War and political conflicts between the Soviet Union and the United States.

The thesis proposed here raises fundamental questions about the nature of the interdependencies in the global political economy. It rejects as inadequate the explanation of migration and refugee flows as being an inevitable result of (1) the dissolution of a century of colonial rule; (2) the postindependent realignment of political and economic forces; and (3) misguided development policies, bureaucratic ineptitude and corruption, and unfavorable climatic conditions. It argues that refugee and migration flows are the result of fundamental structural disorders in an interdependent world system where the weak and the poor bear the burden of policies and institutions imposed and maintained by the powerful and the rich.

REFUGEES IN AFRICA

Defining a Refugee: The Historical Context

Estimates vary, but today some 10 to 15 million people are classified as "refugees." The problems of enumeration are only one reason for the wide range in the estimates. Another is that governments may gain from high or low estimates. A third and often related reason is that governments view refugees as political pawns in the East-West conflict. For some, even the definition of a refugee has ideological overtones. They are unwilling or unable to agree on what constitutes a refugee; consequently, they cannot agree on whom to enumerate as refugees.

The world's current refugee population exceeds that of many individual nations. It is nearly one-third the number of immigrants who went to the United States in the nineteenth century, during the years of peak European immigration. Such figures destroy the usual conception of refugee, which was formed after the First and Second World Wars, when the Western world turned its attention to its uprooted peoples, principally from Europe, who sought to rebuild their lives in the aftermath of war. Many private voluntary agencies and governmental branches made refugee assistance their primary focus. They encouraged governments to formulate codes regarding the status and protection of refugees.

In this process, a "refugee situation" came to be identified as an "individual" phenomenon. Each situation was unique, isolated in and limited to a particular place and time. A particular event could be identified as its cause. The ensuing flow of people was both a tragedy and a crisis, to be met with humanitarian concern and emergency aid. The expectation was that, with such assistance, these single "events" would be resolved and the system, as well as individual refugees, could return to normal.

Normal, however, is exactly what the refugee situation has now become. Since the early 1950s, millions of persons have existed in a homeless limbo. At different times the locations have shifted, from Europe to Asia to Southeast Asia to Africa and most recently to Central America. Individuals and even groups have been resettled, but the flows of refugees continue, until today they seem to constitute not an exception but a permanent feature of our world order. Millions of people are uprooted each year, and many of these are forced to flee their homes, their ancestral environments, their customary ways of living.

These immediate human tragedies in themselves are more than enough to absorb all our energy and attention. A brief glance at the statistics can be overwhelming, granted the reservations on the reliability of the estimates. The United Nations High Commissioner for Refugees estimated about 10 million refugees at the end of 1986, with Pakistan having the greatest number at approximately 2.7 million.[7] Many sources make much larger estimates.

What is unprecedented about the refugee flows at the present time is that they are primarily in the "developing world" rather than in Europe. They flee as populations rather than as individuals. In Africa, they flee on foot, in Southeast Asia they flee both on foot and by boat, in search of refuge in neighboring countries, until such time as they can either return to their homes or find permanent asylum elsewhere. Until that time, most remain uprooted, dispossessed, and homeless.

The Politics of Defining a "Refugee"

International Documents

An appraisal of the refugee situation properly begins by considering how governments define refugees. The conferral of "refugee" status simultaneously establishes legal rights for that person and legal responsibilities on governments. Not surprisingly, governments seek to limit those rights and responsibilities. Unfortunately, ideological considerations and domestic pressures often are more important in determining "refugee" status than the needs of refugees.

An historical note is instructive. Governments of Western Europe and North America developed the international apparatus to respond to refugee needs in the European context following the First and Second World Wars.

After the First World War, the League of Nations responded to the insistence of voluntary agencies caring for Europe's displaced persons and appointed the first High Commissioner for Refugees. Following World War II, the General Assembly of the United Nations, in 1951, created, on a temporary basis, the United Nations High Commissioner for Refugees (UNHCR). The UNHCR had two basic functions: (1) to provide international minimum standards for the recognition and treatment of refugees, and (2) to promote and facilitate either their repatriation or their assimilation into countries of asylum.

The UNHCR's main instruments for achieving these objectives were the 1951 Convention Relating to the Status of Refugees and the 1967 Protocol Relating to the Status of Refugees.[8] Forty African countries have signed the Convention, which has strengthened the rights of refugees across the continent.[9]

These UNHCR documents continue to provide the most widely used definition of a refugee: any person "who owing to well-founded fear of being persecuted for reasons of race, religion, nationality, membership of a particular social group or political opinion, is outside the country of his nationality and is unable, or, owing to such fear, is unwilling to avail himself of the protection of the country."[10] Subsequent articles and documents specify responsibilities which governments have toward those who are granted legal status as refugees.

In 1969 the Organization of African Unity (OAU), reflecting the special problems in Africa, broadened the definition to include "every person, who, owing to external aggression, occupation, foreign domination or events seriously disturbing public order in either part or the whole of his country of origin or nationality, is compelled to leave his place of habitual residence in order to seek refuge in another place outside his country of origin or nationality."[11] The Convention prohibits states from denying asylum and repatriating any person whose welfare would be threatened by return to his country. It also stipulates that the granting of asylum should not be interpreted as an unfriendly act by any other state.

Limitations of the Definitions

Limitations of the official UNHCR definition are well known. They remain because countries conveniently use them for their own purposes. Two limitations especially should be noted. The first relates to the phrase, "well-founded fear of being persecuted." How is this subjective element of "fear" to be established? Moreover, "fear of persecution" or even "persecution" is usually foreign to a refugee's vocabulary. The definition does not allow for the fear that results from war or civil conflict.

The second relates to the specification that the refugee be "outside the country of his or her nationality." The UNHCR guidelines allow "no exceptions to this rule. International protection cannot come into play as long as a person is within the international jurisdiction of his home country."[12]

The principal shortcoming of the definition, however, is that it is based on a concept that had its origin in Europe after World War Two, when the refugee population was relatively stable and distinct. Since then, the vast increase in the scale and complexity of refugee flows has rendered the definition inadequate and the review process inappropriate. As Charles B. Keely points out: "How one defines a refugee implicitly includes an understanding of the determinants of international migration generally and in what way refugees are distinct from other migrants."[13] Changes in the character of international migration since World War Two have, in fact, made the Protocol definition of refugee untenable. Arbitrary distinctions among economic and ideological or political migrants, political exiles, and undocumented aliens produce policy results that are often destructive and inhumane.

The "Excluded" Refugees

Internally Displaced and Victims of Conflict

The UNHCR documents have several other shortcomings. First, they exclude internally displaced persons and extend international protection only to those who have crossed an international boundary. This border stipulation may make sense from a state's point of view; it does not protect individuals who are threatened by a national government or by internal conflict. This requirement is particularly inappropriate in Africa, where arbitrary borders, established by European colonial powers, are frequently a cause of refugee situations.

Second, the documents exclude or fail to consider the victims of military operations. The 1949 Geneva Conventions on the Protection of War Victims considered victims of international armed conflicts. Today, internal military operations, often between groups that are supported and encouraged by external powers, are a principal cause of refugees and displaced persons. In earlier periods, when wars were fought between nations, the control of a population was the end rather than the means of warfare. In many situations today, however, control of a population has itself become the means of fighting the "enemy."

Another significant shortcoming is that they exclude individuals and groups who flee oppressive economic situations (or economic "persecution"). The UNHCR *Handbook* explains that if an individual "is moved exclusively by economic considerations, he is always an economic migrant and not a refugee."[14] The *Handbook* concedes that "the distinction between an economic migrant and a refugee is, however, sometimes blurred...[so that] what appears at first sight to be primarily an economic motive for departure may in reality also involve a political element."[15] This concession does not go far enough.

A more fundamental question relates to the distinction between economic hardship and economic persecution or oppression. Economic hardship describes a situation in which individuals, through "bad luck" or "bad decisions," fail to succeed in what is basically a fair and just system. They wish to migrate to another country to improve their lot. When migration is restricted to "refugees," such individuals may apply for refugee status. However, they correctly are termed *economic migrants.*

On the other hand, economic depression or persecution may also find expression in poverty, both absolute and relative, but they are a consequence of the system itself. For example, in some developing countries, political and economic policies marginalize and impoverish local populations by depriving them of economic resources and political voice. Such situations are found, for example, in Central America and South Africa. They are also present in other areas of the world, without respect to ideologies. They exist in developing countries (DCs) which are oriented toward capitalist as well as communist systems.

In "open" capitalist-oriented DCs, international capital, operating through multinational corporations (MNCs) and in collaboration with local elites, often appropriates the best or potentially most productive resources. For instance, multinational corporations often purchase the most 79 productive agricultural land and develop it to produce crops either for export or for domestic market. Or MNCs may invest in capital-intensive industries, which are oriented toward foreign markets and have limited local employment benefits. In the first instance, they force rural people from the land; in the second, they do not provide nonfarm jobs and incomes sufficient to meet the essential needs of the displaced.[16]

In Communist-oriented DCs, governments may attempt to force local populations to comply with central government and party policies, both political and economic. Although the two systems affect different groups, both may involve economic oppression and persecution. Faced with popular movements for economic and political reform, governments employ military force to maintain "law and order" or to guarantee stability within the population. The victims have a justifiable claim to "refugee" status.

In summary, many more people are "refugees" than those whom the UNHCR Convention and Protocol include in their definition. The excluded fall into three groups: (1) the internally dislocated who are persecuted and unprotected within their own nation; (2) victims of internal military operations and civil conflict; and (3) individuals and groups systematically excluded from economic resources and political rights in their country. It is desirable for individuals and groups to have formal recognition as refugees so that they may claim international asylum and legal rights and so that the world community might address the systems that generate refugees and the underlying causes.

Why People Become Refugees

In analyzing contemporary refugee flows, observers advance different models and typologies. Some attempt to project future refugee flows. Others relate conditions in countries of origin to social and political factors.[17]

In a helpful analysis based on different forms of conflict, Astri Suhrke proposes a typology of several refugee movements:

1. Independence struggles (e.g., Algeria and Angola)

2. Ethnic conflict, with autonomous and separatist dimensions (e.g., Biafra in Nigeria and Eritrea in Ethiopia)

3. Internal ethnic conflict unrelated to separatist or autonomous struggles (e.g., Burundi)

4. Class conflict (e.g., Kampuchea)

5. Internal elite power struggles

6. State terrorism (e.g., Haiti under Duvalier and some Latin American countries)

7. International wars (e.g., World War II and compounding of internal struggles with external intervention, as in Vietnam and Afghanistan)

The principal limitation of Suhrke's typology is that it fails to
identify the relationship of refugee movements to each other and to
more fundamental systemic factors. The conception of the world is
pre–World War II, made up largely of isolated actors, who only mar-
ginally and occasionally are affected by external forces. This typology
is thus consistent with the view expressed in the UNHCR documents,
that refugee situations are either largely unique or limited to area-
specific problems. For this reason, it is less apocalyptic than some
studies of the late 1970s, which projected ever-increasing numbers
of refugees. But Suhrke's typology is misleading. It implies that refugees and refugee flows are due primarily to causes and conflicts that
are either internal to a country or limited to a region and that are
the result of decisions taken by domestic and national actors for
identifiable self-interests. An adequate explanation of the causes of
refugee movements must probe more deeply and relate them to the
world's dominant political and economic systems.

The main refugee flows since the end of World War II are the direct or
indirect result of the conflict between the Soviet Union and the United
States. The conflict between these superpowers takes different forms:

1. Direct military intervention (e.g., the United States in the Dominican
   Republic and Vietnam and the Soviet Union in Afghanistan).
2. Indirect military intervention through satellite or client states (e.g., in
   Central America, the United States used Argentinian military advisers
   and supplies in El Salvador prior to the Falklands war and has since
   created the "Contras" to overthrow the government of Nicaragua. In
   Africa and Latin America the USSR has used Cuba to promote its regional
   interests.)
3. Economic support and pressure, either directly through bilateral aid
   programs or indirectly through multilateral assistance programs such
   as the World Bank and/or the IMF (e.g., the United States has undertaken
   to "stabilize" Central America through the projected Caribbean Basin
   program. The United States has also extended military credits to many
   countries and selectively approves or rejects International Monetary Fund
   (IMF) and World Bank credits and loans to countries, based less on
   economic than on geopolitical criteria—(e.g., it has promoted loans to
   South Africa and Chile and blocked loans to Nicaragua).
4. More general support for economic and political systems compatible with
   the interests of the superpowers, rather than with the developmental
   needs of the poorer countries.

These methods of extending the East-West conflict, however, should not be viewed as separate and isolated from each other, but as elements of a comprehensive approach by which a superpower assists a "friendly" government or attempts to undermine an unfriendly one. The ultimate expression of this policy is the national security state, which has as its principle aim the perpetuation of itself in power and the structuring of the international system along geopolitical lines. Superpowers, as far as they can, manipulate and control internal interests in a direction consistent with and favorable to their own interests. They promote internal elites and class interests accordingly. In turn, they are manipulated by these elites and interests.

The case of Vietnam is illustrative and amply documented. In the Horn of Africa the United States and the Soviet Union have played a role in the generation of hundreds of thousands of refugees. In southern Africa, South Africa is supported by Western interests in the destabilization of the region and has set Mozambique and Angola on fire.

The Refugee Map of Africa

Nearly half the world's refugees are found in Africa, although estimates vary as to the actual number and change from year to year. The UNHCR estimated the 1986 refugee population in Africa at 3.5 million. If internally displaced and hunger migrants are included, some 15 million or more people live uprooted from their homes.

The largest concentration is in the Northeast, the area known as the Horn of Africa. An estimated half a million Ethiopians have fled into neighboring Somalia, and 700,000 have crossed into Sudan. Sudan, one of the poorest countries in the world, and with a civil war of its own, has received an influx of perhaps 100,000 refugees from Chad and 250,000 or more from Uganda. In the western regions of Sudan, 4 to 5 million Sudanese need food assistance.

There are significant refugee flows in other parts of Africa. Some are occasional, if unpredictable. For example, in 1982 Nigeria forcibly repatriated several hundred thousand Ghanaians, many of whom had lived and worked there for many years. Other flows have no end in sight. Civil War in Chad and the prolonged internal conflict in Uganda have created successive waves of refugees into neighboring countries (although refugees are beginning to return to Uganda with promise of stability under the new government).

In southern Africa, South Africa continues to generate new refugees and internally displaced persons. It has created perhaps 3 million internally displaced with its Bantustan or "homeland" policies. Its destabilizing activities against neighboring countries, particularly Angola and Mozambique, have forced several hundred thousand people to flee their homes.[18]

In Africa, as elsewhere, the number of refugees fluctuates with political and economic conditions. For example, when Zimbabwe became independent in 1980, there were an estimated 750,000 refugees and internally displaced persons in a population of less than 6 million. Within a year most had returned to their home areas, and the work of rehabilitation was well underway. One might expect a similar result in Ethiopia, Uganda, and across southern Africa.

CONCLUSIONS

Africa, "the continent on the move," challenges the global community at the deepest level of human values and compassion. This is particularly true of the religious communities, which espouse transcendental values and a stated belief in a fundamental human dignity shared by all persons.

Here I would like to concentrate especially on the religious values of the Christian faith, and specifically the Catholic Church. Forced migrants and refugees challenge the Church at every level of its ministry and its faithfulness to the Gospels. Jesus identified with the migrant and the refugee—"I was a stranger and you took me in." Jesus, through these reluctant migrants and refugees, speaks to us. They are "signs of the times" through whom we encounter the living God. They are the early warning signals of a world in crisis, a global community struggling to be born.

At many levels, the Church in Africa is responding.[19] In many dioceses the Church is hearing their voices and is becoming the Church of the poor. At other levels, the Church's response is uncertain and fragmented.

If this analysis is basically correct in its identification of the underlying causes of the present crisis in Africa, several implications follow for the Church in its ministry to migrants and refugees. In the first instance, the Church at most levels has little awareness of the deep ecological and economic and cultural crises that are rapidly closing in on many rural communities and most countries of Africa. Even if favorable rainfalls occur for the next decade, the crisis will continue. A land area twice the size of India is under direct threat of "desertification," which means that it is becoming a nonproductive wasteland. This is a critical factor for the future of Africa and will delay the prospects of economic recovery. It will be a fundamental reason for the continued generation of reluctant migrants and refugees.

What does this imply for the Church in its ministry? First, perhaps more than any other institution, the Church is uniquely situated to assist communities and countries in this crisis. In many instances, this assistance implied that the Church continue its present forms of ministry, perhaps expanding them and reinforcing them whenever possible. In other instances, the Church must adapt its present ministries to meet the urgent needs of communities in stress. The crisis itself will call the Church to tap all its resources and spiritual strength to support new forms of ministry, particularly in the areas of collaborating with other groups and agencies in helping people in need and in addressing the causes of the present crisis.

But the nature of the Church's presence and assistance will also be important. The Church already is present in many communities that are under stress. Although the Church at the parish level is often deeply involved in supporting local initiatives to improve food production and living conditions, these initiatives will require strengthening, with greater stress on developing self-reliant local communities. Parishes and dioceses will be called to explore methods for greater collaboration, with each other as well as with other agencies and church groups. They will require the support and assistance of the Church at national and regional levels.

Where the Church is not present in areas of greater stress, fidelity to the Gospel requires that it seek to become so. This means being a presence in refugee camps and food distribution centers, wherever that is possible. The Church might strengthen and extend its ministry among migrants in areas of settlement, whether rural or urban, helping them form local communities of support for people under stress. The diocesan and the national churches might develop means of coordinating and supporting this effort wherever possible.

But the poor call the universal Church to yet another form of ministry. This is the ministry of compassion and solidarity. This ministry moves beyond blaming the victims and seeks to probe and analyze the reasons behind the present crisis in Africa. In some areas, this already is occurring. But parishes and dioceses and countries often need support and assistance in comprehending and analyzing these issues, as they seek to relate their response to the justice of the Gospel. Thus, the voices of the poor also speak to the clergy and religious laity, not only in Africa but also throughout the universal Church.

The crisis in Africa is a global crisis. It challenges the Church to develop new forms of solidarity, particularly across the divisions that separate the North and the South. In the face of famine and extensive human suffering which confront peoples and communities in Africa, the Church in the North must ask again and again: Why is it that we cannot stop the arms race? Why is it that we cannot overcome national divisions and create institutions of international cooperation? Why is it that we cannot move beyond the ideologies of legitimation and domination which justify and maintain economic systems and national security states which exploit and oppress the poor?

The crisis in Africa is the crisis of the human spirit. As Pope John Paul II stated in his remarks to diplomats accredited to the Vatican: "Efforts have to be made... through a policy of justice and peace, to get rid of the cause of such a lamentable reality (refugees and famine), which is not an unavoidable one. May our generation take up the challenge!"[20]

The voices of the migrants and refugees continue to raise that challenge. They speak to the universal Church and to each of us from that in-between land where "the twilight of past dreams turns gradually into shadows and expectations fade."[21] In the immediacy of flight they ask for food, shelter, and sanctuary, but they ask for more than this. They wish to build their lives anew either by returning to their home communities or by forming new ones. In the end, however, they plead for the Church to work with them to transform those situations that force them to leave their homes. They ask us to join them in the search for a "community without borders."

NOTES

1. UN Office for Emergency Operations in Africa, "Special Report on the Emergency Situation in Africa: Review of 1985 and 1986 Emergency Needs," New York, January 30, 1986.

2. Noted in *The Guardian,* Manchester, England, March 13, 1986.

3. World Bank, *Toward Sustained Development in Sub-Saharan Africa* (Washington, D.C.: 1984), pp. 10–14.

4. See two recent studies: Independent Commission on International Humanitarian Issues, *Famine: A Man-Made Disaster* (London: Pan Books, 1985); and Lloyd Timberlake, *Africa in Crisis: The Causes, The Cures of Environmental Bankruptcy* (London: International Institute for Environment and Development, 1985).

5. For an excellent review of "labor migration" in Africa, see S. Stichter, *Migrant Laborers* (Cambridge: Cambridge University Press, 1985).

6. Charles H. Wood, "Equilibrium and Historical-Structural Perspectives on Migration," *International Migration Review* 16, no. 2 (1982), pp. 298–319.

7. *Refugees,* no. 1986, pp. 24–25; also see *The World Refugee Survey: 1985 in Review,* pp. 36–40.

8. The 1967 Protocol eliminated the clause in the 1951 Convention restricting refugees to individuals "created by events prior to 1951."

9. Swaziland has signed only the 1967 Protocol.

10. UNHCR, *Handbook,* pp. 6, 11, and 40.

11. Ibid., p. 194.

12. Ibid., p. 88.

13. Charles B. Keely, *Global Refugee Policy: The Case of a Developmental-Oriented Strategy* (New York: Population Council, 1981), p. 13.

14. UNHCR, *Handbook*, p. 62.

15. Ibid., p. 63.

16. See Barbara Dinham and C. Hines, *Agribusiness in Africa: A Study of the Impact of Big Business on Africa's Food and Agricultural Production* (London: Earth Resources Research, 1983).

17. Keely, *Global Refugee Policy.*

18. U.S. Committee on Refugees, 1985, pp. 38–39.

19. See J. G. Donders and S. Smith, *Refugees are People: An Action Report on Refugees in Africa* (Eldoret, Kenya: GABA Publications, October 1985).

20. "A Voice for the Voiceless," January 15, 1983.

21. Ibid.

9

The African Context of Human Rights: Development, Equality, and Justice

Mokwugo Okoye

While no one denies that Africa today faces peculiar problems in the area of human rights, development, and justice, one may still ask: How peculiar, in fact, are African problems, or the people's reaction to them? This chapter explores this question in the context of the link between the African concept of human rights and the regional or global perspectives that shape most of the strategies for human rights implementation in the continent.

THE AFRICAN PREDICAMENT

One may concede that, unlike Europe and the Far East in the past, Africa today is not in a position to use plunder, slavery, colonization, and the brutal exploitation of its own and other peoples to achieve its own development and that the African predicament is not diminished by this narrowing down of options. But the search for appropriate strategies for development is not helped by the kind of foreign criticism that interprets the African problem in terms of an inherent genetic deficiency on the part of the blacks.

It should be stated at the outset that the concept of human rights is not new in Africa. From precolonial times Africans have enjoyed the right to free speech and of sanctuary in temples and in matrilineal homes, as well as the right to participate in public affairs and land use and to receive communal assistance in illness, attack, or bereavement. This is not much different from Harold Laski's formulation of human rights as "those conditions of social life without which no man can seek, in general, to be himself at his best." For Africa, the welfare of the community has always been supreme, although, unlike some European idealist philosophers, Africans did not dispose of the rights of citizens in an arbitrary fashion or treat the state as an absolute moral organism, since they have always had structural devices like age-grade and secret societies, division of function, and customs and taboos that provided adequate checks and balances in the society. Nor did Africans consider the concept of human equality a monstrous fiction that inspired "false ideas and vain expectations into men destined to travel in the obscure walk of laborious life [and] aggravate[d] and emitter[ed] that real inequality which it never can remove."[1] For, in Africa's traditional culture, there was usually no contradiction between personal and communal interest, and the country accepted that both were dependent on each other.

There might be an imprecise definition of individual rights within the traditional culture. Yet a significant characteristic of African customary law is its flexibility, which accounts for the familiar uncertainty and unpredictability of particular decisions in the customary courts in such matters as matrimonial and testamentary causes. One advantage of this flexibility is that there is little risk of crystallizing the law and custom of a particular moment in the development of a community or group of communities. It thereby inhibits future natural development and growth as under a written code that is definitive and self-sufficient in the fields with which it deals. Even if it is true, therefore, as we are sometimes told, that the African mind has a terror of "judgment" of definition and prefers compromise to forcing a decision in favor of one side, this is not invariably so or even intrinsically just. In fact, in the modern period Africans have adopted written constitutions incorporating a bill of rights. They have also taken definite ideological positions on many key issues of vital importance to world peace and security.

To buttress the argument that the African concept of human rights is, and has for many years now been, global, reference may be made to the resolutions of the Conference of Independent African States held at Accra, Ghana, in April 1958 which, inter alia, "proclaimed and solemnly affirm(ed) our unswerving loyalty to the Charter of the United Nations, the Universal Declaration of Human Rights and the Declaration of Asian-African Conference held at Bandung, Indonesia in 1955." (The last-named declaration included "respect for the fundamental human rights and equality of all races and of all nations, large and small, respect for justice and international obligations and peaceful settlement of all international disputes and promotion of mutual interest and cooperation.") Later in the same year, on December 5–12, 1958, the first All-Africa People's Conference, which also met in Accra, similarly recognized the Universal Declaration of Human Rights which, it said, was being flouted in Africa and the Africans were deprived of human rights. The conference, therefore, resolved, among other things, that fundamental human rights (including the freedom of speech, association, movement, worship, and "freedom to live a full and abundant life") be extended to all men and women in Africa and that the rights of indigenous Africans to the fullest use of their lands be respected and preserved. The conference specifically condemned racial discrimination and the political policies of territories like South Africa which base their minority rule of the majority on apartheid.

Following the examples of the European Convention of Human Rights (adopted in 1951) and the American Convention on Human Rights (signed on November 22, 1969, but effective July 18, 1978), the Organization of African Unity (OAU) adopted the African Charter on Human and Peoples' Rights in 1981 which, as in most other parts of the world, is as yet mostly on paper. For example, while respect for human rights may be a "legally required duty" for members of the Organization of American States, as the Charter stipulates, and while the UN Charter (Article 56) requires that "all members pledge themselves to take joint and separate action in cooperation with the Organization for the achievement of the purposes set forth in Article 55" (requiring universal respect for, and observance of, human rights and fundamental freedoms for all without distinction as to race, sex, language, or religion), even UN Security Council members like Britain and the United States have often, with the firm support of France and West Germany, vetoed majority resolutions of the Council to impose mandatory sanctions on apartheid South Africa for its obnoxious racist policies. They have, on the other hand, imposed discriminatory immigration laws on their "colored" visitors, just as in the mid–1930s they connived at the fascist Italian invasion of Ethiopia under the cover of benevolent neutrality. Neither former President Ronald Reagan's "constructive engagement" approach nor the Commonwealth Eminent Persons Group's offer of an olive branch to the apartheidists has shown any sign of bringing about a peaceful change in the South African system.

Without doubt most African countries, since a few years after independence in the 1960s, have been faced with many complex problems, especially in the areas of political stability, social security, balance of trade, civil war, drought, pest infestation, mass unemployment, and shortage of basic commodities (including food and urban housing). These problems have left the people with a heritage of social indiscipline, of relying more on their wits than on the rule of law, and living as if there is no tomorrow. There has been a precipitate fall in the demand for and prices of Africa's primary export commodities (including minerals and cash crops). This decline has affected imports that are so essential to development, particularly spare parts and industrial raw materials, leading to excess industrial capacities in a situation of scarcity of finished products. Moreover, the level of the foreign exchange reserves has fallen to its lowest ebb ever. A severe housing shortage in the towns, a debilitating debt burden (up to $170 billion by the end of 1986), and glaringly inefficient public utilities characterize the urban sector of the economy in many countries. At the same time, drought, civil strife, primitive production techniques, and exploitative market structures have worsened the food situation in the face of rising population.

Unfortunately for Africa, most of the development ideas that were being peddled in academic, business, and political circles in the post–World War II period as the cure-all for the problems of economically backward countries seemingly offered little understanding or agreement as to why poverty should remain so prevalent in a prodigiously productive age. Thus, neither industrialization nor self-reliant agriculture has been completely successful in postwar Africa in raising the living standard of the people and fostering social and political stability.

Industrialization, which was touted as the key to development and the symbol of maturity, has often resulted in mere import substitution (sometimes accompanied by a loss of quality, with no gain in prices) and neglect of agriculture. Self-reliance, sometimes seen as the sure way to the preservation of national independence and avoidance of humiliation at the hands of foreign aid-givers, has mostly failed in a world which technology is steadily making more interdependent every day and in which no nation, whatever its wealth or power, could be truly self-reliant.

Other hopes that "trade, not aid" and even commercial and technical cooperation among the developing countries, or that massive capital infusion from the developed countries, will have a "trickle-down" effect on the lower orders have not materialized in the light of decreasing foreign aid and investment. In the meantime millions of the people are living in wretched, inhuman conditions as others are dying from causes that could have been prevented with the aid of modern science. Besides, these new countries have felt the devastating effects of the current economic recession in the industrialized countries, with its accompanying protectionism directed against the raw materials and manufactured goods of the developing countries; the unrelenting subversive activities of the intelligence agencies and MNCs in the new countries, especially those under radical leadership (e.g., Patrice Lumumba's Congo, Nkrumah's Ghana, and Samora Machel's Mozambique); and misguided economic policies that have not been favorable to savings and investment.

Of course, development, like life itself, is a dynamic and very complex process; it is always beset with a number of problems, especially in a new country. Africa's colonial inheritance, its externally oriented capitalist economy, and its elitist political system have resulted in many contradictions and center-periphery dichotomies and a dependency syndrome. There is, for instance, the existing imbalance between the urban and rural sectors, between the rich and poor, and even between regions. "The contrasts of wealth and poverty in many developing countries," noted Judith Hart, former British Labor minister of overseas development, in 1973, "probably exceeds those of any other civilization at any other time in human history. In their human and social effects they certainly exceed those of Western European countries at the time of the Industrial Revolution, so vividly described by Marx and Engels; and, to some extent, of Western feudalism, in that extreme disparities of wealth are unaccompanied by the paternalism of feudalism."[2] Thus, extreme inequalities exist in many spheres of African society: a dynamic modern sector adjoining a primitive sector of stagnation and ever deepening misery; an air-conditioned Mercedes Benz next to hand carts, luxury skyscrapers towering over shanty towns.

There is inequality not only in wealth and income, but also in technology and productivity, as between the large foreign multinational companies operating huge automated factories, mines, or plantations and the small-scale indigenous activities; between luxurious residential universities and rural illiteracy; between the most modern hospitals and the village babalawo or medicine-man. The dualism is often reinforced by a division along ethnic or religious lines, with its repercussions on legal, electoral, and power-sharing activities and decisions.

It is part of the dilemma of developing societies that the solution of one problem creates another. Thus, decreasing the death rate tends to lead to overpopulation, developing irrigation canals spreads bilharzia, improving the army leads to coups d'etat by ambitious young officers, and opening low-quality colleges produces incompetent teachers and bureaucrats, while increasing the national wealth, say, from export of mineral resources like oil or copper, results in the intensification of social stratification corruption, and conspicuous, wasteful consumption by the new rich and in rising incidence of crime and alienation among the deprived poor. As the U.S. Presidential (Peterson) Commission declared in 1971: "Development implies change—political and social, as well as economic, and such change, for a time, may be disruptive."[3] Perpetual political instability, cultural disintegration, brain-drain or the evaporation of intellectual capital is thus the assured fate of most developing countries, and it is impossible for them and their primitive institutions to educate, in the widest sense of the word, the people needed to solve these difficult problems.

Yet real development involves a structural transformation of the economy, society, politics, and culture. This change will permit a redirection of science and technology, the self-generating and self-perpetuating use and development of the people's potentialities, and improvement in the machinery of administration and productive institutions so that the rising demands of society can be met. The result will be widespread education and literacy, a relative freedom from external bondage and exploitation, a fair and equitable distribution of social wealth, and the presence of a ruling elite strong enough to eliminate the corrupt elements in its own ranks, relatively competent and seriously devoted to public welfare and the reform of existing inequalities.

The achievement of these objectives has been hampered by the continent's structural constraints and by neocolonialist pressures. The social and economic cost for Africa of implementing economic stabilization measures, such as those sponsored by international financial agencies like the International Monetary Fund (IMF), has been very heavy. This casts serious doubts as to their appropriateness or effectiveness even as the investment banks and consulting firms (who moderate these measures) make their huge profits and the national bourgeoisie, tempted by the same profits, get caught in a maze of commitments and obligations to the banks and consulting firms in the hattrick of a massive international game. In this game, the international loan system, rather than constitute a transfer of resources to the less developed world, tends to transfer resources out of the poor countries into the coffers of the private banks in the capitalist Western countries. These transfers are underwritten by taxpayers of the world through national guarantee systems such as the U.S. Export and Import Bank and the IMF. Even a relatively richly endowed and creditworthy country like Nigeria today uses 30 percent (compared to 44 percent in 1984) of its national revenues to service debts owed to Western creditors under a Structural Adjustment Program and Second-tier Foreign Exchange Market scheme. These programs were imposed on the country by the IMF and the World Bank which today exercise a regulatory power over Africa's tariff, tax and trade incentives. In the words of one critic, this policy "simply means more money to develop the USA and Western Europe while at the same time it means less money to satisfy the fundamental needs of our people in the fields of health, education and employment."[4] The same judgment may be applied to countries like Ghana, Guinea, Sierra Leone, Zaire, and Zambia which through IMF directives have been compelled to devalue their currency in the past few years.

Indeed, a recolonization of Africa, as can be illustrated with the tragic case of Zaire seems to be taking place. Of this country, a long-time U.S. Central Intelligence Agency case officer in Africa wrote in 1984 that the United States "has run the country into a debt of $6.2 billion—money that was spent on the multinational corporations, not on the people. In Zaire today, 25 percent of the people are starving, while Mobutu Sese Sekou (the President) has a personal fortune of about $4.5 billion."[5] Similarly, in Liberia, a U.S. Agency for International Development (USAID) Financial Management group supervises the customs duty, import and export, tax collection, and foreign policy of the country. The situation in countries like Chad, Lesotho, and Sudan is not much better. Perhaps the truth is that both the industrialized and nonindustrialized countries are giving more priority and resources to the pursuit of their national glory and security than to development.

HUMAN RIGHTS IN THE GLOBAL CONTEXT

There are perhaps no given sets of prerequisites for economic development, and we have no universally accepted categories of backwardness. What is a hindrance to progress in one setting and at one stage may be helpful under different circumstances. Similarly, the fundamental human rights a people enjoys at any moment are a component of their national sovereignty and, as part cannot be in contradiction of the whole, a country cannot give its citizens what it does not have. One consolation here is that everyone has a hierarchy of needs which are defined by the past, age, environment, education, and "custom deep as frost and deep almost as life itself." Africa's prime concern today is with the issues of race and poverty and their manipulation to the advantage of neocolonialism which inhibits the people's self-actualization. In developed as well as underdeveloped countries, there are reactionary politicians who, when under siege, encourage their poor to turn their discontent on the racial immigrants or minorities in their midst (as happened under the Nazis in Germany or in Uganda under Idi Amin in the 1970s). In the case of the whites whose idea of the Master Race goes back many centuries, a distinguished ethnographer, Dr. Alfred Metraux, has observed:

There exists in the structure of Western civilization a fatal contradiction. On the one hand, it wishes and insists that certain cultural values, to which it attributes the highest virtues, be assimilated by other people. But, conversely, it will not admit that two-thirds of humanity is capable of attaining this standard which it has set up. Ironically, the worst sufferers from racial dogma are usually the people whose intellect most forcibly demonstrates its falseness. By an irony as strange the more capable the so-called inferior races prove themselves of attaining emancipation, the more emphatic grows the assertion of racial dogma, stiffened by the colored races' acquisition of a minimum of political rights or by their emergence as competitors. And the crowning paradox is that, to provide a rational justification for their blind prejudice, appeal is made to our age's gods—science and scientific objectivity.[6]

The human rights record of many African countries is bad enough—abysmally low conditions of living, political repression, rigged elections, wide separation between rich and poor, and widespread corruption, ethnicity, and arbitrary enforcement of the law are obvious examples—but they have no monopoly on these evils. The literature of international human rights organizations like Amnesty International, the UN Commission of Human Rights, and the International Commission of Jurists shows abundant evidence that the infraction of human rights, including the infliction of torture and practice of discrimination against citizens, is not limited to any one country or racial group.

For instance, the United States, whose Bill of Rights goes back to 1791 and whose Supreme Court has condemned capital punishment as inhumane and degrading, nevertheless during its history subjected large segments of its racial or political minorities to lynching, job discrimination, and electronic spying. Today about one-seventh of its population lives below the official poverty level. Moreover, the destabilizing activities of the CIA and MNCs in Third World countries have become notorious.

Even the USSR, which makes so much of equal rights to work, free education, and medicare for all, has been guilty of harassing and detaining nonconformists in its society whose only crime may be questioning the official non-Marxist orthodoxy. Britain, despite its long democratic tradition, has been accused in recent years of torturing political detainees in Northern Ireland and today about 4 million British citizens are unemployed. France, too, has a shameful record of torture and brutality in Madagascar, Algeria, and Vietnam. Women in the West have also not always fared so well. France did not grant women the vote until 1946, while women in Switzerland did not obtain equal rights to the family wealth in the event of divorce until September 1985—and then only by a slim majority of 54.7 percent of the 40.5 percent of its 4 million population who turned out for the polls. Yet all these countries are rated among the most "civilized" in the world.

Countries like Argentina, Brazil, Chile, Greece, Portugal, Poland, Turkey, India, the Philippines, and Indonesia have had occasion to suspend the fundamental human rights provisions of their constitution. Most military regimes, in Africa as elsewhere, simply do not recognize human rights or permit anyone to question the right of the state to arrest or detain a citizen or challenge any of its decrees in the press or law courts, even as apartheid South Africa denies that its black citizens have any right whatever. In South Africa, indeed, where the torture or murder of political detainees is routine, over 10,000 out of the 25,000 political prisoners held without charge, trial or visitation rights in 1986 were sixteen years of age. Denial of human rights there, said Amnesty International in April of that year, "continues daily and has increased remarkably," as had happened in Argentina, Brazil, Guatemala, Indonesia, Kampuchea, and Zaire. Short of the Nazi holocaust itself during World War II, declared U.S. Senator Edward Kennedy in March 1987, "I can think of nothing in modern history that approaches the horror of the brutality in South Africa."[7] On the borderline, lawmakers in many countries dispute the right of citizens, if they so wish, to drug themselves to death or to abort an unwanted or diseased fetus, while in some Third World countries there is a curious tendency for people to condone the blatant abuse of human rights by postulating that the ends of "development" and "political stability" justify the means of tyranny and Machiavellian double-think.

One modern philosopher has even reasoned that most of us owe our comparative freedom today to the relative incompetence and insufficiency of the police force, while some cynics hold that it is the system, real or potential, of one-person-one-vote (where we have it) that complements one-person-one-gun to give us protection against those who would like to suppress us. There may be an iota of truth in these contentions, which helps to explain the fact that, when the chips are down, we have no absolute right to anything, not even to life, liberty, property and the pursuit of happiness that many democratic constitutions celebrate. We owe this anomaly to the ubiquitous virus, accidents, armed robbers, or the perverse arrival of events or circumstances, inflation, or revolution that can deprive us of everything at any time. In any case, right without might, as Ambrose Bierce noted, is often a cipher.

Imperialists throughout history have often given an ironical twist to the glorious ideal of the right of self-determination in order to enslave the weaker races of the world. Like the Romans in their heyday, they usually come as liberators but end up as oppressors. The British and French did so when they divested a defeated Turkey of its Arab colonies after World War I, just as in the nineteenth century the Americans, in the name of a self-serving Monroe Doctrine, established their hegemony over territories in the southern hemisphere liberated from the Spaniards, or the Russians after World War II, after helping to liberate Eastern Europe from the German Nazis. Even today, in spite of the UN Universal Declaration of Human Rights and Declaration on Granting of Independence to Colonial Countries and on Elimination of Racial Discrimination, some colonial powers, like Britain, France, and the United States, still cling desperately to their last posts in Africa and the South Pacific. In other places, national minorities like the Amboines, Balubas, Basques, Durzes, and Kurds who sought—or were forced to seek—the preservation of their freedom in union with their neighbors are discovering, late in the day, that they have indeed lost that for which they embraced integration with their neighbors. And what are we to say about the theory and practice of preventive detention under which citizens can be imprisoned in order to "prevent" them from committing a crime they may never have intended but was speculatively intuited to them by those with reason and power—to remove them from circulation?

Even when we live under the rule of law, which with the Sovereignty of Parliament is said to be the pillar of constitutional government, the rights we enjoy depend largely on the whims of those who make or administer the law. If these do not practice injustice it is probably because, as Plato has Glaucon say in *The Republic,* they realize that others are like that and would practice it, too, at their expense when in a position to do so. This would impel the rulers to contract with all, as a basis of government, and guarantee that none would practice injustice, nor suffer it to be done by others. As for the sovereignty of Parliament, we have frequently seen ingenious and ambitious minds use cajolery or force to defeat Parliament. In most countries Parliament is already weakened in dealing with the executive by the lack of adequate information, by interest conflicts, by the patronage system, and by the time lag between lawmaking itself and its execution. By evading the courts, the will or caprice of the executive has thus been made supreme and unfettered in the land in a situation where, in the words of Professor D. W. Brogan, administration is nine-tenths of the law.

Although there is an old saying that the law is no respecter of persons, implying that we are all equal and none has an advantage over the other under the law, experience seems to support Aristotle's contention in his *Politics* that, "From the hour of their birth some are marked out for subjection and some for command." For even if all people are born equal, in time some *do* outgrow others—in status, wealth, charm, guile, intellect, perseverance, luck, or what you will. Thus, while the symbols of politics in our time may be drawn from popular democratic thought, the reality can often be understood from the viewpoint of elite theories. This means that the power, right, or degree of equality we enjoy depends to a large extent on such factors as our knowledge (of the law's demand or guarantees which, in the nature of things, is never equal), our ability to hire able counsels to defend us when for any reason we find ourselves in the warm embrace of the Criminal Code, and—let us admit it—our status or our "connections" with those who make the law or enforce it.

What is more, there is an element of "luck" in the way we fare with the law. For, ultimately, crime may be no more than discovered wrong, and surely, in the life of many of us, there are dark deeds (not to mention dark thoughts) that merit punishment if we were "caught in the act." Yet, under some fortuitous circumstances, we escape detection, and, so in the eyes of the world, we retain our reputation of innocence. Without these loopholes in the law or its subjective interpretations that enable us and our friends to escape its meshes, the venality or favoritism of those who administer the law, our prisons will have been bursting with thousands of people who today walk our streets as decent citizens.

EQUALITY AND JUSTICE

Justice is often represented as a blindfolded goddess, with a sword in one hand and a scale in the other, who stands impartially between conflicting claims, sees nothing, but weighs everything. Yet, as we read the judgments of our courts, we suspect that some people are able to escape the meshes of the law because of their position in society, their education, their wealth, or their counsel's brilliance in wading through the intricacies of the law. In this connection, the scales seem weighted against the poor or ignorant person. The sophist Thrasymachus in Plato's *Republic* was not far wrong when he suggested that "might is right, and justice is the interest of the stronger" even if it happens sometimes that, as Rousseau remarked later, "the strongest is never strong enough to be always the master."

All this is quite apart from the inequality of punishment for similar crimes which court records in many lands show (such as twenty-one years imprisonment with hard labor in one Nigerian case of stealing a sheep and a paltry fine in another, or ninety-nine years imprisonment in one U.S. case of murder and six months in another). No doubt, the courts have their good reasons for not treating similar crimes the same way, just as constitution-makers in many countries sometimes grant immunity from prosecution to some high officers of state even when this has resulted in the not uncommon phenomenon of a Richard Nixon, Muhammad Zia ul Haq, or Mobutu Sese Sekou toying with the fate of his fellow citizens with impunity.

Courts the world over have traditionally distinguished between, say, first offenders and hardened criminals, between accidental and premeditated crimes. They have recognized extenuating circumstances in some cases, such as provocation, self-defense, neglect, or even ignorance (of the law), despite the fact that it is not a legitimate excuse under the criminal code. In the same way they have considered caution, pardon, fine, or "suspended sentence" for some classes of offenders who otherwise would have ended up in prison. Again, while respecting the supreme majesty of the law, one suspects that even judges must sometimes act from purely personal considerations, such as, for example, their own state of mind at the time, their extrajudicial knowledge of the offender or his or her ethnic, professional, or sociopolitical affiliation, which may mitigate or aggravate the punishment as the case may be. There may also be an instinctive conviction in the mind of a judge that imprisonment—which the offender may well deserve—will mar the career of a promising youngster or public official. Few of us, judges as well as laypersons, can always resist the temptation to forgive Beauty—which proverbially, rides on a tiger—when she comes before us for judgment on any matter. Indeed, male applicants for colleges, jobs, licenses, or contract awards have frequently complained that their women rivals use their sexual power to achieve their ends.

Subjectivism is by no means a monopoly of judges, and each of us has prejudices, and into every act of judgment there enters a passionate contribution of personality. Indeed, social research in many countries has conclusively proved that personal appearance influences our evaluation of others. If academicians of U.S. universities, for instance, could judge undergraduate work—as was discovered in the mid–1970s by investigators like A. G. Miller, David Landy, and Harold Sigali according to the students' appearance or attractiveness—one imagines that some judges, like the rest of us, might also be susceptible to physical beauty, as others might be to bribery, blackmail, or even flattery. The moral of this cautionary tale is, one may suggest, that if enough of us can be persuaded that our perception of others may be distorted by appearance or ingrained prejudice, rather than guided by the innate quality of things, we will at least be predisposed to humility and skepticism in dealing with our fellows when called on to pass judgment on them.

One feature of social life that also has a bearing on justice is that, ironically, the more law you have, according to an old quip, the more offenders. A situation may exist in which we can have much law but little justice or in which the lawmakers are themselves lawbreakers and there is a double standard in law enforcement. One implication of this is that we can sometimes reduce the number of criminals in our society merely by scrapping some of our nonessential laws, such as those against sedition, drug and currency trafficking, loitering, and poaching (adolescent fun in traditional African society, as was social criticism, sometimes carried on by means of song, fable, or the *egungun* masquerade). What is more, many criminologists have recognized the socioeconomic basis of much crime. There is some truth in the contention of the ancient Chinese sage Mencius that, "if beans and millet were as plentiful as fire and water, such a thing as a bad man would not exist among people."

As a people who have been conditioned by centuries of communal culture, Africans should not continue to tolerate gross inequality and discrimination between citizens on the basis of their sex or ethnic origins. Nor should they allow a few people to monopolize the instruments of production for their private gain. For justice, as we know it, is not limited to what happens in the law courts but extends to the whole web of relationships between person and person, between group and group. It is difficult for those who have no home, no food, no job, or no access to the best elements of culture that their age or society has to offer, to have a feeling that justice exists for all. Culture implies an ethos, a set of values, rituals, and beliefs shared by a people, a style of behavior and aesthetics, an intellectual ferment that is productive of creative effort, and a way of understanding and dealing with self and others. As the word implies, it connotes a cultivation of life to which African communalism is profoundly relevant.

The relationship between liberty or equality and justice is a curious one. Empirically, freedom has many limitations, which made Rousseau exclaim in the opening paragraphs of his *Social Contract* that the individual is born free but everywhere is in chains.[8] Thus, apart from the laws of nature which bind us, the citizen of most modern states is circumscribed today by blasphemy, sedition, slan-

der, obscenity, contempt, libel, and official secrets acts. In spite of
the American, French, Russian, and other historic revolutions, or
the UN Declarations of Human Rights, a person may be too low,
ignorant, or poor to know or to enjoy any of those "inalienable" rights
spelled out in many constitutions. For freedom has a hollow sound
to an outcast, a jobless, ignorant, friendless, or hungry man who,
rightly or wrongly, feels himself unwanted and unprovided for in the
scheme of things in his community, or who has, in Arnold Toynbee's
expressive phrase, the consciousness—and the resentment that this
consciousness inspires—of being disinherited. Freedom, of course,
can never be total in the absence of any certainty about our im-
mortality and omnipotence. We only have the delusive *feeling* that
we are free, which carries with it the readiness to fight for its preservation. This does not necessarily imply that all is vanity, since
even a subjective state of mind can upturn the logic of events and
create a new reality, literally out of nothing.

Perhaps in the ultimate analysis, freedom is a very personal thing,
and one measures one's personal freedom by the opportunity which
may be enjoyed in society for real life and the pursuit of happiness—
the opportunity to be educated and obtain a job according to qualifications, without regard to creed or social status, to have easy
access to recreation, health, and welfare services on equal grounds
with others. It was Marx who pointed out that the kingdom of freedom actually begins only where drudgery, enforced by hardship and
by external purposes, ends. Long before him, Aristotle observed that
"the first principle of all action is leisure. . . . For the proverb says
truly, There is no leisure for slaves." Perhaps the whole mechanism
of the universe militates against equality. The law (as some eighteenth-century English social critic would say) punishes a person
who steals a goose from the common but lets the greater felon loose
who steals the common from the goose. For a while, theoretically,
the net of the law spreads so wide that no sinner may hide from its
sweep or any child of wrong sneak through its meshes. Some big
fishes have sometimes escaped from its wondrous webs of mystery.

The law in its majestic equality may forbid the rich as well as the
poor to sleep under bridges or steal bread, yet the outcome for both
is almost predetermined by their circumstances. For, while a rich
man may have difficulty entering the Kingdom of Heaven, as the
Christian Bible assures us, he certainly will find it relatively easier
than the poor to escape the meshes of the law or to enter the higher
councils of state or industry. In this world, as Lenin observed, "right
is nothing without an apparatus capable of enforcing the standards
of right."[9]

Admittedly, we are not all equal—either in our talent or our taste, in any cross-section of time. However, we are equal in our total existence, and despite the aberrations of nature or of the law, the doctrine of equality has inspired the best human instincts throughout history. Of course, we are always confronted with certain inevitable contradictions that exist between the related ideals of liberty and equality. For though we can prevent one person from having more money, education, or political power than another, by legislation, we cannot prevent anyone from making a better use of money, education, or opportunities. Nor can we equalize wit, charm, strength of will, beauty, courage, foresight, or spiritual talent. Even if, as the philosophical anarchist Herbert Read conceded, the products of the community's labor were eventually more or less equally divided, "the sharing of this wealth would not produce a uniformity of desire." A human society giving full opportunity for the education and development of the mind (which only requires time and space to differentiate itself) has no need to fear a reign of intellectual uniformity and stupidity which is usually "created by conditions of poverty and lack of leisure."[10]

In this way, "equality of opportunity," which is often touted as the epitome of democracy, presupposes inequality, since "opportunity" in essence means opportunity to rise to a higher level than one's fellows in a stratified society. But perhaps equality of opportunity also presupposes equality, for it implies that the inequalities embedded in this stratified society have to be counteracted in every generation so that individuals can really develop their personal abilities. Today, as a result of the democratic revolution, most people believe that all should be equal before the law, including the constitution which, as the rule of conduct and mirror of communal ideas, derives its formal sanction from the sovereign philosophy. It is the community that sustains the state which is not an end in itself but only a means to social well-being and the symbol of our mutual dependence and control. By this token it cannot, therefore, be above morality even in the defense of its own security. Since the seventeenth century, humankind has come to accept that, while human rights are maximized in the collectivity, a state that cannot guarantee to its citizens these basic human rights cannot morally claim any valid allegiance from them. As Sancho Panza, in Cervantes' famous satire *Don Quixote*, told the carver of Barataria, "And now, give me something to eat or else take your government; for a trade that does not feed its master is not worth two beans."

CONCLUSIONS

We have argued that development is a dynamic and complex process whose prerequisites or objectives may differ from place to place.

Nonetheless, perhaps a few of its general characteristics can be indicated. Development offers the people a particular constellation of means by which they can obtain a better life and create or improve their material, moral, and intellectual conditions of life which are related in some way to a perceived need for esteem. Development will ultimately free them from servitude to nature, to ignorance, to other people, to institutions, and to beliefs that are considered oppressive. This means that, while it can be expressed in terms of growth of output, development must also entail the enhancement of the quality of life, the provision of work, education, and medicare for all, as well as the equitable distribution of income and the fruits of development. The establishment of human rights is often contingent on the mobilization and coordination of all available hands and resources for an all-round and even development, as well as the introduction of social security for all, including education and medicare at all levels, full employment, sickness, and maternity and old age benefits. It involves the association of labor with management in industry aimed at increased output and equitable sharing of the fruits of labor; the abrogation of all discrimination against citizens in school enrollment, job placement, and law enforcement on the basis of tribe, religion, sex or status; recognition of freedom of the press; provision of housing with cheap rental for all; establishment of civic centers for all communities equipped with the best in modern culture; and the introduction of proportional representation for all contending forces in society (including unassimilated minorities) at all levels of government.

To safeguard basic human rights, many modern nations have also entrenched them in the constitution and have established an independent judiciary and separation of powers which allow the various agencies of government to check one another. They have instituted the system of ombudsman or public complaints commission whose task is to investigate wrongdoing or abuses of power by public officials, or as the Swedish who instituted the system in 1809 put it, "to investigate wrong doing and to tell the truth derived from such investigation and further, when this is called for, to prosecute or call for the prosecution of civil servants who have committed errors or shown negligence."[11] But above all, these countries have, over time, fostered the freedom-loving spirit in their people and have encouraged zestful, popular participation in the government.

For they realize that courts and constitutions alone cannot guarantee liberty for a people; true liberty, said U.S. Judge Learned Hand in 1944, lives in the hearts of men and women, and when it dies there, no constitution, no law, and no court can save it or do much to help it. Popular consciousness is thus a powerful element in the preservation of liberty, which makes education basic to democracy. "To know one's rights," stated the director-general of Unesco, Amadou-Mahtar M'Bow in 1978, "is a step towards obtaining their recognition. For the men and women who are aware, at this moment, that they still have to struggle, sometimes at the risk of their lives, to try to exercise their basic rights, could not do so with any hope of success unless they could draw comfort and moral and intellectual inspiration from the certainty that the principles underlying these rights are now adopted by the whole international community."[12]

Today in Africa, as elsewhere around the world, people are undoubtedly more aware of their rights than ever. In the empirical world we live in, however, there is all the difference between a positive right and a normative right, between what is and what ought to be, between the realm of fact and the realm of morality. Yet there can be little doubt that, as someone has remarked, "the moral claims of today are often the legal rights of tomorrow." The violations of human rights that are still perpetrated every day show that the need for action is no less now than it was before the Universal Declaration of Human Rights in 1948. In fact, it may be greater. The strategy for action must include widespread publicity of all infractions of human rights and popular protests on behalf of the victims. Such action must focus both on the level of international law (e.g., for the abolition of torture, detention without trial, and the death penalty) and on the level of human solidarity with those who suffer. International agreements alone cannot guarantee the protection of human rights, and public opinion must provide the momentum needed to ensure that such agreements are respected regardless of the tangle of power politics. That is why we must be ready to intervene wherever fundamental human rights are violated. As the Brazilian journalist Vladimir Herzog declared in 1975 shortly before he died in prison, "If we lose our capacity to be outraged when we see others subjected to atrocities, then we lose our right to call ourselves human beings."[13]

Every right carries with it an obligation to respect the reciprocal rights of others as well as the duty, as the UN Charter (Article 29) reminds us, to preserve public order, public morality, and the general welfare of the community. For the state to command our services and obedience, it must give us protection under the laws. Fortunately, in all the changing scenes of life, human emotions can be trusted to elevate human rights above all arbitrary statutes whenever there is a studied and blatant attempt to deny such rights. In spite of the myth-making powers and the huge machinery of coercion at the disposal of the modern state, revolution remains the ultimate court of appeal for an oppressed people, a state of affairs which in the end tempers every despotism and keeps alive the hope for democracy.

NOTES

1. Edmund Burke, *Works*, vol. 5 (London: 1952), pp. 180–81.

2. Judith Hart, *Aid and Liberation: A Socialist Study of Aid Politics* (London: Victor Gollancz, 1973), p. 42.

3. *Report of the U.S. Presidential Commission: U.S. Foreign Assistance: A New Approach* (Washington, D.C.: U.S. Government Printing Office, March 1970).

4. Tunde Fatunde, "The American Award," *The African Guardian* 2, no. 14 (April 1987).

5. John Stockwell, in an article in *Harper's Magazine*, September 1984.

6. Alfred Metraux, in *Unesco Courier*, July 1950; cited in Michael Leirie, *Race and Culture* (Paris: Unesco, 1958), p. 30.

7. Quoted in *The Guardian,* Lagos, March 28, 1987.

8. J. J. Rousseau, *Social Contract*, Book 1 (1762) (London: Penguin Books, 1968), p. 49.

9. V. I. Lenin, *The State and Revolution*, vol. 4 (1917).

10. Herbert Read, *Anarchy and Order* (London: A Condor Book, Souvenir Press, 1974), p. 88.

11. See Alfred Bexelius, *The Swedish Institutions of the Justitie Ombudsman* (Stockholm: Swedish Institute, 1965), p. 2.

12. From an opening address to the International Congress on the Teaching of Human Rights, Vienna, 1978.

13. Quoted in the *Daily Times,* Lagos, June 18, 1981.

10

Some Impressions of the Ghanaian Version of Black Feminism

Stanlie James

A recent phenomenon in the United States is the nascent evolution of a new perspective called Black Feminism, which seeks to analyze the nature of the oppression experienced by black women and to find ways to overcome this oppression. Oppression, which Stephanie Urdang defines as dominance and exploitation, refers to a "lack of control over one's own destiny and lack of possibility to fulfill one's potential. The key to oppression is the victim's cooperation in its perpetuation."[1]

Black Feminism argues that women have experienced oppression in their roles as workers by classism, as blacks by racism, and as women by patriarchy. Each of these systems of dominance and exploitation is so intertwined with the others that they have developed and are nurtured by the sustenance they provide to each other. Together, they have combined to have a devastating impact on the lives of black women. Pauli Murray, in comparing the lives of black and white American women, has stated that the black woman "remains single more often, bears more children, is in the labor market longer and in greater proportion, has less education, earns less, is widowed earlier and carries a relatively heavier economic responsibility as family head than her white counterpart."[2]

Sexism, racism, and classism can be viewed as a multidimensional phenomenon linked by a common modality of operation—the objectification process. The "sex-gender system is the place to discern the objectification process at work in its basic form and is therefore the role model for objectification of all social relationships."[3] The prototype of this process is the establishment of a masculine ideology and power and has been described by Catharine A. MacKinnon in the following manner:

Men *create* the world from their own point of view, which then *becomes* the truth to be described. . . . *Power to create the world from one's point of view is power in its male form.* The epistemological stance, which corresponds to the world it creates, is objectivity. The ostensibly noninvolved stance, the view from a distance and from no particular perspective, apparently transparent to its reality. It does not comprehend its own perspectivity, does not recognize what it sees as a subject like itself, or that the way it apprehends the world is a form of subjugation and presupposes it. The objectively knowable is object. Woman through male eyes is sex object, that by which man knows self as one as man and as subject.[4]

This power to establish an ideology and thus create "truth" is the ability to define humanity—that is, to determine which people are deemed worthy to be considered as full human beings. Those who exhibit characteristics such as race, class, or gender—or any combination of these—have often arbitrarily been subjected to objectification which in turn has provided a rationale for oppression.

Elizabeth Fiorenza, a feminist theologian, has shed light on the above by utilizing an Aristotelian conceptualization of patriarchy. She suggests that society is analogous to the patriarchal household which was sustained by slave labor. Thus, patriarchy is defined as "a male pyramid of graded subordinates and exploitations which specifies women's oppression in terms of class, race, country or religions of the men to whom 'we belong.' "[5]

This conceptualization of patriarchy recognizes that women are not the only group oppressed, objectified, or defined as "the other"; races and other groups are also categorized as "the other" and thus subjected to domination. Therefore, women of color, and/or Third World women, from this definition can be considered to be doubly or even triply oppressed. They occupy the bottom rungs of what could be characterized as a patriarchal pyramid. That is, they are objectified because of gender, because of race, and again because of class.

In response to this triple oppression, some black women have devoted considerable energy and thought to the development of a new social movement—Black Feminism. Alice Walker, who has coined the term *womanist* to refer to Black Feminists or feminists of color, has defined this perspective in the following manner:

From the black folk expression of mothers to female children. "You acting womanish", i.e., like a woman. Usually referring to outrageous, audacious, courageous, or willful behavior.... Interchangeable with another black folk expression: "You trying to be grown." Responsible. In charge. *Serious*... Committed to survival and wholeness of entire people, male *and* female. Not a separatist.... Traditionally universalist.... Loves struggle. *Loves* the folk. Loves herself. Regardless.... Womanist is to feminist as purple to lavender.[6]

Although black women in the United States appear to be the vanguard in the development of the Black Feminist perspective, women in other parts of the world are also concerned with this issue. Chikwenye Okonjo, a Nigerian writer, in a review of literature written by contemporary black women, more clearly defines the womanist perspective. She views it as a "widespread and distinct praxis" and argues that the difference between the feminist and the womanist perspective is that the feminist is concerned specifically with eradicating patriarchy and/or establishing utopia away from the patriarchy. African and Afro-American women "as a group... are distinct from White Feminists because of their race, because they have experienced the past and present subjugation of the black population along with present-day subtle (and not so subtle) control exercised over them by the alien, Western culture." Thus, the womanist must not only be conscious of and concerned about sexual issues, but she must also "incorporate racial, cultural, national, economic and political consciousness into her philosophy."

Okonjo goes on to argue that

Black women... are not limited to issues defined by their femaleness but attempt to tackle questions raised by their humanity. Thus the womanist vision is racially conscious in its underscoring of the positive aspects of Black life. The politics of the womanist is unique in its racial-sexual ramifications; it is more complex than white sexual politics, for it addresses more directly the ultimate question relating to power: how do we share equitably the world's wealth and concomitant power among the races and between the sexes.[7]

Although the multidimensional issue of gender, race, and class oppression has not been specifically addressed by the international community, ultimately Black Feminism can be viewed as an integral aspect of the twentieth-century international movement to establish and protect human rights. This movement developed out of a recognition that oftentimes states have denied the humanity of some of their citizens, thereby limiting the rights of some individuals because they failed to conform to their definition of humanity. In response to the above, much effort has been devoted to defining equality, which Warren McKean has described as "the view that unless there is a reason for it, recognized as sufficient by some identifiable criterion, one man should not be preferred to another."[8] Under international law, this principle of equality has usually been equated with or stated in the negative as nondiscrimination. In the 1949 report entitled *Main Causes and Types of Discrimination*, the UN secretary general described discrimination as "any conduct based on a distinction made on grounds of natural or social categories which have no relation either to the individual capacities or merits or to the concrete behavior of the individual person."[9]

The effort to establish the principle of equality or nondiscrimination has been promulgated in the various UN documents such as the Universal Declaration of Human Rights, the UN Charter, and the Covenants that declared women and people of color to be equal and supported the intention to eradicate sex-based and color-based discrimination. This commitment was strengthened by the adoption of the UN Convention to Eliminate Racial Discrimination and the UN Convention on the Elimination of All Forms of Discrimination Against Women.

The purpose of the above is to establish a just society. A just society is envisioned as one that actively implements and protects the traditional first- and second-generation civil and political, and social, economic, and cultural rights. In addition, the newer, less well-defined third- and fourth-generation rights such as the rights to development and peace and to satisfy basic human needs are also incorporated in this vision of a just society.

Black Feminists envision a society built on the principle of nondominance,[10] one that incorporates the norm of nondiscrimination and equality for all. In summary, the Black Feminist perspective is characterized by

1. Its emphasis on analyzing the triple oppression experienced by black women
2. Its insistence that black women will no longer cooperate in the perpetuation of their own exploitation
3. Its assertion that black women will struggle to overcome dominance particularly in the areas of gender, class, and race in an effort to control their own destinies and to fulfill their own potential

Proponents of Black Feminism argue that a confrontation is beginning to develop between Black Feminism and other social movements. While other movements such as the civil rights and antiracist movements in the United States were concerned with changing societies, they have not adequately addressed the crucial issues of concern to black women either within their values or their programs. Even more disconcerting to Black Feminists is that both the Western and socialist feminists have also failed to incorporate the crucial issues of concern within their analyses. Bell Hook in *Feminist Theory: From Margin to Center* has summarized the problem:

Privileged feminists have largely been unable to speak to, with, and for diverse groups of women because they either do not understand fully the interrelatedness of sex, race and class oppression, or refuse to take inter- relatedness seriously. Feminist analyses of women tend to focus exclusively on gender and do not provide a solid foundation on which to construct feminist theory. They reflect the dominant tendency in western patriarchal minds to mystify women's reality by insisting that gender is the sole deter- mination of women's fate.... Although Socialist feminists focus on class and gender, they tend to make a point of acknowledging that race is im- portant and then proceed to offer an analysis in which race is not consid- ered.[11]

This chapter is based on research that is concerned with devel- oping a more comprehensive understanding of the theory and prac- tice of Black Feminism. A basic question to be addressed is whether this is only an American phenomenon or one that can be found in other parts of the world. Thus, it is a pioneering study that hopefully will lay the basis for future in-depth studies of the international ramifications of a Black Feminist movement.

Ghana, in particular, provides a compelling example of the diver- gence that exists between the perception and reality of women's lives. Forty-four percent of its population is comprised of the Akan groups, including the Ashante and the Fanti ethnic groups. The Akans are notable for their matrilineal societies in which descent is reckoned through the women. Women have traditionally been considered to wield considerable influence, especially because of the Queen Mother's crucial role in the choice of chiefs and her responsibility and right to advise or admonish the chief. At various times throughout their history, women have served as chiefs, of whom the most famous was probably Yaa Asantewa, the Ejisu Queen Mother who led her people against the British in the Anglo Ashante War of 1900–1901. Later Ghanaian women—particularly the market women—were con- sidered to be politically influential as they provided monetary support for Nkrumah as he rose to power.

This chapter seeks to provide some preliminary impressions of women in Ghana after a short research visit. During this visit, efforts were made to ascertain whether a Ghanaian feminist consciousness was developing and if so, if it had any similarity to its Black Feminist counterpart in the United States. With the help of the National Council on Women and Development (NCWD) to identify and provide an introduction to activist women, twenty-two formal interviews were conducted. The respondents were women from various walks of life, including education, government, business, trading, and journalism. They all shared a commitment to bringing about change for women within Ghanaian society.

Ghana has adopted both international and national legislation that purports to protect the rights of women. Ghana has ratified the UN Supplementary Convention on the Abolition of Slavery, the Slave Trade, and Practices Related to Slavery which require the prohibition of bride's wealth and the inheritance of a widow's property by her late husband's family. She has also ratified the Convention on Nationality of Married Women which is concerned with women's loss or acquisition of nationality resulting from marriage or dissolution of marriage resulting from her husband's change in nationality during marriage. In addition, Ghana has also adopted the International Labor Organization (ILO) Convention (No. 100) Concerning Equal Remuneration of Men and Women Workers for Work of Equal Value and the ILO Convention (No. 111) Concerning Discrimination in Respect to Employment and Occupation.[12] Recently, Ghana has also become one of the few African nations to become signatory to the omnibus UN Convention on the Elimination of All Forms of Discrimination Against Women. Finally, Ghana is also a party to the Banjul Charter which prohibits discrimination on the basis of sex and provides for respect of "the integrity of the person."

In the 1950 constitution and the 1957 independence constitution, Ghanaian women were granted the right to vote as well as the right to stand for election. These rights at present are irrelevant, not only for women but also for men, as Ghana is now ruled by the dictatorship of the Peoples National Democratic Council (PNDC) and elections have not been held in recent years. Women are becoming more visible in appointed governmental capacities. For example, women are in such visible positions as chairperson of the Environmental Protection Agency, undersecretaries of the ministries of health and education, and executive secretary of the Committee for the Defense of the Revolution (CDR). Admittedly, many of these positions could be viewed as an extension of the traditional Ghanaian role of women as wives and mothers. However, the fact remains that there is some representation of women in high governmental offices.

Possibly in response to the ratification of the previously mentioned UN conventions, legislation has been passed which purports either to protect women or to establish equality. It is debatable as to whether this legislation has helped or exacerbated the problems of women.

For example, one such piece of legislation has been the Labour Decree (1967) NLCD 157, a portion of which is concerned with maternity benefits for the working woman. To summarize, this act provides maternity leave for women of up to six weeks before the birth of a baby and up to six weeks after the birth. The leave can be extended if there are difficulties surrounding the birth or if it is a multiple birth. While on leave, her job is protected, and she receives at least 50 percent of her base salary. Upon her return if she is nursing, she is allowed an hour a day during working hours for this purpose.

On the face of it, this piece of legislation appears to be wonderfully accommodating to the woman who is combining a career with motherhood. But the impact of the legislation has been negative. What has happened partially as a result of this decree is that employers feel it is unproductive to employ a woman who would get pregnant and that it is more economical to employ a man. Thus, a law that was intended to be protective of women has instead led to discrimination against women. H.J.A.N. Mensa-Bonsu has stated:

Even a quick look at these provisions . . . would show that an employer who employs a woman would lose her maximum services for the better part of a year-and-a-half whenever she undertakes procreation. In addition to these provisions, a woman who becomes temporarily unfit for duty due to ill health after delivering a baby is given extra protection. She cannot be . . . dismissed without directives from the Chief Labour Officer. To compound the problem, there is no limit to the number of times a woman might avail herself of these provisions.[13]

This same decree contains another provision that prohibits the employment of women on the night shift and in underground work. It was apparently designed to protect women, but again, it operates in such a way that it discriminates against them. Thus, if women wanted to do underground work, they could not do so. If, for example, a woman was in line for a promotion that would require underground or night work, it would be denied to her by law. Moreover, factories that operate twenty-four hours a day often pay night workers more than day workers. Hence, the idea of equal pay for equal work is negated.[14]

Labor regulations are covered by Legislative Instrument 632 of 1969. Among its provisions is one that does not allow employment of women at a lower rate for identical or substantially identical jobs.

Although it defines identical jobs, it does not give guidelines for ascertaining what is identical. It does indicate that differences in rates of pay based on length of service, seniority, or any other factor other than sex would not constitute a failure to comply with regulations.[15]

The final piece of legislation to be mentioned here is the Law of Intestate Succession (1985) PNDCL 111. The law provides some protection for women married under customary law in that it confers a specific interest in the estate of a dead husband. Furthermore, if unmarried mothers are able to establish the acknowledgment of a child by a deceased father, the child automatically shares in the proportion of the intestate's property which the law assigns to children. Childless women, however, are only entitled to three-sixteenths of the deceased husband's property, whereas the husband who is a widower would be entitled to one-half of the deceased wife's property. The impact of this law has yet to be determined, but it is clear that there are advantages and disadvantages.[16]

From this summary of a few of the laws enacted in Ghana, it is clear that some effort has been made to establish and protect the rights of women. However, it is also clear that, perhaps unintentionally, some of this legislation has had a negative impact on women. When asked if they had experienced discrimination, eleven of the women said no, three were not sure, while seven said they had experienced discrimination. In the working environment, all agreed that equal pay for equal work was the rule. Most of those who felt they had experienced discrimination in the workplace described it as "subtle." For example, one woman mentioned that she was blocked in efforts for promotion because her boss felt that, though qualified, others might misconstrue the promotion as being the result of a nonexistent extracurricular liaison between the two. In that situation, she was given the responsibility of the extra work without the reward of the promotion or additional pay. After much unsuccessful protest, she finally quit and found employment elsewhere. Another who had been a headmistress in a coeducational school recalled that when she applied for a new position as an assistant to the headmaster in another school, her ability to discipline boys was questioned because she was a woman.

The existence of discrimination in social environments was also mentioned. For example, one woman recalled that at a family gathering at the death of a family member, an elderly woman tried to speak. The men told her she must shut up because no woman should speak in such a situation. Another woman recounted an incident in which her brother had been unfairly arrested for illegal parking. Because she had witnessed the incident, she went with him to the police station to try to explain the circumstances. She was told repeatedly that she must shut up because no woman could possibly provide any relevant testimony.

These examples of discriminatory behavior experienced by women are the result of the traditional Ghanaian conceptualization of the role of women in that society. This role has been summed up by Miranda Greenstreet, director of the University of Ghana's Institute of Adult Education, as the "Motherhood Myth." Greenstreet stated in an interview that the Motherhood Myth

implies that the Ghanaian woman fulfills herself completely in addition to all other things she might do when she has become a mother and she has had her children. Maybe mostly when she becomes a grandmother when in the local language it means "she is now a mother."

Because you are a mother, you get a lot of assistance from your own mother and extended family. But when you are a grandmother that's when you go around nursing your children—at least your daughter's children.

We are anxious to get partners, to have children. And because of the lack of social insurance—the lack of support in old age—children tend to be the main support of the parents when they are old. And, therefore, you struggle to support your children.

However much money you have had in the world, however much you have had in terms of your education, your profession, if you haven't become a mother, then you have not really fulfilled everything.[17]

When asked what they felt were the most serious problems encountered by Ghanaian women, a variety of responses were given, including such things as disease, health care, social resources, and illiteracy. However, this chapter will confine itself to brief comments on the three most commonly mentioned problems. Almost every woman interviewed mentioned marital and family problems, economic problems, and education.

In Ghanaian society, adults are expected to be married. *The Ghanaian Fertility Survey 1979–80* indicated that, by the age of thirty-four, 99.2 percent of the women were married or had been previously married. The proportion of women in polygamous marriages was 34.5 percent.[18] Polygamy per se was not necessarily perceived as a problem by Ghanaian women if it were conducted in the traditional manner. That is where legally married cowives shared responsibilities for the family and the household, and were treated equally and provided for by the husband in question. However, there was also agreement that the way in which these relationships were being conducted today was wrong and detrimental to the healthy development of the family. Instead of marriages that were openly accepted and respected, men were involved in "married affairs" or else married one woman under the ordinance and the other(s) under customary law.

The problem with this arrangement, as the women explained it, was that the man had divided loyalties and was not providing the necessary support, guidance, or time for the children involved. As one woman stated, "even if you are married, you are a single parent." Thus, women find themselves shouldering most of the responsibility of caring for children. This necessity to be both father and mother means that women must find jobs that will allow them to adequately support their families.

This brings us to the second problem most often mentioned, that of economics. Mrs. Comfort Engman, chairperson of Women's World Banking, Ghana, provided a summary of the overall economic situation in Ghana. She stated that the main problem is proverty. "Our country itself is poor. What Ghana receives for her labor is very low indeed. We are a monocrop economy. We have not got to a stage to where our exports are manufactured goods. We are living below poverty level. Very few of us get enough to spare."[19]

In an article entitled "Occupations of Women in Ghana," Kodwo Ewusi established that the most important economic activities for women in Ghana were in the areas of agriculture, commerce, and manufacturing. In agriculture, women are mostly food crop farmers who have largely not benefited from either government extension programs or loan schemes being advanced to farmers. Although cocoa farming is the most important cash crop activity, the involvement of most women is as laborers and especially as head loaders of cocoa from farms to towns for fermentation. On the other hand, the men's involvement is more likely to be in farm ownership or management. By 1970, women accounted for 84.6 percent of the employment in the commerce sector; however, the bulk of their activities was in the area of petty trading or hawking. The accessibility to commercial loans to expand their activities was limited by lack of collateral. Finally, in 1970 women outnumbered men in the manufacturing sector largely because 66,000 food sellers were reclassified from the commercial sector. Incidentally, this area includes bread bakers and seamstresses as well. Their access to governmental assistance is also limited. Ewusi sums up women's economic activities by stating: "(E)xcept for a few success stories, women are mostly engaged in small-scale, low productivity and low income earning activities."[20]

The third problem to be briefly mentioned is that of education. Grace Nartey, former executive secretary of National Council on Women and Development (NCWD), has stated:

The thought is still lurking in Ghanaian males and women that "oh a girl will get married so she doesn't need all that education." A woman is channeled into the service sector and into trading. Girls are not getting as much information as they need. Girls must help their mothers and they are not allowed much freedom so they don't have much access to information.[21]

Miranda Greenstreet agreed with this assessment and also stated that "Historically . . . there have been less opportunities for women in terms of available places in school. Then there has been this idea that if income is limited you should give the option to males."[22]

According to the March 1987 *Quarterly Digest of Statistics,* enrollment of girls in schools continues to lag behind that of boys, and the further one goes up the ladder of education, the bigger the gap. The 1983–1984 figures show that there were 780,214 boys and 734,083 girls enrolled in primary schools. The middle school enrollment was 345,780 boys to 234,201 girls; the secondary enrollment from grades 1 through 6 was 92,706 boys to 33,563 girls, and finally, university enrollment was 6,524 boys to 1,439 girls. Thus, while the proportion in primary school enrollment was 55.7 percent male to 44.3 percent female, by the university level the proportion was 82.9 percent male to 18.1 percent female.[23]

Kate Abbam, editor and publisher of *Obaa Sima,* the only woman's magazine in Ghana, discussed the impact of illiteracy and lack of education on women. She stated: "women . . . may not understand government policy and some of the laws that have passed may not be filtered down to them. When I say illiteracy you know that she may not know about primary health care, personal hygiene, family planning, all these things that come under that."[24]

This quick summary of a few of the serious problems Ghanaian women are facing leads one to ask the question, "What is being done about it?" For purposes of this research, we may ask, "Has a Ghanaian feminist consciousness begun to develop and, if so, what qualities make it unique?"

From the interviews conducted with women active in various organizations, it was clear not only that they are cognizant of the overwhelming problems they face, but also that they are involved in seeking remedies at the individual, community, and national levels. For example, the Federation of Ghanaian Women Lawyers (FIDA), devotes Wednesdays to providing free legal advice to women who need it. The Ghana Association for the Welfare of Women commissioned a report on female genital operations prevalent in the North and is actively working to end that practice.[25] The Zonta Club of Accra has adopted a village and is in the process of trying to sink a well to provide clean drinking water. They have also built a multi-purpose center in the village to house classes on prenatal and post-natal care, and for childbirth and literacy classes (among other things). The YWCA provides leadership training courses for women, nursery care for children of working mothers, and classes to teach young women how to establish and run creches. Other organizations such as the various church women's fellowship groups have, for example, adopted women's wards in hospitals and provided them with privacy screens, night gowns, buckets, cutlery, and dishes.

The NCWD has itself been deeply involved in a variety of projects, including the development of appropriate technology for gari making and fish smoking. The chorker smoker that they were instrumental in designing has been recognized as the most efficient new appropriate technology in this area and has been recommended for use all over Africa. The NCWD has also actively lobbied either to change or make new laws to benefit women. Most recently, they were deeply involved in the development of the new intestate succession law.

These projects are especially important at the individual and community level, but they are piecemeal efforts. Between 1966 when Ghana's first republic was overthrown and the coup d'etat of December 31, 1981, which brought in the PNDC for the second time, no mass women's organization existed in Ghana. The only national organization in existence was the NCWD. It was established by the National Redemption Council (NRC) decree 322 on February 20, 1975, in response to a UN resolution calling on member states to establish appropriate governmental machinery to more fully integrate women into development and to eliminate discrimination against women. The decree mandated NCWD:

1. To advise government on all matters relating to women
2. To research the problems of women
3. To act as a national body for cooperating with national and international organizations on matters relating to women

The PNDC government has issued numerous pronouncements about the need to elevate the status of women and to encourage women to aspire to equality. In a 1982 rally in Bolgatanga, for example, the PNDC chairman, Flight Lieutenant Jerry John Rawlings, presented a rifle to a woman to symbolize the emancipation of womanhood in Ghana and then called on women to accept the challenge to become equal to men.

These public pronouncements have led to the growth of several national women's organizations, including the Federation of Ghanaian Women and the All Women's Association of Ghana. But perhaps the most important but least understood organization to develop has been the 31st December Women's Movement, established in May 1982. Its president is Nana Konadu Agyeman-Rawlings, wife of the PNDC chairman.

From 1982 to 1986, there was an uneasy coexistence between the 31st and the other women's organizations, particularly the NCWD. This situation ended in June 1986 when the NCWD was dissolved and replaced by an interim management committee composed of women, some of whom were also members of the 31st. The current executive secretary who was appointed by the government and given the status of secretary of state is also a member of the 31st.

Originally, it was unclear as to whether or not the 31st was an organization formed to struggle for women's rights independently of the government or whether it was a government organization. However, with time it has begun to exhibit characteristics that seem to indicate it is a governmental organization. For example, the statements of the leadership are always within the context of making the 31st December Revolution work. Furthermore, the members have not been mobilized to struggle for specific women's issues that are outside of the government's plans for women. Their mass actions have included, for example, women marching to the castle to thank the government for passing such laws as the Intestate Succession Law which they described as favorable to women and children. Recently, the 31st issued a statement supporting the 1987 PNDC budget, calling it the best since independence.[26]

Regardless of the fanfare surrounding the 31st and the NCWD, it should be noted that the PNDC has not established education programs to inform the people about the new laws, nor has the machinery been established to enforce these laws.[27]

In Ghana, as in other parts of the Third World, women are the poorest of the poor. The fact that women suffer the highest rates of illiteracy and are less likely to complete the educational process has severe ramifications for them, their families, and indeed Ghanaian society generally. This lack of education severely hampers their employment prospects, which in turn limits their ability to provide for their families both financially and socially. In addition, women suffer from norms and customs that are uniquely problematic to them. These include genital operations, traditional widowhood and inheritance laws, and lack of control over their bodies owing to poor access to information on birth control and stringent abortion laws.

Nonetheless, women in Ghana, for the most part, have not consciously identified themselves as feminists; in fact, the term itself seems to make them uneasy. This is true of even such committed activists as former Supreme Court Justice Annie Jiajie who so ably served as Ghana's representative to the UN Commission on the Status of Women for sixteen years. She felt that the feminist movement, as it existed in the Western world, was irrelevant to women in the Ghanaian society.[28] Obviously, illiterate women had little or no awareness of the feminist movement, but those who were aware were not impressed. One woman stated that she felt the Western feminists were either struggling to become surrogate men or were wasting time on such irrelevant issues as whether or not God was female.[29]

Although few would characterize themselves as feminist, both literate and illiterate women were cognizant of and deeply distressed by their plight and committed to a responsibility for bringing about change, especially through the legislative process. But they were also aware that legislation—difficult as it is to achieve—is a necessary, though not sufficient, condition for the kind of change that is needed. Along with the legislation, they recognize the need for massive education programs available to all so that women can be made aware of legal changes in order to make informed choices about available options, especially with regard to norms and customs that some women might find constraining.

The problems of Ghanaian women are an integral aspect of the international movement to establish and protect human rights. The crucial issue of concern is the problem of underdevelopment and the necessity to satisfy basic human needs. There is, for example, a necessity for access to clean pipe-borne water, adequate health care, and preventative medicine in the form of hygiene and sanitation. Because hunger and malnutrition lurk ominously close to every door, it is critical that appropriate technology be developed and implemented expeditiously so that adequate incomes can be generated for the care of families. In addition, extensive literary campaigns must be mounted so that crucial information is easily available to the entire population. Thus, the struggle, as defined by Ghanaian women, is one in which no one segment of the population (i.e., male) would benefit to the detriment of the others. Rather, it is one in which the potential of all—women, men, and children—is fulfilled so that the development of their society becomes a reality.

NOTES

1. Stephanie Urdang, *Fighting Two Colonialisms: Women in Guinea Bissau* (New York: Monthly Review Press, 1979), p. 1.

2. Pauli Murray, "The Liberation of Black Women," in Mary Lou Thompson, ed., *Voices of the New Feminism* (Boston: Beacon Press, 1970), p. 99.

3. Arthur Brittan and Mary Maynard, *Sexism, Racism and Oppression* (New York: Basil Blackwell, 1984), p. 216.

4. Catharine A. MacKinnon, "Feminism, Marxism, Method and the State: An Agenda for Theory," in Nannerl O. Keohane, Michelle Z. Rosaldo, and Barbara C. Gelpi, eds., *Feminist Theory: A Critique of Ideology* (Chicago: University of Chicago Press, 1982), pp. 23–24.

5. Elizabeth S. Fiorenza, *Bread not stone: The Challenge of Feminist Biblical Interpretation* (Boston: Beacon Press, 1984), p. 5.

6. Alice Walker, *In Search of Our Mothers' Gardens: Womanist Prose* (New York: Harcourt Brace Jovanovich, 1983), pp. x–xii.

7. See Chikwenye Okonjo's excellent article, "Womanism: The Dynamics of the Contemporary Black Female Novel in English," *Signs: Journal of Women in Culture and Society* 11, no. 1 (1985), pp. 63–80.

8. Warren McKean, *Equality and Discrimination Under International Law* (Oxford: Clarendon Press, 1983), p. 285.

9. See UN docs. E/CN. 4Sub.2/40/rev. 1, as quoted in McKean, *Equality and Discrimination*, p. 286.

10. For a definition and discussion of the concept of nondominance, see George W. Shepherd, "Non-Dominance: The Material and Moral Basis," Paper, Graduate School of International Studies, University of Denver, n.d.

11. Bell Hook, *Feminist Theory: From Margin to Center* (Boston: South End Press, 1984), p. 14.

12. Rhoda Howard, "Women's Rights in English-Speaking Sub-Sahara Africa," in Claude E. Welch and Ronald I. Meltzer, eds., *Human Rights and Development in Africa* (Albany: State University of New York, 1984).

13. H.J.A.N. Mensa-Bonsu, "The Subtle Effect of Legislation on Women and Childbearing," Unpublished paper, 1985.

14. Ibid.

15. E. Tsikata, "Ghana: Women in Mass Organizations—1982–87," Paper presented to seminar on the Post Colonial State and National Development, April 21–23, 1987, Legon, Ghana.

16. Mensa-Bonsu, "The Subtle Effect of Legislation."

17. Personal interview with Miranda Greenstreet, May 13, 1987.

18. Central Bureau of Statistics in Collaboration with the World Fertility Survey, *Ghana Fertility Survey, 1979–80: Background, Methodology and Findings*, vol. 1 (Accra, Ghana, 1983).

19. Personal Interview with Comfort Engman, April 24, 1987.

20. Kodwo Ewusi, "Occupations of Women in Ghana," in National Council on Women and Development Proceedings on the Seminar of Ghanaian Women in Development (September 4–8, 1978), vol. 1.

21. Personal interview with Grace Nartey, April 22, 1987.

22. Personal interview with Miranda Greenstreet, May 13, 1987.

23. Statistical Survey, *Quarterly Digest of Statistics*, March 1987 (Accra, Ghana, 1987).

24. Personal interview with Kate Abbam, May 5, 1987.

25. See Dr. John Kardi, *The Practice of Female Circumcision in the Upper East Region of Ghana: A Survey Report* (Accra, Ghana: Ghanaian Association for Women's Welfare, September 1986).

26. Tsikata, "Ghana."

27. Ibid.

28. Personal interview with Justice Annie Jiajie, April 9, 1987.

29. Personal interview with Kate Abbam, May 5, 1987. In this interview she also added that in Ghanaian traditional religion, God was both male and female.

11

Human Rights and Militarism in Nigeria

S. O. Alubo

Two laws. Two justices. One law and one justice protects the
man of property, the man of wealth. . . . Another law, another
justice silences the poor, the hungry, our people. . . . In the court
of imperialism, there has and will never be justice (nor human
rights) for the people.

—Dedan Kimathi

The interests of international capital and of the international
and national political institutions which sustain it are incompatible with the realization of human rights.

—Vicente Navarro

Human rights are often conceived in the narrow legalistic sense of
the right to life, freedom of association, and freedom of speech. At
other times they are regarded as the benevolent characteristic of
particular governments such as the Carter administration in the
United States and Nigeria's current "human rights—open government" of General Babangida.

Even with this conception, human rights like other social facilities
and rewards exist within a particular political economic context.
Yet, the context of human rights is hardly examined in its discourse.
Furthermore, even within the legalistic straitjacket, the arguments

are truncated and not carried to their logical conclusions. Would the right to life, for instance, entail the provision of material bases for sustaining life, i.e., employment, adequate wages, and protection from harm at work? Or would it be limited to the "thou shalt not kill" type of proscriptive injunction?

In this chapter we will look beyond this legalistic orthodoxy to an examination of the structural processes in society which sustain life and its social features, including human rights. In doing so, we have elected to examine human rights under military rule in Nigeria, because in its twenty-eight years of political independence, the military has been in power for some seventeen years. In fact, military intervention in politics has attracted considerable scholarship.[1] There is, however, no consensus as to whether the military are modernizers (old wine in new skin) or revolutionaries. Whichever label is more appropriate need not detain us here. Suffice it to say that the military has charted the course of, and left its imprint on, the annals of Nigeria's postindependence history.

The primary thesis of this chapter is that the issue of human rights is inextricably tied to structural processes in society rather than to the benevolence or malevolence of individual governments. Let us begin by laying out the political economic context within which human rights exist in its various forms. Just what is the structure of Nigeria's political economy, and how does this structure affect human rights? If we take these structures as given, does a particular government make a difference?

The issue of human rights under the military rule in Nigeria is examined against this background. While examples are drawn from past military regimes, the major focus will be on the Babangida self-styled "human rights—open government." Even with this label, to what extent can this regime pursue human rights when these run counter, as they must, to the logic of Nigeria's neocolonial economy? We conclude that human rights under capitalism, including its aberration, neocolonialism, is a class issue and has to be resolved within the broader ambit of the struggle for a more *humane* society. It cannot be guaranteed just by legal provision or the benevolence of any regime.

THE POLITICAL-ECONOMIC CONTEXT OF HUMAN RIGHTS IN NIGERIA

However conceived, human rights do not exist in a vacuum but rather within a given political economic reality.[2] The purpose of this section is to detail the political economy of contemporary Nigeria.

Nigeria was formally annexed into the capitalistic world market during colonialism. To some extent, this annexation antedates colonialism as European traders began to purchase precious metals, agricultural produce, and slaves as far back as the seventeenth century.[3] The resulting social order changed the mode of existence from subsistence to peasant agriculture as production was now for the market. To further enhance the new mode of production, taxes (payable in the newly introduced money) were introduced. This meant that emphasis now shifted to cash crops like cocoa, ground nuts, cotton, oil palm, and soya beans; all needed raw materials to feed European industries.

The state also created produce marketing boards as outlets for these cash crops. Other sectors of the economy like manufacturing and distribution were dominated by European companies.[4] Later, these businesses were joined by finance capital.

It is this externally dictated and directed economy that was inherited at independence. The economy contained a contradiction, however: On the one hand Nigeria was independent, and on the other the material basis for that independence lay outside its control. As Hamza Alavi[5] and other postcolonial state theoreticians[6] have argued, this contradiction permeates most Third World countries and is not unique to Nigeria.

But no state would risk jeopardizing its sources of revenue. Moreover, there are pressures, even if subtle, from the home countries of investors to ensure that a good government gets to power. In practical terms, these links meant that the real control of the state apparatus was from outside, a fact which General Obasanjo, a former Nigerian head of state, seemed to understand. He described Nigeria as a "trading post."[7] This term suggests that policy decisions originate not necessarily out of consideration for the governed but more from the interests of these investors.

This is not to suggest, however, that the domestic bourgeoisie is completely powerless. Actually, this class has continued to grow in strength through the protection of the state and within the state apparatus. The state has created several credit facilities such as agricultural, industrial, and mortgage banks, as well as the necessary legislation to prop up the domestic bourgeoisie.[8]

But as Leigh has argued, power and wealth cannot be divorced for long.[9] One of two things normally happens: Power will either take over wealth, or wealth will purchase power. This contradiction is resolved through what Terisa Turner has called the commercial triangle—an intimate alliance between middlemen in the private sector, representatives of multinational corporations who own and control major economic activities, and government officials who (nominally) control the state apparatus.[10]

The picture painted is one of merchant capital, though some manufacturing also takes place.[11] This process of production links the indigenous bourgeoisie more closely with foreign partners in the quest for technology and "expertise." The interests of this class and those of foreign investors are therefore fused. It is in this respect that it has been argued that the state in Nigeria protects capital in general, regardless of ownership.[12] This confluence of interests means that the dominated classes confront the state at two ends. This configuration frustrates attempts to successfully challenge, let alone change, existing relations of production. In this way, class struggles assume a militaristic character and the state often represses dissent and threatens "law and order."[13]

In recent times, the pursuits of these interests have taken the form of neglect of popular welfare through a wage freeze in the face of inflation, commercialization of welfare services (e.g., increased school and hospital fees), and privatization. Regarding education and medical services, these have been priced out of reach of the majority.[14] Furthermore, the government only recently (February 1987) restated its policy not to review wages even as prices have more than quadrupled, particularly since the inception of the Second-tier Foreign Exchange Market (SFEM) as part of the so-called Structural Adjustment Program (SAP).

The continued popular diswelfare is ironic because the military justified the overthrow of Shehu Shagari in 1983 by pointing to intolerable unemployment figures, high inflation, and the gradual decimation of social services. The problems were blamed on "corrupt and inept" leadership.[15] In this way, the crisis of the Nigerian economy is reduced to a problem of its managers rather than its structures.

Just before his overthrow, Shagari began to negotiate for a loan of $2 billion from the IMF. This negotiation continued throughout the Buhari regime (December 1983 to August 1985). When General Babangida took over, he promised to break the IMF deadlock.[16] But probably for political expediency, the Babangida government put the IMF loan issue to a popular debate, which purportedly formed the basis for its eventual rejection. This rejection apparently stemmed from unacceptable conditions such as rationalization of the public sector and 60 percent devaluation of the naira.[17] But even before Babangida, the preceding regime (which came to power bemoaning the high unemployment and decimated social services) had already fulfilled most of the IMF requirements. Thus, local government areas (along with their bureaucratic complements) were reduced from over 900 to 304. Furthermore, across the country employees in the public service were retrenched. The Babangida regime has continued these austerity measures in the form of more retrenchment, higher school, hospital, and other levies, and salary cuts. The naira was also allowed to float in order to enable it to find a "realistic value." Besides this devaluation in disguise, SFEM was introduced in September 1986 and has effectively devalued the naira by over 400 percent.

It may thus be seen that, even as the IMF loan was rejected, ostensibly because of unacceptable conditionals, these same conditions have been implemented several times over without the loan, probably at the behest of foreign creditors. This situation may be likened to that involving a woman who refuses induced labor in preference for normal delivery and then must have a Caesarean operation.

Economic recovery is the raison d'etre of the Babangida coup. When he took office, he imposed economic emergency measures (freezing wages and taking any action to revive the economy), initially for fifteen months. As part of this emergency, salaries were reduced by 2 to 20 percent, depending on a person's annual salary. To confer legality on this unilateral pay cut, a special decree (No. 37, 1986) was promulgated empowering the government to deduct workers' wages for purposes of reviving the economy. Midstream the period was extended to 1988, an apparent indication that the economy is still "comatose" and could not be revived. Retrenchments have continued along with privatization and cuts in social benefits even to the hitherto "untouchables" like Nigerian diplomats.

Unable to resolve unemployment problems, the Babangida regime has devised ingenious solutions, one of which is its exportation, via the newly created Technical Service Corps (the Nigerian brand of Peace Corps, VSO, CUSO). It has also, by fiat, abrogated the minimum wage law. The government's Directorate of Employment now recruits graduates for a paltry N200/month—over 50 percent less than the going rate. Moreover, it has amended the minimum wage act so that the minimum wage is no longer obligatory for employers with a labor force of under 500.

The same contradictions apply to social services. Regarding medical services, for example, when President Babangida himself took ill, he flew to Paris, a testimony that Nigeria's hospitals may still be "consulting clinics." Yet transforming hospitals from mere consulting clinics was part of the reason for the Babangida coup. The issues of class privileges and confidence in Nigeria's social services cannot be discounted as a major determinant of his choice of location for medical treatment.[18]

As the contradictions of Babangida's policies have illustrated, the structures of society rather than good intentions ultimately determine government policy, including human rights. It is against this background that human rights and militarism must be correctly interpreted and understood.

HUMAN RIGHTS AND MILITARISM: AN EXCURSION

In Nigeria, there are adequate legal provisions for human rights within the constitution (see Chapter 4) and other laws. These rights include the traditional triad of freedom from discrimination, the right to due process of law, and access to social services, including medical care.

Under the Buhari regime, several sections of the constitution were suspended. Decree No. 2 of 1984, for example, permits the state to arrest and detain without trial, for up to six months, anyone considered to be a security risk. Several Nigerians were detained under this decree, most of whom were released when Babangida came to power. Another "oppressive" Draconian law was Decree No. 4 which stipulates a jail term of up to two years for embarrassing the government. Two journalists were sentenced to jail for contravening this decree.

When Babangida came to power, Decree No. 4 was immediately repealed, and all those detained under it were unconditionally released under the new regime's human rights banner.[19] He also released most of the people held under state security decree and promised to review the case of detained politicians, most of whom had been in detention for over one year without trial. These initial steps won the new regime mass following and accolades. The Babangida human rights government has retained Decree No. 2, however, and has invoked it to detain people.

But beyond repressive decrees, how has the Babangida regime fared with respect to human rights? To answer this question, let us turn to the traditional trinity. But rather than a constricted conception, these provisions are examined against the material bases in which they exist.

It is incontrovertible that all persons have a right to life. But just what does this right mean? We argue that this right cannot be restricted to the proscription against taking life through "open" murder. More fundamental is the right to sustain life which includes the right to employment, to adequate reward and wages, and to protection from harm. Within this broader conception none of the several postcolonial governments, including the Babangida regime, could be said to truly uphold human rights.

Since Babangida came to power, Nigerians have continued to lose jobs through retrenchment and rationalization and the various SAPs (which really *sap* the people). For those lucky to have jobs, wages and salaries have fallen several times below the cost of living. Survival has been rendered more precarious by the withdrawal of the petroleum subsidy, privatization, and commercialization of welfare. As we discussed above, the Babangida regime has further undermined wages through the so-called stipends and the amendments to minimum wage legislation.

These various SAPs have begun to translate to morbidity and mortality problems. With reference to children's disease and death, the recent communique from the Pediatric Association of Nigeria illustrates that diseases such as cancrumois, which were hitherto confined to textbooks, are now commonplace in Nigerian hospitals. Furthermore, the current epidemic of nutritional diseases—accounting for one-half of all children's admissions to teaching hospitals in 1986[20]—was last experienced during the civil war.[21] These conditions and other recent epidemics like yellow fever and tuberculosis are directly traceable to SAP, the major plank in Babangida's economic recovery program.

But when the means of sustaining life are severed through retrenchment, unemployment, and diswelfare, violence is committed. In fact, as Friederich Engels long ago illustrated, the restriction of wages below cost of living, dangerous conditions of work, as well as conditions of near or actual starvation do, in fact, constitute murder.[22] That the Babangida economic program is designed to sacrifice the underclasses on the altar of debt slavery and accumulation seems clear. Hence, in the continuous *sapping* of the dominated classes, several concessions (e.g., promises of free land, tax holidays, avenues for profit repatriation, and privatization) are being made to business. Herein lies the violence of SAP. Indeed, as Vincente Navarro has argued:

It is correct to define as violent that set of class relations that puts property and the right to accumulate property over the right of life and freedom from harm, however *impersonal, indirect and unintentional* those relations may be. And it is equally correct to define those economic and political institutions that sustain and replicate the right to life and freedom from harm as violent institutions.[23]

It may thus be seen that it is a contradiction in terms to refer to the Babangida regime as one that truly upholds the right to life.

The same contradiction exists between declared intentions and the practice of freedom of association. Just what happens when the goals of associations contravene those of accumulation? And does not the freedom of association also extend to dissenting organizations? In reality, the exercise of their freedom is the largesse of a particular regime—it is to be given and withdrawn at will. Thus, following strikes and protests, the Buhari regime outlawed several associations, including the Pilots Labor Union, National Students, and Medical Associations.[24]

How has the "humanist" regime of Babangida fared with respect to freedom of association? Like other governments, this regime is intolerant of dissent, as illustrated by the massacre of students at Ahmadu Bello University (ABU) in May 1986.[25] In that incident police went to quell a peaceful protest with live bullets and incurred many casualties. The commission of inquiry subsequently appointed to investigate the crisis found the university administration "blameless" in the whole melee. The government also rejected the recommendation that future use of live bullets in quelling students protests be prohibited.

To protest the ABU killings, the Nigerian Labor Congress (NLC) planned a sympathy rally for June 4, 1986. But the government interpreted this protest as a challenge to its "legitimacy" and vowed to meet this challenge "with all resources at its disposal." It is noted here that even during the civil war there were limits to the use of resources at government disposal. Specifically, tanks were rolled and stationed in NLC offices, and MIG jets and Jaguar fighters roared through the skies. Across the country, labor leaders were detained to preempt the march, and some were charged in court for subversion. These charges were later dropped as part of the government's show of magnanimity.

In its continued assault on freedom of association, the Babangida regime promulgated a special decree in 1986 which excised the Association of Staff of Universities Union (ASUU) and other senior staff associations from membership in the Nigerian Labor Congress. Following the ABU crisis, the regime also banned student unions in all institutions of higher learning in Nigeria. In a similar manner, all religious organizations in institutions of higher learning were banned for twelve months, beginning March 1987. This ban was sequel to religious disturbances in parts of Kaduna State.

The same restrictions are placed on freedom of expression and are sometimes carried to absurd limits. During the last days of the Buhari regime, for instance, the government slapped a ban on *political* discussions. The humanist regime of Babangida has continued this trend, as illustrated in the white paper to the Abisoye Report (FGN, 1986) which stated that some lecturers are "not teaching what they are paid to teach" and should be "flushed out." Contrary to what this allegation may suggest, it is not that those employed to teach chemistry are teaching theater arts. At stake here is the right to dissenting opinion and the liberty to express it.

Perhaps the most blatant violation of this right is the proscription of *Newswatch* magazine. The government of General Babangida explained that *Newswatch* illegally obtained and published (ordinarily this is called a "scoop" in journalism) the Report of the Political Bureau which was being studied by the government. As punishment for this "illegality"—though without due process of law—the magazine was banned for six months. A special decree of 1987, No. 6, was subsequently promulgated, with retrospective effect to confer the necessary legality on the apparently illegal ban.

In effect, then, the government *is* the law and can hardly contravene the law. If and when it does, the laws are changed (e.g., Decree No. 2 was amended in 1986 to extend the period of detention from three to six months) or new ones are enacted, as we saw with the decree enabling the deduction of workers salaries. Nigeria's information minister, Tony Momoh, acknowledges this fact:

Whether the proscription [of *Newswatch*] is legitimate or not is a legal question, if [the] proscription is not legitimate or unpopular, it does not mean that it is not legal. If the books do not make it legal, it could be made legal. There will be a law to deal with the *Newswatch* situation.[26]

In other words, the issues transcend the rule of law. More fundamental is the law itself—whose law? This is the significance of our opening epigram.

HUMAN RIGHTS IN AN INHUMAN SOCIETY

We have illustrated that, contrary to the humanist label and rhetoric, the Babangida regime is yet to truly uphold human rights. We have lodged this failing not in the evil nature of the regime, but in the internal logic of the working of capitalism within which unemployment, squalor, and starvation coexist with profit maximization and accumulation. The inherent contradictions of capitalism, especially its underdeveloped form, become particularly glaring when one examines the balance sheet of corporations. It is ironic that the same corporations that closed down factories or retrenched workers, ostensibly for sluggish business, continue to make windfall profits, even with decreasing turnover.[27] Indeed, the structures of neocolonialism and the continued pillage of Nigeria require a repressive government. For several of the anti-people programs can only be implemented by such a regime. At the end of the day, therefore, "class power relations are what determine the rights of citizens within society. The individual's right will depend on what class position he or she holds within (Nigeria's) class structure."[28]

Our central thesis has been that individual governments do not make a difference. The neocolonial system is patently inhuman. Given present structures, individual regimes, whatever their label and rhetorics, are necessarily and ultimately repressive. The difference might be in the style of repression and violation of human rights. Thus, while we have concentrated here on military regimes, similar cases of flagrant violations can be documented during the civilian era. A minimum tally of these cases must include the Black Maria deaths when 50 of 68 detainees suffocated to death in a police van; the deportation of Shugaba; and the Bakalori Massacre. The Bakalori Massacre has been widely described as "a monument of police brutality and state repression."

Clearly, the issue of human rights cannot be resolved separately from the class question. To do differently is to pursue an illusion: human rights in an inhuman society.

NOTES

1. See I. Ayu, "To Adjust or to Smash Imperialism in Africa: Militarism and the Crisis," Paper presented at the International Conference on Economic Crisis and Austerity Measures and Privatization in Africa, Ahmadu Bello University (ABU), March 11–17, 1985; B. Beckman, "The Military as Revolutionary Vanguard: A Critique," *Positive Review Monograph*, 2–1, 1986; O. Odetola, *Military Regimes and Development* (Boston: Allen and Unwin, 1982); S. Tyoden, "The Military and the Prospect for Socialist Construction in the Third World: Some Preliminary Observations," Presented at a conference on Nigerian Economy and Society Since the Berlin Conference, ABU, Zaria, November, 1985.

2. Most of this section is a revision of S. Alubo's original manuscript for the Port Harcourt Conference, 1987.

3. See B. Onimode, *Imperialism and Underdevelopment in Nigeria* (Lagos: Macmillan, 1983), and W. Rodney, *How Europe Underdeveloped Africa* (Dares Salaam: Tanzanian Publishing House, 1972).

4. A. Abba et al., *Nigerian Economic Crisis* (Zaria: Gaskiya Corp., 1985).

5. Hamza Alavi, "The State in Post Colonial Societies: Pakistan and Bangladesh," *New Left Review* 59–81 (July-August 1973).

6. B. Beckman, "Bakolon; Peasants vs. State and Capital," *Nigerian Journal of Political Science* 4, nos. 1, 2 (1985): 76–104.

7. I. Eteng, *Myths and Fallacies in Nigeria Development* (Port Harcourt, Nigeria: University of Port Harcourt, 1979), pp. 48–78.

8. S. Alubo and U. Ogbe, "The 1986 Yellow Fever Epidemic in Nigeria: A Materialist Analysis," Unpublished paper, 1987; and S. Othman, "Classes,

Crises and the Coup: The Demise of Shagari's Regime," *African Affairs* 83–33 (1984), pp. 441–61.

9. B. Onimode et al., *Multinational Corporations in Nigeria* (Ibadan: Les Shraden, 1983).

10. T. Turner and P. Badru, "Class Contradictions and the 1983 Coup in Nigeria," *Journal of African Marxists* 7 (1985), pp. 4–21.

11. Abba et al., *Nigerian Economic Crisis,* and S. Othman, "Classes, Crises and the Coup."

12. B. Beckman, "Whose State? State and Capitalist Development in Nigeria," *Review of African Political Economy* 23 (1982), pp. 37–51.

13. S. Alubo, "The Political Economy of Doctors' Strikes in Nigeria," *Social Science and Medicine* 22, no. 4 (1986), pp. 467–77.

14. S. Alubo, "State Violence and Health in Nigeria," Unpublished paper, 1987.

15. Turner and Badru, "Class Contradictions."

16. I. Babangida, "Why We Struck," *Newswatch,* September 9, 1986, pp. 18–19.

17. B. Usman, *Nigeria Against the IMF* (Kaduna: Vanguard, 1986).

18. Alubo, "State Violence and Health."

19. Babangida, "Why We Struck."

20. A. Onipede, "Life Rough for Babies," *Sunday Tribune,* February 15, 1987.

21. Alubo and Ogbe, "The 1986 Yellow Fever Epidemic in Nigeria."

22. Friederich Engels and Karl Marx, *Collected Works* (New York: International Publishers, 1975).

23. V. Navarro, "The Economic and Political Determinants of Human (including health) Rights," in Navarro, ed., *Imperialism, Health, and Medicine* (Farmingdale, N.Y.: Baywood, 1981), pp. 53–76.

24. Alubo, "The Political Economy of Doctors' Strikes."

25. ASUU, *The Killings at ABU* (Zaria: 1986).

26. Quoted in the *Guardian,* April 12, 1987, p. 3.

27. Usman, *Nigeria Against the IMF.*

28. Ibid.

12

Human Rights and Self-Reliance in Africa

Mark O.C. Anikpo

INTRODUCTION

Since the early 1960s, various aspects of human rights as they relate to national and regional development have been on the United Nations (UN) agenda. It was not until 1982, however, that the UN General Assembly declared emphatically that the right to development is "an inalienable human right."[1] This declaration is understandably premised on the notions of respect for human dignity and social justice. By implication, the UN declaration on human rights and development presupposes that it is the primary responsibility of any human group to solve the problems of their society using their own resources, intelligence, decisions, and capabilities, with or without outside help.

It is also noteworthy that the persistence of the development debate on the UN human rights agenda is consequent on reports monitored by the UN Commission on Human Rights from African and other Third World Nations who are becoming more persistent in their demand for justice in their relationships with the industrialized nations of Europe and North America. For Africa, in particular, centuries of devastating association with the rest of the world have led to the necessity for an alternative development strategy in dealing with the multiple problems of the Continent.

The strategy of "self-reliance" at national and regional levels has already been proposed by the Organization of African Unity (OAU) and the Economic Community of Africa (ECA) in the document usually referred to as the Lagos Plan of Action (LPA). The new strategy would involve a "partial delinkage of Africa from the global trading system and enlarged emphasis on intra-African trading. Interactive agricultural and industrial development within a network of strong sub-regional frameworks."[2] This is to ensure a durable foundation for self-sustained development based on the resources, talents, and expectations of Africans.

The sentiments expressed in the LPA are also implied in the Banjul Charter or the African Charter on Human and Peoples' Rights in which the OAU, in 1981, articulated the African concept of human rights to reflect the African concern for the right to development. This concern had earlier been expressed in the OAU establishment Charter adopted in 1983. African and Malagasy heads of state and government assembled at Addis Ababa, Ethiopia, had unanimously declared;

Convinced that it is the inalienable right of all people to control their destiny; conscious of the fact that freedom, equality, justice, and dignity are essential objectives for the development of the African peoples; dedicated to the general progress of Africa; persuaded that the Charter of the United Nations and the Universal Declaration of Human Rights, and to the principles of which we reaffirm our adherence, provide a solid foundation for peaceful and positive cooperation among states.[3]

There is therefore a mutual compatibility between human rights and self-reliant development. It is not merely that the protection of human rights provides a stable and peaceful framework for development; both uphold the utilization of and respect for local resources and capabilities.

George Shepherd's[4] analysis of the Banjul Charter and the self-reliance strategy provides some useful insights into the genesis of this relationship. In his own words, "the discovery of African and other Third World Peoples' unfavorable position within the world system is the basis for the growing awareness of a third generation of rights. These people have taken their place in a world dominated by the rivalry of the two super-powers and have felt the need to formulate specific statements of the rights threatened by this situation." Hence, in the Banjul Charter, the OAU declares that "it is henceforth essential to pay particular attention to the right to development and that civil and political rights cannot be dissociated from economic, cultural and social rights in their conception as well as universality, and that the satisfaction of economic, social and cultural rights is a guarantee for the enjoyment of civil and political rights."

The question that inevitably arises is: Given the UN Declaration on Human Rights and Development, and Africa's decision to make self-reliance a development strategy within the framework of people's economic, social, and cultural rights, what is hindering the implementation of this decision? An adequate answer to this question will entail a comprehensive analysis of the African political economy. The emphasis will be on the historical dialectical relationships arising from internal class configurations and external interventions from the economically and militarily more powerful nations of Europe and North America. A number of scholars such as Samir Amin,[5] Walter Rodney,[6] and Claude Ake[7] have provided useful analyses of Africa's political economy. Using the Marxian model of historical materialism, they have focused on the economic structures arising from colonialism and neocolonialism which hold Africa in a dependency relationship with West European and American nations. They have also provided the impetus for further investigations into the dynamics of the structural relationships between Africa on the one hand and Europe and America on the other.

An attempt is made here to extend the insights offered by the political economy paradigm into the sociocultural realm in order to understand the more subtle dimensions of the African economic and political crisis. The focus is on how neocolonial imperialism, through intellectual subversion, undermines Africa's efforts to pursue a self-reliant development strategy. The central thesis is that the declaration of human rights is not a design to help Africa achieve self-reliance, but rather an indication of the pressure which African nations have been able to put on the international community to face the reality of an unjust global social order. It attempts to show that the conflict of interests that results in human rights violations is the necessary negation for the intensification of the struggle for global social justice by the oppressed peoples of Africa and the rest of the world.

THEORETICAL CONSIDERATIONS

It is perhaps necessary to clarify some of the theoretical issues in this analysis. Despite the recognition of the dual sources of the African development dilemma in terms of internal and external influences, the international orientation of the human rights question shifts the focus of the analysis to a consideration of the external or imperialist sources of the African crisis. It may be difficult for some people to understand how African underdevelopment is a consequence of global imperialist manipulations. It may be even more difficult to appreciate the idea that the subjugation of Africa, which has made it impossible for African states to provide the basic necessities of life for millions of their citizens, is a human rights problem rather than an abstract political miscalculation. To such people, it is perhaps easier to explain the inability of Africa to achieve self-reliance in terms of localized factors, such as corrupt leadership, drought, desertification, low intelligence, disease-ridden environment, and cultural inertia.

Other people, however, would take a global view of localized phenomena, especially when they affect a whole Continent. Their objective is not necessarily to establish common indices and units of measurement, but, while recognizing the influence of cultural specificities, to examine the historical and structural interconnections (if any) of seemingly isolated events and social conditions. The appreciation of such global linkages may require an ideological orientation that views such social conditions as the product of antagonistic class relations in which the rich and politically powerful groups oppress and exploit the poor and weak ones. The ethical or humanitarian undertones behind such considerations are obvious. But in international relations, morality is not a major factor in decision-making or policy formulations. Indeed, when morality clashes with national or class interests, the latter often prevail, paving the way for economic and military power to emerge as the final arbiter in the operation of any social order. Morality is not part of the "realism" of world politics. It is against this background that one can make sense out of the notorious violations of human rights and the intellectual imperialism that undermined the achievement of a self-reliant development strategy in Africa.

What this implies is that discussions on human rights have an undeniable undertone of morality or political expediency. Premised on the philosophical tripod of liberty, equality, and fraternity, the notion of human rights presupposes that all men and women have some inherent potentialities which, as individuals and groups, they are obliged and free to use in solving the problems of their environment. By its ethical connotation, it abhors injustice, especially as expressed in inhuman brutality, exploitation, and obstruction. At times, such discussions not only reflect political naïveté, but also make a mockery of scientific analysis. Yet, they reflect a certain phenomenological reality without which the scientific endeavor tends to relapse into crude empiricism.

This chapter is written not necessarily to persuade Africa's detractors to voluntarily and fraternally respect the Continent's right to solve its problems its own way, but rather as a kind of pedagogy for the oppressed. The debate on human rights is necessary, not that by itself, as Shepherd hopes, it "will provide the entire world with a more profound basis on which to build policies in areas such as Africa."[8] Rather, since such policies can only be determined by the logic of capitalist development, the sharpening of consciousness which such debates bring about provides the only meaningful basis for the struggle toward achieving and protecting human rights. As Osita Eze has already noted, historical evidence reveals that "any progressive shift in the nature and scope of human rights protected or promoted has generally resulted from a struggle between the privileged and the oppressed."[9] J. Maritain makes exactly the same point when he affirms that, "In human history, no 'new' right, I mean no right of which common consciousness was becoming newly aware, has been recognized in actual fact without having to struggle against and overcome the bitter opposition of some 'old rights.'"[10] What we call human rights are, therefore, those concessions forced on the dominant classes in both national and international affairs. Although such rights can be traced to the historical development of the civil society, they invariably evolve side by side with other social forces that tend to stifle them. For instance, the development of property relations as recorded from the time of the early Greeks generated a simultaneous development of class exploitation and imperialist encounters. Whatever rights the human mind, in the course of societal development, had conceived as inalienable to the individual or the group had been so recognized because they were hitherto denied to numerous individuals and groups in society and had to be demanded and invariably fought for.

This is not the place to review in detail the historical evolution of the various generations of rights. In the first place, other authors have discussed the subject adequately.[11] Moreover, the debate on human rights seems to have progressed beyond such historical anthology. Suffice it to say that the concern with people's rights in Africa raises one of the unresolved controversies in the human rights debate: that is, the issue of how appropriate the West European focus on individual rights is in the African context. Although Western individualism makes sense in an environment where groups of people are not enslaved or oppressed by virtue of their collective identity, it fails as a basis for human rights in situations where colonialism and neocolonialism have held groups in emasculating bondage, rendering them impotent as individuals.

It is not correct to argue that the African concept of human rights in the group or community context has developed because the community gives identity to the individual. The obvious teleological posture of such a concept makes it analytically unacceptable. This concept of human rights in contemporary Africa fails to distinguish the revolutionary demand for group action from the teleological notion of proprietary personality vested in the *genos* or *polis* in Homeric and Aristotelian Greece. It also fails to distinguish the collective imperative of self-reliance as a development strategy from the "European socialist idea of the state as the validator of law and rights."[12] While the African concept of community rights has an ideological resemblance to European socialism, it is more of an attempt to reconcile the bigotry of ancient Greek selective citizenship and the exploitative individualism of modern Euro-American liberal democracy. It is a recognition by the people of Africa and their respective national governments that no meaningful conditions of life can be achieved on the continent, even at the individual level, as long as the continent remains under imperialist influence.

Ake sums up the discrepancy as follows:

In the African context, human rights have to be much more than the political correlate of commodity fetishism which is what they are in the Western tradition. In that tradition, the rights are not only abstract, they are also ascribed to abstract persons. The rights are ascribed to the human being from whom all specific determinations have been abstracted: the rights have no content, just as the individuals who enjoy them have no determination and so do not really exist.[13]

Euro-American societies may require the legalistic concept of rights to mediate in the atomistic model of their social organization. In Africa, however, where the majority "still live and think in organised wholes—family, clan, lineage or ethnic group,"[14] such individualism has limited value. It is also in this context that one has to understand the strategy of self-reliance as an alternative development strategy for Africa.

THE LAGOS PLAN OF ACTION (LPA) AND SELF-RELIANCE

In response to the worsening conditions of life in Africa following the decade of political independence (1960–1970), the OAU released two documents that forcefully articulated the right of African nations to independent self-reliant development. These were the Banjul Charter and the Lagos Plan of Action already mentioned. While the Banjul Charter tried to clarify the focus of human rights on the group rather than the individual, the LPA elevated the right to development from a request to a demand. It attempted to crystallize the theoretical and methodological implications of self-reliance for Africa. However, since its adoption, the LPA has been subjected to orchestrated ridicule which has undermined its merits even as an intellectual effort to understand and recommend solutions to the problems of Africa. It is to this intellectual distortion that this analysis is directed in order to explain why self-reliance seems to have become an unrealistic African dream.

Despite destructive criticisms and apparent rejection, three features of the LPA must be acknowledged as unique. First, the LPA is an historical moment in the developmental efforts of African nations. It emerged at a period when all the economic indicators on the Continent were pointing downwards, and when the forces of imperialism, mostly in the form of neocolonialism, had descended on the continent in all their vehemence. This is clearly reflected in the following Preamble to the LPA.[15]

The effect of unfulfilled promises of global development strategies has been more sharply felt in Africa than in the other countries of the world. Indeed, rather than result in an improvement in the economic situation of the continent, successive strategies have made it stagnate and become more susceptible than other regions to the economic and social crises suffered by the industrialized countries.

. . . . . .

We view with distress, that our continent remains the least developed of all the continents; the total Gross Domestic Production of our countries being only 27 per cent of the world's per capita income averaging US $166.

. . . . . .

We view, with disquiet, the over-dependance of the economy of our continent on the export of basic raw materials and minerals. This phenomenon had made African economies highly susceptible to external developments and with detrimental effects on the interests of the continent.

It was the first time the regional organization had released a pointedly challenging document. Despite any shortcomings the LPA may have had, the document heralded a new consciousness in the attempt to understand and deal with the African underdevelopment crisis on a permanent basis.

Second, the LPA is a genuine attempt by Africans to spell out their problems and to tackle these problems. This recognition by African leaders that it was time they took control of their own destinies is also reflected in the Preamble to the LPA, as follows:

Thus, following a series of in depth considerations of the economic problems of the continent by our Ministers and by groups of experts, we adopted at our 16th Ordinary Session, held in Monrovia, Liberia, in July, 1979, the "Monrovia Declaration of Commitment of Heads of State and Government of the OAU" on the guidelines and measures for national and collective self-reliance in economic and social development for the establishment of a new international economic order.

The Declaration recognized "the need to take urgent action to provide the political support necessary for the success of the measures to achieve the goals of rapid self-reliance and self-sustaining development and economic growth." It spelled out specific guidelines to achieve the stated objectives. Critics, however, argued that these guidelines were not specific enough to serve as a blueprint for practical action.

Third, the LPA, regardless of whether its guidelines were appropriate and whether or not they were going to be implemented, was an intellectual affront against imperialist exploitation. Indeed, its call for self-reliance has more far-reaching implications than a mere strategy for development. It involved the reordering of the world system economically, politically, and ideologically.

Economically, self-reliance would mean for Africa a total control of the Continent's resources in such a way that Africa might have to delink, however partially, from the orbit of global capitalism. It would further mean the closure of sources of cheap labor and raw materials needed for the continued replenishment of Euro-American capitalism. It could result in an equitable balance of trade between Africa and the industrialized countries which could raise the level of accumulation in Africa and simultaneously reduce the profit margin for others.

Such an alteration of the long-established lines of economic advantage would shake the foundations of the capitalist world, which has exploited Africa's resources since colonial times. Herein lies the political consequence of self-reliance in Africa. A self-reliant Africa will be better able to make decisions affecting international relations without the retaliatory economic measures that such decisions could provoke from aggrieved superpowers. Enhanced economic and political rights for Africa will be certain to break the dominance of European and American powers in world affairs. It is therefore not in their economic and political interests that Africa should become self-reliant.

It is perhaps the ideological implication of self-reliance that makes it more openly a target of vigorous criticism. As already indicated, the search for self-reliance is a consequence of neocolonial imperialism manifested visibly in the capitalist operations of multinational corporations and the secret wars of the CIA.[16] At the time self-reliance was mooted as an idea, capitalism had demonstrated an incapacity to raise productive forces in Africa. The continuous decline in existential conditions, while adopting reformist strategies of capitalist development, forced many Africans to rethink the appropriateness of capitalism for Africa. As demonstrated first in the request for a New International Economic Order (NIEO) and later in the Banjul Charter and the LPA, African nations were slowly but surely awakening to the imperative of an alternative to capitalist development.

Probably because of the need to steer clear of the existing and conflicting ideological labels, African leaders avoided the use of "socialism" to identify their search for an independent development strategy. But, as Ekekwe[17] clearly stated, even as defined in the LPA, self-reliance was a demand for an ideological umbrella. Under this umbrella new concepts and strategies will not only mean something to those concerned, but will also place in the control of African and all dependent peoples all the means of production within their territories, provide guidance for political leadership, and restore human dignity to all those humiliated and dehumanized by both internal and external oppressors. The socialist sentiments implied in such a search are unmistakable. Self-reliance was a search for the goals usually enunciated in socialism and was unquestionably anti-imperialistic. It would thus be correct to argue that the search for self-reliance, as an alternative development strategy, is the result of the unfulfilled hopes of capitalism in Africa and the inability or unwillingness of the United Nations to enforce its human rights declarations as they affect development in Africa.

Despite the ideological resemblance of self-reliance to socialism, there is still a difference introduced by the historical gap that separates the two. Since self-reliance is essentially a struggle against neocolonial imperialism, its strategies are likely to be influenced, not only by the history and culture of the African societies, but also by the new methods of capitalist exploitation, and the new class configurations within the continent. Thus, the struggle for self-reliance has the dual fronts set by neocolonial imperialism and internal compradorial classes that operate within the African countries. Above all, self-reliance deals with the question of internal reconstruction after the confrontation with imperialist forces because it aims at the total mobilization of the masses to use their own resources and capabilities to solve their problems by themselves. This effort includes restructuring the social relations of production for the socialization of productive forces and equitable distribution of collectively produced wealth.

THE BERG REPORT AS INTELLECTUAL IMPERIALISM

The LPA may not have spelled out in comprehensive detail the technicalities involved in achieving self-reliance, but this is hardly a justification for denying even its heuristic value. Neither does it explain why the African nations that signed it failed to implement its recommendations. While African leaders and intellectuals must be blamed for succumbing to imperialist propaganda, the distortion of self-reliance as a concept and the consequent eclipse of the LPA by the World Bank-sponsored Berg Report must be held largely responsible for the ambivalence of African nations toward the self-reliance strategy.

The World Bank report, *Accelerated Development in Sub-Saharan Africa: An Agenda for Action* (otherwise known as the Berg Report),[18] epitomizes the subtle form of opposition to and violation of Africa's right to self-reliant development. Its opposition is so subtle that it may be lost in the sophisticated academic garb that conceals its human rights violation. It is a typical demonstration of the attitude of superiority that has characterized Euro-American relationships in which the industrialized nations of Europe and North America have consistently refused to respect Africa's right to self-determination.

It will be recalled that the LPA, which was in the making for several years, was finally signed on April 29, 1980. According to Robert Cummings in the Foreword to *The Lagos Plan of Action vs. the Berg Report,* "The Lagos Plan of Action constitutes the first comprehensive continent-wide formulation and articulation of the preferred long-term economic and development objectives of African countries."[19] In 1981, the World Bank presented a draft copy of the Berg Report to the OAU leadership. The Report, prepared by a team of World Bank "experts" on African affairs, is alleged to have been initially requested by African finance ministers. In the late 1970s, these leaders, like most other Africans, were so disillusioned with the continent's deteriorating economic conditions that they asked for expert advice on how to avert the looming collapse of African economies. It should be mentioned here that these same economic considerations, during this same period, fired the series of meetings initiated by African planning ministers which eventually culminated in the birth of the LPA. According to Browne and Cummings, The Berg Report "is an analytical, basically economic document which examines specific policies currently being pursued in Africa and either approves or denounces them in terms of their presumed effectiveness in the development process."[20]

Compared to the LPA, the Berg Report contains two striking features that have made it one of the most harmful documents on African development. The first deals with the scope and time frame of their respective recommendations. While the LPA projects into the distant future and recommends strategies that may take a long time to be effected but will solve the development problems of Africa once and for all, the Berg Report was concerned with short- and medium-term measures to deal with immediate problems such as the export of Africa's primary products and obtaining loans to finance development projects. The Berg Report favored external dependence and by implication rejected the LPA call for self-reliance.

The second dividing line between the two documents is related to the first. While the LPA clearly places the blame for African underdevelopment on the rich industrialized countries of the West, "Berg chose to place the major blame for Africa's economic deterioration on the improper policies pursued by many African nations and offered policy prescriptions which were in many cases politically difficult for African leadership to implement."[21] What baffles the critical observer of international affairs is the zeal and self-declared compassion with which some UN agencies offer both solicited and unsolicited development recommendations to African nations, while all the requests by these African nations, based on their own perceptions of their problems, are invariably turned down or vetoed at UN assemblies. One also wonders why this compassion is never translated into "debt forgiveness," or at least interest-free loans.

The only way to make sense out of these apparent contradictions is to view such actions against the background of national, racial, or class interest defense. As already indicated, it will not be in the interests of Euro-American nations that control the United Nations for Africa to become self-reliant. At the same time, when confronted with the illogic of their inconsistency, the injustice in their dealings with Africans, and the persistent demands of the African nations for a just social order, they reluctantly or grudgingly make concessions that add to the list of rights enjoyed by the victims of oppression.

The Berg Report has come and gone. Its rejection by Africa and its later repudiation by its sponsors are demonstrations of a new consciousness of Africa's right to self-determination and self-reliant development. For the collective opposition they receive as a group from the industrialized countries of Europe and North America, the African concept of human rights will make sense only in the collective context of people's rights or group rights as against individual rights. In terms of ensuring that this group right to development is accepted and respected globally, one would argue that unless and until a new world order that recognizes the dignity and wishes of

Africans emerges, the demands and struggles are likely to continue
as the surest guarantee for the protection of both individual and
group human rights in Africa.

CONCLUSIONS

For too long, the rich and powerful nations of Europe and North
America, through their international organizations such as the
World Bank, the International Monetary Fund, Unesco, and the
USAID, have posed as champions of African development. They recommend and organize all forms of "aid" for Africa. In health, industry, agriculture, education, and development planning, they
send their "experts" on African affairs to conduct research, the findings of which are meant to guide African nations along Western-
defined paths to development.

Despite their prescriptions for the African underdevelopment dilemma, African economies have continued to decline, leading to serious social and political problems all over the continent. Instead of
viewing the African crisis in the context of the global capitalist orbit
within which African economies have been entangled, these "experts" still insist that the problems of Africa are internal and can be
solved by short-term measures such as taking loans from the World
Bank and IMF to fund development projects under conditions imposed by the lending bodies.

One does not need to be a radical Marxist critic to understand the
folly of asking African nations to continue a development approach
that has spelled doom for their economies since World War II. It may
perhaps take a critical ideologue to see that beyond the facade of aid
and evangelism and research is an imperialist plot to keep Africa
perpetually subjugated for the continued strengthening of capitalism in the developed countries.[22] The critic also finds that invariably
the so-called assistance to Africa takes the form of a subtle but flagrant
violation of Africa's right to self-reliant development. An analysis of
the Berg Report against the background of the Lagos Plan of Action
and its call for self-reliance as an alternative development strategy
in Africa reveals that the Berg Report is a subtle affirmation that
Africans do not know the problems of their Continent and cannot
deal with these problems by themselves. It is also an affirmation that
the developed countries of the world will continue to use their power
positions in world affairs to stifle and violate Africa's right to independent development.[23] It is recognized that the acquisition of such
rights invariably involves a struggle by an oppressed group, which
needs the right, against a privileged group.

NOTES

1. Ved P. Nanda, "Development and Human Rights: The Role of International Law and Organizations," in George W. Shepherd and Ved P. Nanda, eds., *Human Rights and Third World Development* (Westport, Conn.: Greenwood Press, 1985), p. 290.

2. See Robert Browne and Robert Cummings, *The Lagos Plan of Action vs. The Berg Report: Contemporary Issues in African Economic Development* (Richmond, Va.: Brunswick Publishing Co., 1984), Charts 1 and 2.

3. Quoted in N.S.S. Iwe, *The History and Contents of Human Rights: A Study of the History and Interpretation of Human Rights* (New York: Peter Lang, 1986).

4. George Shepherd, Jr., "The Tributary State and People's Rights in Africa: The Banjul Charter and Self-Reliance," in *Africa Today* (Special Double Issue—December 1986).

5. See Samir Amin, *Imperialism and Unequal Development* (Brighton, Eng. and New York: Harvester Press and Monthly Review Press, 1977).

6. See also Walter Rodney, *How Europe Underdeveloped Africa* (London: Zed Press, 1962).

7. Further issues of Africa's political economy are also analyzed in Claude Ake, *A Political Economy of Africa* (London: Longmans, 1987).

8. Shepherd, "The Tributary State."

9. Osita Eze, *Human Rights in Africa: Some Selected Problems* (Nigeria: Macmillan Nigeria Ltd., 1984), p. 1.

10. Iwe, *The History and Contents of Human Rights.*

11. Ibid.

12. Shepherd, "The Tributary State."

13. Claude Ake, "The African Context of Human Rights," in *Africa Today* 34, nos. 1 & 2, (1987), p. 10.

14. Ibid.

15. The LPA is the report of an ECA Joint Committee which was adopted in Lagos, Nigeria, in 1981 as the blueprint for Africa's economic development from 1980 to 2000. (Addis Ababa: OAU, 1980). The Berg Report contradicted most of the recommendations of the LPA. See Appendix A.

16. Bob Woodward, *Veil: The Secret Wars of the CIA, 1981–1987* (New York and London: Simon and Schuster).

17. Eme Ekekwe, "Self-Reliance and National Development: Ideological and Economic Crises" (unpublished conference paper, University of Port Harcourt, Nigeria, 1985).

18. Elliot Berg, et al., *Accelerated Development in Sub-Saharan Africa* (World Bank Report, 1981).

19. Browne and Cummings, *The Lagos Plan of Action.*

20. Ibid.

21. Ibid., p. 23.

22. Adebayo Adedeji and Timothy Shaw, *Economic Crises in Africa: African Perspectives on Development—Problems and Potentials* (Boulder, Colo.: Lynne Rienner Publishers, Inc., 1985).

23. Peter Dunigan, "Africa from a Globalist Perspective," in Gerald Bender et al., ed., *African Crisis Areas and U.S. Foreign Policy* (Berkeley: University of California Press, 1985), p. 291.

Selected Bibliography

Abacha, S. Text of speech announcing overthrow of Shagari. *Daily Times*, December 31, 1983.

Abba, A. et al. *Nigerian Economic Crisis*. Zaria: Gaskiya Corp., 1985.

Abbott, G. C. "Rhetoric and Reality." *International Journal* 34, no. 1 (Winter 1978–1979).

Achebe, Chinua. *The Trouble with Nigeria*. Enugu, Nigeria: Fourth Dimension Publ., 1983.

Achtemeier, E. "Righteousness in the Old Testament." *Interpreter's Dictionary of the Bible*, vol. 4. Nashville, Tenn.: Abingdon Press, 1962.

Adedeji, Adebayo. "Africa: Permanent Underdog?" *International Perspectives* (March-April 1981).

———. "The Lagos Plan of Action: Main Features and Some Other Related Issues." Keynote Address to the International Conference on the OAU, ECA, and LPA and the Future of Africa, Ile-Ife, March 1984.

———. "Perspectives of Development and Economic Growth in Africa Up to the Year 2000." In *What Kind of Africa by Year 2000?* Addis Ababa: OAU, 1979.

———, and Timothy Shaw. *Economic Crises in Africa: African Perspectives and Development—Problems and Potentials*. Boulder, Colo.: Lynne Rienner Publishing, 1985.

Afigbo, A. *Ropes of Sand: Studies in Igbo History and Culture*. Oxford: Oxford University Press, 1981.

Ajayi, J. F. Ade and Ian Espie. *A Thousand Years of West African History*. Ibadan: Ibadan University Press, 1965.

Ake, Claude. *A Political Economy of Africa*. London: Longmans Group, 1987.

———. *Revolutionary Pressures in Africa*. London: Zed Press, 1978.

Akinyemi, A. B., P. D. Cole, and Walter Ofonagoro, eds., *Readings on Federalism*. Lagos: Nigerian Institute of International Affairs, 1979.

Alavi, Hamza. "The State in Post-Colonial Societies: Pakistan and Bangladesh." *New Left Review* (July-August 1973).

Ali, Major-General Ibrahim. International Symposium on The Militarization of Africa. SIPRI, Stockholm, November 10–12, 1986.

Alubo, S. "The Political Economy of Doctors' Strikes in Nigeria." *Social Science and Medicine* 22, no. 4 (1986), pp. 467–77.

———. "State Violence and Health in Nigeria." Unpublished paper, 1987.

———, and U. Ogbe. "The 1986 Yellow Fever Epidemic in Nigeria: A Materialist Analysis." Unpublished paper, 1987.

Ameluxen, C. "Marriage and Women in Islamic Countries." *Human Rights Case Studies* 2 (1975), p. 89.

Amin, Samir. *History of Capitalism in West Africa*. London: Penguin, 1978.

———. *Imperialism and Unequal Development*. New York: Monthly Review Press, 1977.

———. *Unequal Development*. New York: Monthly Review Press, 1976.

Amnesty International. *Background Paper on Ghana*. London: Mimeo, 1974.

———. *Human Rights in Uganda*. New York, 1986.

———. *1986 Report*. London, 1986.

Anifowose, Remi. *Violence and Politics in Nigeria: The Tiv and Yoruba Experience*. New York: Nok Publishers International, 1982.

Appadorai, A. *The Substance of Politics*. New Delhi: Oxford University Press, 1975.

Ardayfio, Elizabeth. "Women and Urban Marketing in China." Selected Papers and Speeches from the Association for Women in Development Conference, April 25–27, 1985, Washington, D.C.

Arnold, Hugh M. "Africa and the New International Economic Order." *Third World Quarterly* 11, no. 2 (April 1980).

Aron, Raymond. *Peace and War*. New York: Free Press, 1962.

ASUU. *The Killings at ABU*. Zaria: 1986.

Ayu, I. "To Adjust or to Smash Imperialism in Africa: Militarism and the Crisis." Paper presented at the International Conference on Economic Crisis and Austerity Measures and Privatization in Africa, ABU, March 11–17, 1985.

Babangida, I. "Why We Struck." *Newswatch*, September 9, 1986.

Ball, Nicole. "Defense and Development: A Critique of the Benoit Study." *Economic Development and Social Change*, no. 31, April 1983.

———. "Military Expenditure, Economic Growth and Socio-Economic Development in the Third World." Conference paper No. 3 of the Swedish Institute of International Peace Research.

———. "Security Expenditure and Economic Growth in Developing Countries." *Pugwash Annals, 1985*. London: Macmillan, 1986.

———, and Milton Leitenberg. *Disarmament, Development and Their In-*

terrelationship. Los Angeles: Center for the Study of Armament and Disarmament, California State University, 1980.

Baran, F. "The Commitment of the Intellectual." In *The Longer View*. New York: Monthly Review Press, 1966, p. 8.

Bassey, Chief Andrew. *A People's Struggle for Survival*. Calabar: Associated Publishers and Consultants, Ltd., 1980.

Baynham, Simon, ed. *Military Power and Politics in Black Africa*. London: Croom Helm, 1986.

Beckman, B. "Bakolon: Peasants vs. State and Capital." *Nigerian Journal of Political Science* 4, nos. 1, 2 (1985).

———. "The Military as Revolutionary Vanguard: A Critique." *Positive Review Monograph*, 2–1, 1986.

———. "Whose State? State and Capitalist Development in Nigeria." *Review of African Political Economy* 23 (1982).

Bend-Dak, Joseph D. "Some Directions for Research Toward Peaceful Arab-Israeli Relations." *Journal of Conflict Resolution* 16, June 1972.

Bender, Gerald, James Coleman, and Richard Sklar. *African Crisis Areas and U.S. Foreign Policy*. Berkeley: University of California Press, 1985.

Benoit, Emile. *Defense and Economic Growth in Developing Countries*. Lexington, Mass.: Lexington Books, 1963.

———, Max F. Millikan, and Everett E. Hagen. *Effect of Defense on Developing Economies, Main Report*, Vol. 2, ACDA/E–136. Cambridge, Mass.: MIT Press, 1971.

Berg, Elliot, et al. *Accelerated Development in Sub-Saharan Africa*. Washington, D.C.: World Bank, 1981.

Bexelius, Alfred. *The Swedish Institutions of the Justitie Ombudsman*. Stockholm: Swedish Institute, 1965.

Bhagwati, J. N., ed. *The New International Economic Order: The North-South Debate*. Cambridge, Mass.: MIT, 1977.

Biener, Henry, ed. *The Military Intervenes*. New York: Russell Sage Foundation, 1967.

Bloom, A. "Human Rights in Israel's Thought: A Study of Old Testament Doctrine," *Interpretation* 8 (1954).

Bollen, Kenneth A. "Political Rights and Political Liberties in Nations, An Evaluation of Human Rights Measures, 1950 to 1984." *Human Rights Quarterly* 8 (November 1986).

Bonkovsky, F. O. *International Norms and National Policy*. Grand Rapids, Mich.: Eerdmans, 1980.

Boro, Major Isaac Jasper Adaka, and Tony Tebekaemi, eds. *The Twelve-Day Revolution*. Benin City: Idodo Uweh Publishers (Nig.), Ltd., 1982.

Brett, E. A. *Colonialism and Underdevelopment in East Africa*. New York: Nok, 1973.

Brittan, Arthur, and Mary Maynard. *Sexism, Racism and Oppression*. New York: Basil Blackwell, 1984.

Brown, Neville. "Underdevelopment as a Threat to World Peace," *International Affairs* 47, no. 2 (April 1971).

Browne, Robert, and Robert Cummings. *The Lagos Plan of Action vs. The*

Berg Report: Contemporary Issues in African Economic Development. Richmond, Va.: Brunswick Publishing Co., 1984.

Brunner, Emil. *Man in Revolt: A Christian Anthropology.* Ed. O. Wyon. Cambridge, Eng.: Lutterworth, 1939.

Bryde, Brun-Otto. *The Politics and Sociology of African Legal Development.* Frankfurt am Main: Alfred Metzner Verlag, 1976, p. 68.

Bull, Hedley. *The Anarchical Society.* London: Oxford University Press, 1980.

Cabral, Amilcar. *Return to the Source: Selected Speeches.* Ed. Africa Information Service. New York: Monthly Review Press, 1973.

Campbell, Horace. "The Dismantling of the Apartheid War Machine." *Third World Quarterly* 9, no. 2 (April 1987).

Carr, E. H. *The Twenty Years Crisis.* New York: Harper and Row, 1964.

Carter, Gwendolyn. *Continuity and Change in South Africa.* Los Angeles: Cross Roads Press, 1986.

Cervenka, Zdenek. Report on the International Symposium on The Militarization of Africa, November 10–12, 1986.

Chand, H. *Nigerian Constitutional Law.* Modinager, India: Santosh Publishing House, 1982.

"Coup in Nigeria." *Daily Times,* January 1, 1984.

Cutrufelli, Maria Rosa. *Women of Africa: Roots of Oppression.* London: Zed Press, 1983.

Dahrendorf, R. *The New Liberty: The BBC Reith Lectures.* London, 1975.

Davis, Angela. *Women, Race and Class.* New York: Random House, 1981.

Dewar, David. "Urban Poverty and City Development: Some Perspectives." Carnegie Conference Paper No. 163. Saidru: University of Cape Town.

Dimitryevic, Vojin. "The Right to Development." Paper prepared for International Studies Association, 23rd Annual Convention, 1986.

Dinham, Barbara, and C. Hines. *Agribusiness in Africa: A Study of the Impact of Big Business on Africa's Food and Agricultural Production.* London: Earth Resources Research, 1983.

Donders, J. G., and S. Smith. *Refugees Are People: An Action Report on Refugees in Africa.* Eldoret, Kenya: GABA Publications, October 1985.

Donnelly, Jack. "In Search of the Unicorn: The Jurisprudence and Politics of the Right to Development." *California Western International Law Journal* 15, no. 3 (Summer 1985).

———. "Recent Trends in UN Human Rights Activity: Description and Polemic." *International Organization* 35, no. 4 (Autumn 1981).

Duboff, R. B. "Converting Military Spending to Social Welfare: The Real Obstacles." *Quarterly Review of Economics and Business* 12 (Spring 1972).

Ejiofor, Lambert U. *Africa in World Politics.* Onitsha: African Educational Publishers (Nig.), Ltd., 1981.

Engels, Friedrich. *The Origin of the Family, Private Property and the State in Light of the Researches of Lewis H.I. Morgan.* New York: International Publishers, 1972.

Evans, Peter. *Dependent Development: The Alliance of Multinational,*

State and Local Capital in Brazil. Princeton, N.J.: Princeton University Press, 1979.

Ewusi, Kodwo. "Occupations of Women in Ghana." National Council on Women and Development, Vol. 1, September 4–8, 1978.

Eze, Osita C. *Human Rights in Africa: Some Selected Problems.* Lagos: Nigerian Institute of International Affairs, in cooperation with Macmillan Nigerian Publishers, 1984.

———. "Human Rights, Legal Rights or Social Rights." In *Human Rights Education in Nigeria,* eds. L. A. Jinadu, and U.M.O. Ivowi. Lagos, Nigeria: Nigeria National Commission for Unesco, 1982.

———. "The Right to Health as a Human Right in Africa." In *Right to Health as Human,* ed. Réné-Jean Dupy. The Hague: Sigthoff and Nordhoff, 1979.

———. *Society and the Rule of Law.* Owerri, Nigeria: Totan Publishers, 1987.

———. "Theoretical Perspectives and Problematics." In *Society and the Rule of Law,* ed. Osita C. Eze.

———. "Toward a Positive Conception of Human Rights." Paper presented at the International Conference on Human Rights Education in Rural Environments, organized by the Department of Jurisprudence.

Falola, Toyin, ed. *Britain and Nigeria: Exploitation or Development?* London: Zed Press, 1987.

———. *State, Class, and Society in Nigeria.* Ibadan: Heinemann, 1987.

———, and Julius Ihonvbere. *The Rise and Fall of Nigeria's Second Republic, 1979–1984.* London: Zed Press, 1985.

Fanon, Franz. *The Wretched of the Earth.* New York: Grove Press, 1965.

Faroq, Hassan. "Solidarity Rights: Progressive Evolution of International Human Rights Laws." *Human Rights Annual,* Vol. 1 (New York: New York University Press, 1983.

Fatunde, Tunde. "The American Award." *The African Guardian* 2, no. 14 (April 1987).

Federal Republic of Nigeria. *Public Service Review Commission Main Report.* Lagos: Federal Ministry of Information, Printing Division, 1974.

Foy, Colm. "Crackdown in Kenya." *Afric-Asia,* no. 40 (April 1987).

Fromkin, D. *The Independence of Nations.* New York: Praeger, 1981.

Gandar, M., and N. Bromberger. "Economic and Demographic Functioning of Rural Households in the Mahlabatini District." *Social Dynamics* 10, no. 2 (1984).

Gervasi, Sean. "Breakdown of the United States Arms Embargo." In *U.S. Military Involvement in South Africa,* ed. Western Massachusetts Association of Concerned African Scholars. Boston: South End Press, 1978.

Ghana Fertility Survey, 1979–80: Background Methodology and Findings. Vol. 1, First Report. Accra, Ghana: Central Bureau of Statistics, in Collaboration with the World Fertility Survey, 1983.

Giddings, Paula. *When and Where I Enter: The Impact of Black Women on Race and Sex in America*. New York: William Morrow and Co., 1984.

Gillomee, Herman. "Afrikaner Nationalism and the Fable of the Sultan's Horse." *Energos,* no. 13 (1986).

Gilmour, D., and A. Roux. "Urban Black Unemployment and Education in the Eastern Cape." Carnegie Conference on Poverty, Paper 120, University of Cape Town, 1984.

Gonidec, P. *Les Droits Africains: Evolution et Source.* Paris: R. R. Pichon and R. Durand Auzias, 1978.

Green, R. H. "Basic Human Rights/Needs: Some Problems of Categorical Translation and Unification." *The Review* 24–27 (1980–1981).

Greenstreet, Miranda. "Social Change and Ghanaian Women." *Canadian Journal of African Studies* 2 (1972).

————. "Various Salient Features Concerning the Employment of Women." National Council for Women and Development, Background Papers, September 1978.

Gutkind, P.C.W., and Peter Waterman, eds. *African Social Studies: A Radical Reader.* New York: Monthly Review Press, 1977.

Gutierrez, Gustavo. *A Theology of Liberation: History, Politics and Salvation.* Maryknoll, N.Y.: Orbis Books, 1973.

Gutteridge, William. *Military Institutions and Power in the New States.* London: Pall Mall, 1962.

————. "Undoing Military Coups in Africa." *Third World Quarterly* 7, no. 1 (January 1985).

Hansen, J.D L. "The Child Malnutrition Problem in South Africa." Carnegie Conference Paper No. 208. Saidru: University of Cape Town, 1973.

Hart, Judith. *Aid and Liberation: A Socialist Study for Aid Politics.* London: Victor Gollancz, 1973.

Hatch, John. *Africa Emergent: Africa's Problems Since Independence.* Chicago: Henry Regnery, 1974.

Haughey, John C., ed. *Faith That Does Justice.* New York: Paulist Press, 1977.

Headley, Bernard D. "Behind a Manley Victory in Jamaica." *Monthly Review* (February 1987).

Henkin, Louis. "Rights Here and There." *Columbia Law Review* 81, no. 8 (December 1981).

————. *The Rights of Man Today.* Boulder, Colo.: Westview Press, 1978.

Herz, J. H. "Political Realism Revisited." *International Studies Quarterly* 25, no. 2 (June 1981).

Hodges, Tony. *Angola to the 1990s: The Potential for Recovery.* London: Economic Intelligence Unit, 1987.

————. *The Roots of a Desert War.* Westport, Conn.: Lawrence Hill and Co., 1983.

Hoffman, S. *Primacy of World Order: American Foreign Policy Since the Cold War.* New York: McGraw-Hill, 1979.

————. "Theory and International Relations." In *International Politics and Foreign Policy,* ed. J. N. Rosenau. New York: Free Press, 1969.

Hook, Bell. *Ain't I a Woman: Black Women and Feminism*. Boston: South End Press, 1981.

———. *Feminist Theory: From Margin to Center*. Boston: South End Press, 1984.

Hooker, M. B. *Legal Pluralism: An Introduction to Colonial and Neo-Colonial Laws*. Oxford: Clarendon Press, 1975.

Howard, Rhoda. "Women's Rights in English-Speaking Sub-Sahara Africa." In *Human Rights and Development in Africa*, eds. Claude E. Welch and Ronald I. Meltzer. Albany: State University of New York Press, 1984.

Human Rights Monitor. *Africa Today* 34, nos. 1 & 2 (1987).

Hunt, Alan. *The Sociological Movement in Law*. London: Macmillan, 1978.

Ihonvbere, Julius O. "Economic Crisis and Militarism in Africa: Responses and Options." Mimeo. University of Port Harcourt, May 1987.

———, and Toyin Falola, eds. *Nigeria and the International Capitalist System*. Boulder, Colo.: Lynne Rienner, 1988.

———, and Amechi Okolo, "The International Environment and Africa's Deepening Crisis: A Critique of the OAU's Lagos Plan of Action and the African Poverty Programme for Economic Recovery." Mimeo. University of Port Harcourt, 1987.

———. *Problems of Development in Africa* (forthcoming).

Ikime, Oboro. "Towards Understanding the National Question." *Africa Events*, (April 1987).

Independent Commission on International Humanitarian Issues. *Famine: A Man-Made Disaster*. London: Pan Books, 1985.

International Studies Quarterly 25, no. 2, June 1981.

Iwe, N.S.S. *The History and Contents of Human Rights: A Study of The History and Interpretation of Human Rights*. New York: Peter Lang, 1986.

Janowitz, M. *The Military in the Political Development of New States*. Chicago: University of Chicago Press, 1964.

Jinadu, A. L. *Human Rights and U.S. African Policy Under President Carter*. Lagos: NIIA, 1980.

Johnson, J., ed. *The Role of the Military in Underdeveloped Countries*. Princeton, N.J.: Princeton University Press, 1962.

Johnson, R., *How Long Will South Africa Survive?* London: Macmillan, 1977.

Kardi, John. *The Practice of Female Circumcision in the Upper East Region of Ghana: A Survey Report*. Accra: Ghanaian Association for Women's Welfare, September 1986.

Keely, Charles B. *Global Refugee Policy: The Case of a Development-Oriented Strategy*. New York: Population Council, 1981.

Klare, Michael T. "The Reagan Doctrine." *Inquiry*. Washington, D.C.: Institute for Policy Studies, March-April 1984.

Kyemba, H. *State of Blood*. London: Corgi Books, 1977.

Lee, J. M. *African Armies and Civil Order*. London: Chatto and Wendus, 1969.

Legum, Colin. "The Impact of Militarization on the Natural Resources of Africa." *African Contemporary Record*. New York and London: Africana, 1986.

———. *African Contemporary Record*. New York and London: Africana, 1986.

Leirie, Michael. *Race and Culture*. Paris: Unesco, 1958.

Levi, W. "The Relative Irrelevance of Moral Norms in International Politics." in *International Politics and Foreign Policy*, ed. J. N. Rosenau. New York: Free Press, 1969.

Limbard, Jan. "Power in the Market Economy." *Focus on Key Economic Issues*, no. 34. Johannesburg: Mercabank, 1984.

Lloyd, D. *Introduction to Jurisprudence*. London: Butterworths, 1978, pp. 291, 292.

Lock, Peter. "Armaments Dynamics: An Issue in Development Strategies." *Alternatives* 6, no. 2 (July 1980).

Luckham, Robert. "Armaments, Underdevelopment and Militarization in Africa." *Alternatives* 6, no. 2 (July 1980).

Luthuli, Albert. *Let My People Go, An Autobiography*. London: Fontana Books, 1963.

MacKinnon, Catharine A. "Feminism, Marxism, Method and the State: An Agenda for Theory." In *Feminist Theory: A Critique of Ideology*, eds., Nannerl O. Keohane, Michelle Z. Rosaldo, and Barbara C. Gelpi. Chicago: University of Chicago Press, 1982.

Madunagu, Edwin. *The Tragedy of the Nigerian Socialist Movement*. Calabar: Centaur Press Ltd., 1980.

Magubane, Bernard. "South Africa: A Luta Continua." Paper presented at the biennial conference of the African Association of Political Science, Addis Ababa, Ethiopia, May 13–15, 1985.

Manifesto of the Unity Party of Nigeria, Lagos, 1983.

Marable, Manning. *How Capitalism Under-developed Black America: Problems in Race, Political Economy and Society*. Boston: South End Press, 1983.

Markakis, John. "Military Regimes in Africa." Paper presented to the seminar on Conflict Formation and Militarism in the Third World. Oslo, May 28–29, 1986.

Markovitz, I. *Power and Class in Africa: An Introduction to Change and Conflict in African Politics*. Englewood Cliffs, N.J.: Prentice-Hall, 1977.

Marmorstein, Victoria. "World Bank Power to Consider Human Rights Factors in Loan Decisions." *Journal of Law and Economics* 13 (1978).

Marx, Karl. "Communist Manifesto." Pamphlet, 1870.

Mazrui, A. A. "World Culture and the Search for Human Consensus." In *On the Creation of a Just World Order*, ed. S. H. Mendlevitz. New York: Free Press, 1975.

Mbeki, Thabo. "South Africa: The Historical Injustice." In *Conflict and Change in Southern Africa*, eds. Douglas G. Auglin, Timothy M. Shaw, and Carl G. Widstrand. Washington, D.C.: University Press of America, 1978.

Mbiti, John S. *African Religions and Philosophy*. London: Heinemann, 1970.

McCarthy, T. E., J. B. Marie, S. P. Marks, and L. Sirois, *Human Rights Studies in Universities*. Under the supervision of Karel Vasak. Paris: Unesco, 1978.

McGrath, Mike. "Global Poverty in South Africa." *Social Dynamics* 10, no. 2 (1984).

McKean, Warren. *Equality and Discrimination Under International Law*. Oxford: Clarendon Press, 1983.

Mensa-Bonsu, H.J.A.N. "The Subtle Effect of Legislation on Women and Childbearing." Unpublished paper, 1985.

Metraux, Alfred. In *Unesco Courier*, July 1950.

Midgley, E.B.F. *The Natural Law Tradition and the Theory of International Relations*. London: 1975.

Miranda, Jose. *Marx and the Bible*. Ed. John Eagelson. Maryknoll, N.Y.: Orbis Books, 1974.

Morris, Colin. *The Unyoung, the Unpoor, and Uncolored*. London: Zed Press, 1962.

Mott, Stephen. *Biblical Ethics and Social Change*. New York: Oxford University Press, 1982.

Murray, Pauli. "The Liberation of Black Women." *Voices of the New Feminism*, ed. Mary Lou Thompson. Boston: Beacon Press, 1970.

Museveni, Yoweri. "Address to the 22nd OAU Summit, Addis Ababa, 28–30 July, 1986." *Africa Magazine*, September 1986.

Nahmani, Haying Simha. *Human Rights in the Old Testament*. Tel Aviv: Chachik, 1964.

Nanda, Ved. "The United States Armed Intervention in Grenada—Impact on World Order." *California Western International Law Journal* 14, no. 3 (Summer 1984).

Nardin, T. "Distributive Justice and the Criticism of International Law." *Political Studies* 29, no. 2 (September 1981).

Nattrass, Jill. "South Africa's Status in the International Development States." *Indicator SA* 1, no. 1, 1983.

———. "The Year 2000 from the 1986 Viewpoint." *Energos*, no. 13 (1986).

Navarro, Y. "The Economic and Political Determinants of Human (including health) Rights." *Imperialism, Health and Medicine*. Farmingdale, N.Y.: Baywood, 1981.

Nduru, Moyigahorokoto. "Sudan: Sharia by Another Name." *Afric-Asia*, no. 40 (April 1987).

"Newswatch Proscribed." *National Concord*. Lagos. April 1987.

Nnoli, O., ed. *Path to Nigerian Development*. Dakar: Codesing, 1981.

Nobel, Peter. "The Concept of Peoples and the Right to Development in the African (Banjul) Charter on Human and People's Rights." Paper prepared for a research project, Refugees and Development in Africa. Uppsala, Sweden: Scandinavian Institute of African Studies, October 1984.

———. *Refugee Law in the Sudan*. Uppsala: Scandinavian Institute of African Studies, 1982.

Ntalaya, Nzongola, and Ilunga Kabondo. *The Crisis in Zaire: Myths and Realities*. Trenton, N.J.: Africa World Press, 1986.

Nwabueze, B. O. *Constitutionalism in Emergent States.* London: C. Hurst and Co., 1973.

———. *The Presidential Constitution of Nigeria.* London: C. Hurst and Co., in association with Enugu: Nwamife Publishers, 1982, pp. 30–35.

Nwankwo, G. O. *The New International Economic and World Monetary System.* Lagos: NIIA, 1976.

Nyerere, Julius. "Stability and Change in Africa." Address reproduced in *Africa Contemporary Record* 2, (1968–1970).

OAU. *The Lagos Plan of Action for the Economic Development of Africa, 1980–2000.* Geneva: International Institute for Labor Studies, 1981.

Ojudu, Babatunde. "Nigeria: Morning Yet on Human Rights Day." *African Concord,* June 9, 1987.

Okolo, Amechi. "Dependency in Africa: States of African Political Economy." *Alternatives* 98 (Fall 1983).

Okonjo, Chikwenye. "Womanism: The Dynamics of the Contemporary Black Female Novel in English." *Signs: Journal of Women in Culture and Society,* 11, no. 1 (1985).

Ollawa, Patrick E. *Participatory Democracy in Zambia: The Political Economy of National Development.* Elms Court, Devon: Arthur H. Stockwell, 1979, pp. 157–60.

Onimode, B., et al. *Multinational Corporations in Nigeria.* Ibadan: Les Shraden, 1983.

Onipede, A. "Life Rough for Babies." *Sunday Tribune,* February 15, 1987.

Onwu, N. "The Current of Biblical Studies in Africa." *Journal of Religious Thought* 41, no. 2 (Fall/Winter 1984–1985).

———. "The Distorted Vision: Reinterpretation of Mark 8:22–26 in the Context of Social Justice." *West African Religion* 29, nos. 1/2 (1980).

———. "The Social Implications of Dikaiosune in Saint Matthew's Gospel." Ph.D. Thesis, University of Nigeria, Nsukka, 1983.

Plamenatz, John. *Man and Society—A Critical Examination of Some Important Social and Political Theories.* Vols. 1 and 2. London: Longman Group, 1978.

Pollis, Adamantia. *Socialist and Third World Perspectives on Human Rights.* New York: Praeger, 1982.

Power, Jonathan. *Amnesty International: The Human Rights Story.* Oxford: Pergamon Press, 1981.

Pratt, Renate. "Human Rights and International Lending: The Advocacy Experience of the Task Force on the Churches and Corporate Responsibility (TCCR)." Toronto: University of Toronto, Development Studies Programme. Working Paper no. 15, February 1985.

Price, J. H. *Political Institutions of West Africa.* 2nd ed. London: Hutchinson and Co. Publishers, 1975.

Read, Herbert. *Anarchy and Order.* London: A Condor Book, Souvenir Press, 1974.

Roberts, Pepe. "Debate on Feminism in Africa." *Review of African Political Economy,* nos. 27 and 28 (1985).

Rodney, W. *How Europe Underdeveloped Africa.* London: Zed Press, 1962.

Rogers, Barbara. *The Domestication of Women: Discrimination in Developing Societies.* New York: Tavistock Publications, 1983.

Rothstein, R. L. "The North-South Dialogue: The Political Economy of Immobility." *Journal of International Affairs* 34, no. 1 (Spring/Summer 1980).

Rousseau, J.J. *Social Contract.* Book I, 1762. London: Penguin Book, 1968.

Safilios-Rothschild, Constantina. *Women and Social Policy.* Englewood Cliffs, N.J.: Prentice-Hall, 1974.

Sandbrook, Richard. *The Politics of Basic Needs: Urban Aspects of Assaulting Poverty in Africa.* Toronto: University of Toronto Press, 1982.

Savage, Michael. "The Cost of Apartheid." *Third World Quarterly* 9, no. 2 (April 1987).

Seidman, Ann. *The Roots of Crisis in Southern Africa.* Trenton, N.J.: Africa World Press, 1985.

———. *South Africa and Multinational Corporations.* Westport, Conn.: Lawrence Hill and Co., 1977.

Shepherd, George W., Jr. *Anti-Apartheid: The Struggle for Liberation in South Africa.* Westport, Conn.: Greenwood Press, 1977.

———. *The Trampled Grass: Tributary States and Self-Reliance in the Indian Ocean Zone of Peace.* New York: Praeger, 1987.

———, and Ved P. Nanda, eds. *Human Rights and Third World Development.* Westport, Conn.: Greenwood Press, 1985.

Sherman, Richard. *Eritrea: The Unfinished Revolution.* New York: Praeger, 1980.

Simkins, Charles. "How Much Socialism Will Be Needed to End Poverty in South Africa?" Paper presented at the Conference on Apartheid in South Africa, University of York, October 1966.

SIPRI. *Southern Africa: The Escalation of a Conflict.* New York: Praeger, 1976.

———. *Yearbook.* Stockholm: 1986.

Sivard, Ruth L. *World Military and Social Expenditures, 1977.* Leesburg, Va.: WNSE Publications, 1977.

Sklar, Richard L. *Nigerian Political Parties: Power in an Emergent African Nation.* New York: Nok Publishers International, 1983.

Smith, Adam. *An Inquiry into the Nature and Causes of the Wealth of Nations.* Chicago: Encyclopaedia Britannica, 1952.

Stichter, S. *Migrant Laborers.* Cambridge: Cambridge University Press, 1985.

Stockwell, John. *Harper's Magazine.* September 1984.

Straus, Leo. *Natural Right and History.* Chicago: University of Chicago Press, 1971.

Study Mission to South Africa. *South Africa: Change and Confrontation.* July 3–11, 1980, to Committee on Foreign Affairs, U.S. House of Representatives. Washington, D.C.: U.S. Government Printing Office, 1981.

Suboff, R. B. "Converting Military Spending to Social Welfare: The Real Obstacles." *Quarterly Review of Economics and Business* 12 (Spring 1972).

Sweezy, Paul M. "The Present Global Crisis of Capitalism." *Monthly Review* 29, no. 11 (April 1978).

Tambo, Oliver. "Certainties and Uncertainties: Strategic Options for International Companies." *Sechaba* (July 1987).

———. *Forward to Peoples' Power*. Harare: Ministry of Information and Broadcasting, 1986.

———. "South Africa Freedom Day." *Selected Writings on the Freedom Charter, 1955–1985*. London: ANC, 1985.

"The Freedom Charter." Congress of the People, Kliptown, South Africa, June 26, 1955.

Thomas, Clive. *The Rise of the Authoritarian State in Peripheral Societies*. New York: Monthly Review Press, 1984.

Timberlake, Lloyd. *Africa in Crisis: The Causes, The Cures of Environmental Bankruptcy*. London: International Institute for Environment and Development, 1985.

Trivedi, R. N. "Human Rights, Rights to Development and the New International Economic Order: Perspectives and Proposals." In *Development, Human Rights and the Rule of Law: Report of a Conference Held in the Hague, April 27, - May 1, 1981*. Oxford: Pergamon Press, 1981.

Tsikata, E. "Ghana: Women in Mass Organizations—1982–87." Paper presented to seminar on the Post-Colonial State and National Development, April 21–23, 1987, Legon, Ghana.

Tucker, R. W. *The Inequality of Nations*. London: Robertson, 1977.

Turner, T., and P. Badru. "Class Contradictions and the 1983 Coup in Nigeria." *Journal of African Marxists 7*, (1985), pp. 4–21.

Tyoden, S. "The Military and the Prospect for Socialist Construction in the Third World: Some Preliminary Observations." Presented at a Conference on Nigerian Economy and Society Since the Berlin Conference. Zaria: Ahmadu Bello University, 1985.

Udo-Inyang, D. S. *The Man, Sir Justice Udo-Udoma*. Calabar: Wusen Press Ltd., 1985.

Umezurike, U. O. *Self-Determination in International Law*. Hamden, Conn.: Archon Books, 1972.

Unesco. *Human Rights, Human Needs and the Establishment of a New International Economic Order*. Doc. 55 78/conf.

Unobe, E. "Government Lawlessness During the First Four Years of Nigeria's Second Republic," eds. Mohammed, S. and T. Edoh. In *Nigeria: A Republic in Ruins*. Zaria: ABU, 1986.

UN General Assembly, *Study on the Relationship Between Disarmament and Development*. New York: United Nations, 1982.

UN Office for Emergency Operations in Africa. "Special Report on the Emergency Situation in Africa: Review of 1985 and 1986 Emergency Needs." New York, January 30, 1986.

U.S. Arms Control and Disarmament Agency. *World Military Expenditures and Arms Transfers 1972–82*. Washington, D.C.: ACADA Publication, 1984.

Uno, Edet. *Struggle for Redemption: Selected Speeches of Mohammed Abubakar Rimi.* Zaria: Northern Nigerian Publishing Co., 1981.

Urdang, Stephanie. *Fighting Two Colonialisms: Women in Guinea Bissau.* New York: Monthly Review Press, 1979.

Usman, B. *Nigeria Against the IMF.* Kaduna: Vanguard, 1986.

Van den Berghe, Pierre. *Race and Ethnicity: Essays in Comparative Sociology.* New York: Basic Books, 1970.

Verhelst, T. G., ed. *Legal Process and the Individual: African Source Materials.* Addis Ababa: Centre for African Legal Development, Faculty of Law, Haile Selassi I University, 1965, pp. 31–32, preamble to Jogolose Constitution of 1963.

we Thionglo, Ngugi. *Detained.* Nairobi: Heinemann, 1977.

————. *Petals of Blood.* London: Heinemann, 1977.

Wiking, Staffan. *Military Coups in Sub-Saharan Africa (How to Justify Illegal Assumption of Power).* Uppsala: Scandinavian Institute of African Studies, 1983.

Wilfong, Marsha, ed. "Towards a Common Testimony." *The Reformed World* 39, no. 5 (1987).

Wilmot, Patrick F. *Sociology, A New Introduction.* London: Collins International Text Books, 1985, Chapter 4.

Wilson, Francis. *Labour in South African Gold Mines.* Cambridge: Cambridge University Press, 1972.

————. "South African Poverty Major Issues." *Social Dynamics* 10, no. 2 (1984).

Wiredu, Kwasi. *Philosophy and an African Culture.* Cambridge: Cambridge University Press, 1980.

Wolfers, Michael. *Politics in the Organization of African Unity.* London: Methuen and Co., 1976.

Wood, Charles H. "Equilibrium and Historical-Structural Perspectives on Migration." *International Migration Review* 16, no. 2 (1982).

World Bank. *Accelerated Development in Sub-Saharan Africa: An Agenda for Action.* Washington, D.C.: 1981.

————. *Toward Sustained Development in Sub-Saharan Africa.* Washington, D.C.: 1984.

Wright, C.J.H. *Human Rights: A Study on Biblical Themes.* Bramcote: Grove Books, 1979.

Index

About the Contributors

S. O. ALUBO is Professor of Sociology, University of Jos, Nigeria.

MARK O.C. ANIKPO is Senior Lecturer in Sociology, University of Port Harcourt, Nigeria. He is the author of *Poverty in Africa: An Introduction to the Sociology of Underdevelopment* (1987) and *Peasants and Politicians in the Nigerian Food Crisis* (1987).

ZDENEK CERVENKA is Senior Research Associate, The Scandinavian Institute of African Studies, Uppsala, Sweden. He has coauthored with Colin Legum *The Horn of Africa in Continuing Crisis* (1979) and *The Unfinished Quest for Unity* (1973).

OSITA EZE is Professor and Dean of the College of Legal Studies, Iwo State University, Okigwe, Nigeria, and author of *Human Rights in Africa: Some Selected Problems* (1984).

JULIUS O. IHONVBERE is a Lecturer in Political Science, University of Port Hartcourt, Nigeria. He is editor with Toyin Falola of *Nigeria and the International Capitalist System* (1988) and *The Rise and Fall of Nigeria's Second Republic, 1979–1984* (1985).

STANLIE JAMES is Assistant Professor, Afro-American Studies and Center of African Studies, University of Wisconsin, Madison, Wisconsin.

OBED O. MAILAFIA is a Lecturer at the National Institute of Policy and Strategic Studies, Kuru, Jos, Nigeria.

OKWUDIBIA NNOLI is Professor of Political Science, University of Nigeria, Nsukka, Nigeria. He is the editor of *Path to Nigerian Development* (1981) and *Self-Reliance and Foreign Policy in Tanzania: The Dynamics of the Diplomacy of a New State, 1961–1971* (1978).

MOKWUGO OKOYE is Retired Chief, Enugu, Cross River State, Nigeria and author of *Point of Discord: Studies in Tension and Conflict* (1973) and *The Growth of Nations* (1978).

NIENANYA ONWU is Professor of Theology, Department of Religion, University of Nigeria, Nsukka, Nigeria.

MICHAEL J. SCHULTHEIS is Director of Jesuit African Refugee Service, Nairobi, Kenya, and author of *The Structure of a Global Justice Issue.*

GEORGE W. SHEPHERD, JR., is Professor of International Relations, Graduate School of International Studies and Director of the Consortium on Rights Development, University of Denver. He is the author of *The Trampled Grass* (1987) and coeditor of *Human Rights and Third World Development* (1985).